10^{00}

LODGING IN SPAIN'S MONASTERIES

Inexpensive Accommodations
Remarkable Historic Buildings
Memorable Settings

Eileen Barish

Monasterio de la Oliva, page 396

Lodging in Spain's Monasteries

by Eileen Barish

ANACAPA PRESS

P.O. Box 8459, Scottsdale, AZ 85252
Tel: (800) 638-3637

www.monasteriesofspain.com

ISBN #1-884465-17-X
Library of Congress Catalog Card Number: 2002-190103
Printed and bound in the United States of America

Also by Eileen Barish
Lodging in Italy's Monasteries
www.monasteriesofitaly.com

While due care has been exercised in the compilation of this directory, we are not responsible for errors or omissions. Information changes and we are sorry for any inconvenience that might occur. Inclusion in this guide does not constitute endorsement or recommendation by the author or publisher. It is intended as a guide to assist in providing information to the public and the listings are offered as an aid to travelers.

SPECIAL SALES

Copies of this book are available at special discounts when purchased in bulk for fund-raising and educational use as well as for premiums and special sales promotions. Custom editions and book excerpts can also be produced to specification.
For details, call 1-800-638-3637.

Monasterio De Iranzu, page 404

CREDITS

Author — Eileen Barish
Publisher and Managing Editor — Harvey Barish
Senior Researcher — Francesca Pasquini
Editorial Assistant — Phyllis Holmes
Cover Design — David Johnson
Book Layout — José Cardeña

PHOTO CREDITS

The author and publisher are greatly indebted to the people and organizations that so generously supplied the photos for this book. First and foremost we would like to thank the monasteries, convents and casas that provided the photos used to illustrate their institutions. We are also grateful to the Spanish Government Tourist Board in Los Angeles who offered their extensive photography files and supplied all of the other photos of Spain shown in this book.

Santuario de San Miguel de Aralar, page 420

ACKNOWLEDGEMENTS

This book would not have been possible without the diligent efforts of Francesca Pasquini, our research manager and colleague. From the onset, her determination and thoroughness was apparent in every stage of the project. Not only did she carefully document the research data accumulated from hundreds of interviews, but she filled her reports with insight into Spain, its customs, traditions, geography, linguistics and enchanting peculiarities. The fact that she gave birth to a baby during the research phase of this book says it all. Thank you Francesca. And welcome to Romeo, a darling baby boy. Understanding the consuming nature of research, we are grateful to Dario Pasquini for his patience and assistance.

Special thank you to Phyllis Holmes, a dedicated assistant who can always be counted upon.

Since nothing in life is possible without love and encouragement, I am eternally grateful to Harvey, my number one champion. And to Nona, Kenny, Chris and especially to Katie for always believing.

Eileen Barish

HOW TO USE THIS GUIDE

This book is an introduction to hundreds of Spain's monasteries, convents and casas that extend hospitality to guests. It is organized as follows:

Section One: Monasteries offering hospitality to all

These establishments welcome everyone regardless of religion, with or without a spiritual purpose. Listings in Section One describe the monastery, its setting, history, architecture, artwork, products made by the order, folklore and surrounding tourist sites. It provides all the information you'll need to make an informed lodging decision and the wherewithal to reserve a room including:

Accommodations
Type and number of rooms, indicating private or shared baths.

Amenities
Meals and facilities available to guests.

Cost of lodging
Lodging and meal rates are approximate. Some rates are quoted on a per person basis while others are per room. When no rate is given, the monastery or convent either requests only a donation or reserves the right to determine the rate when reservations are made, depending on the number of people, number of meals and time of the year.

Directions
Directions to each location are provided by car and public transportation.

Contact
Information includes the person in charge of hospitality, address, telephone, fax and where available, website and email address, as follows:

Contact person ....Madre Hospedera

Name of Monastery.............................Monasterio Santa María La Real

Address..........................Apartado 50, Ctr. Madrid-La Coruña, km 129

Zone, City, (Province),Country...............05200 Arévalo (Ávila), Spain

Tel/Fax..Tel: 920/300231, Fax: 920/328006

Website...www.planalfa.es

Email address... ocsoavi@planalfa.es

How to make a reservation
A sample reservation letter in Spanish and English is included on pages 12 & 13.

Section Two: Monasteries offering hospitality for spiritual endeavors
These establishments welcome guests specifically for retreat, vocation or other spiritual purposes. Listings in Section Two include the basic contact information necessary to make a reservation.

Table of Contents

• Admire centuries-old cathedrals and palaces.

• Explore ancient alcázars and battlemented castles

• Visit the famous white towns of Andalucía

• Hike in the Picos de Europa

• Investigate prehistoric caves

• Play in the surf on the Costa del Sol

Monasterio de San José
page 207

Spend a night or a week at a monastery and come away filled with the essence of Spain, its history, art, architecture and local traditions

Monasterio Inmaculada Concepción
page 201

Awaken each morning to church bells ringing out over sleepy villages and walled towns. Mingle with the townspeople at the daily market. Enjoy a glass of sangria in a friendly cafe. People watch from an atmospheric plaza. Leisurely stroll the medieval quarters and cobblestone streets. Admire centuries-old houses and palaces that stand side by side, as charming today as they were hundreds of years ago.

Open to all, regardless of religious denomination, lodging at monasteries is an untouched Spanish adventure. A *new* approach to travel based on a centuries-old tradition of hospitality. Whether you prefer the sophistication of a city or the quaintness of the countryside, each of the monasteries described in this guide represents a singular experience in a unique setting. An experience that will linger long after you've returned home.

But perhaps most remarkable is the low cost of accommodations and meals. It is extremely inexpensive to spend the night at a monastery. Rates range from a voluntary donation to an average of $20 per night. And many monasteries serve meals for just a few dollars more. Others have kitchens and dining rooms where guests may prepare their own food. What is common to each is cleanliness, graciousness, beauty and a sense of unhurried, uncrowded tranquility.

Monasteries are an integral part of Spain's history and heritage and are emblematic of Spain's diverse culture. There are monastery locations to suit every traveler. Choose a location in a secluded village backdropped by snow-capped mountains. Reserve a room in an ancient city still enclosed by 13th century walls or a tiny hamlet overlooked by a massive fortress. There are monasteries on the enchanted Canary and Balearic islands and others just a stone's throw from a fabled beach.

Àvila, page 193

More than just lodging particulars, history-laced vignettes offer insight into the little known villages surrounding the monasteries, information not readily found in guide books. You'll learn about places unspoiled by tourism, places that have remained unchanged for centuries.

What's in a name? Monastery, convent (hermitage, sanctuary), or casa, what's the difference? Historically, monasteries housed monks whereas nuns resided in convents. A casa is a guest house owned and generally managed by an order. Over the centuries, much has changed and the gender of the order in residence and its designation as monastery or convent is no longer gender specific.

Monastic orders have traditionally offered hospitality to travelers. This book introduces you to that remarkable travel resource and to a custom that allows you to immerse yourself in another time and place. One that only a handful of people have enjoyed. Staying at a monastery is a rewarding experience but it is important to remember that a monastery is not a hotel and should be regarded accordingly.

Lodging in Spain's Monasteries was researched through personal interviews with each institution. The monasteries described in Section One offer hospitality to all visitors.

San Millán de Suso y Yuso
page 366

The information necessary to plan a trip is included: rates, address, telephone, fax (and where available, email address and website), contact person and description of accommodations. A sample reservation letter in Spanish and English will help you make your travel arrangements. You can book reservations by letter but faxing and telephoning may prove more effective. When calling or faxing, be certain to take into account the time difference and avoid waking someone in the middle of the night. For those institutions that offer email portals, we suggest emailing your requests.

Section Two is a listing of monasteries that offer hospitality to guests who would like to sample the religious life or experience a time of spiritual retreat. All pertinent contact information and special requirements are provided.

English/Spanish Reservation Form Letters

To make a reservation by mail or fax, the sample letter is appropriate. It is suggested that you write in both English and Spanish and make your reservations well in advance. Just fill in the blanks indicated by {brackets} with your specific travel information.

The English to Spanish translation guide on the next page will assist you in composing your reservation letter.

Reservation Form Letter - English Version

{Date}

Padre Hospedero
Monasterio de Santo Domingo
45300 Ocaña (Toledo), Spain

Dear Padre Hosperdero:

I would like to reserve {number of room(s) and choice i.e. one double room with private bath}. I would like to stay at your institution for a total of {indicate number - 1, 2, 3 etc.} nights beginning {day, month, year} until {day, month, year}.

Please contact me and let me know if the above reservation request can be arranged. Please also include the cost of the room and what deposit, if any, is required. As soon as I hear from you, I will send you a check. If possible, please respond in English.

Thank you for your kindness and courtesy. I look forward to visiting your institution. Best regards.

(Signature)

Your Name
1234 Any Street
Santa Barbara, California 93101, United States
Tel: (805) 555-1234, Fax: (805) 555-2345
Email: yourname@aol.com

Reservation Form Letter - Spanish Version

{Date}

Padre Hospedero
Monasterio de Santo Domingo
45300 Ocaña (Toledo), Spain

Estimado/os Padre Hosperdero:

Me dirijo a ustedes con el fin de solicitarles tengan a bien reservarme {indicate number and type of rooms - i.e. double with provate bath} habitación doble con baño privado en vuestra Institución por un total de {indicate number of nights} noches a partir del día {day, month, year of arrival} hasta el {day, month, year of departure} inclusive.

Os ruego me respondáis a la mayor brevedad si es factible dicha reserva, el coste de la misma y si es necesario enviar un depósito, importe que os haré llegar tan pronto como tenga vuestra respuesta a través de cheque o transferencia bancaria. Por último, si es posible, os agradecería me respondáis en inglés.

Agradeciendo vuestra colaboración y con la esperanza de poder visitar vuestra Institución, os envío un cordial saludo.

(Signature)

Your Name
1234 Any Street
Santa Barbara, California 93101, United States
Tel: (805) 555-1234, Fax: (805) 555-2345
Email: yourname@aol.com

Days
Monday - Lunes
Tuesday - Martes
Wednesday - Miercoles
Thursday - Jueves
Friday - Viernes
Saturday - Sábado
Sunday - Domingo

Months
January- Enero
February - Febrero
March - Marzo
April - Abril
May - Mayo
June - Junio
July - Julio
August - Agosto
September - Septiembre
October - Octubre
November - Noviembre
December - Diciembre

Room Options
Single Room/
Habitación individual
Double Room/
Habitación doble
Triple Room/
Habitación triple
Quadruple Room/
Habitación cuádruple

Bath Options
Private Bath/
Baño privado
Shared Bath/
Baño compartido

SECTION ONE

Monasteries Offering
Hospitality to All

Casa Vicente Pallotti
page 110

ANDULUCÍA

CONVENTO INMACULADA CONCEPCIÓN
Clarisse Nuns

The convent is quartered in Alhama, a pretty town on the route connecting Granada and Málaga. Sited at the foot of the Sierra de Almijara, it has wonderful views of the surrounding mountains. Founded in 1556, it is inhabited by a community of Clarisse nuns who were forced to leave their original convent during the religious suppressions. The nuns bought the complex from Franciscan monks who once lived there. During the Spanish Civil War of 1936-39, the building and church were nearly destroyed by a fire. Although the compound has been completely restored, its artwork and much of its originality were lost. "As a former Franciscan institution, it is all very simple," said one of the nuns.

A picturesque spa town, Alhama de Granada (Al hamma means hot springs), is perched atop a deep, grassy-banked gorge. The town's center is of Muslim origin, its narrow, twisting streets constitute an engaging setting. Noteworthy architecture includes an Arab fortress, the Gothic-Isabelline style House of the Inquisition, the Renaissance structure of Pósito and an age-old synagogue. The 16th century Iglesia del Carmen is ornamented by fine stone carving; its terrace offers dramatic views of the terrain. A Roman bridge signals the turn to the spa and the locale of the Roman and Moorish baths where warm spring waters have been channeled since Roman times.

The area above and west of the convent comprises numerous towns nestled between rolling hills and rivers, towns that perpetuate a rich historical heritage. Loja boasts a collection of remarkable monuments: Alcázaba fortress, the neoclassical Mausoleum of Narváez, the 16th century Gothic-Mudéjar Church of La Encarnación and the Church of San Gabriel. Loja is known as the city of water for its abundance of springs, fountains and pillars of great artistic merit.

The town of Montefrio is defined by tiled rooftops and pretty, whitewashed houses running up to a steep crag. It is home to an Arab fortress and the dome-topped neoclassical Iglesia de la Encarnación. A couple of miles beyond town is Hipo-Nova (site of megalithic dolmens), the ruins of an Iberian acropolis and intriguing Visigoth tombs.

Granada is thirty miles south of the convent. Its unique history has bestowed it with an harmonious grandeur embracing Moorish palaces and Christian Renaissance treasures. The Moors crossed the Strait of Gibraltar in 711 and settled in what was then a small Visigoth town on Alhambra Hill. They erected walls and laid the foundation for the prosperous civilization that followed. As the last Moorish kingdom on the Iberian peninsula, it possesses great symbolic value. The city has been shaped by its hills, where the old districts in the Albaycín and Alhambra were founded. They abound with quaint nooks and incredible landscapes.

Alhambra

Majestically positioned in the foothills of the snowy Sierra Nevada, a mountain range of fourteen peaks more than 9,800' high, Granada is acclaimed for its Alhambra, citadel of the Moorish kings of Spain. A dominating force, the complex represents a true expression of the once flourishing culture and is considered the finest example of Moorish architecture in Spain.

Comprised of two main parts, the Alcázaba and the Nasrid Palace, the Alhambra is enveloped by ramparts and towers. The palace is a structure of elegantly proportioned rooms and courtyards, its interior emblazoned with honeycomb and stalactite vaulting. The walls are covered with geometric designs of infinitesimal detail and intricacy executed in marble, alabaster, glazed tile and carved plaster. The halls and chambers surround a series of open courtyards including the Court of Lions where arcades rest on one hundred and twenty-four slender white marble columns. Once the harem, it was built by Muhammad V. A fountain at

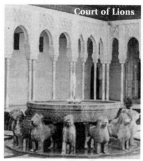
Court of Lions

the center of its patio rests on twelve namesake marble lions. In the early 19th century while living in the palace, Washington Irving immortalized this Moorish jewel in his book, *Tales of the Alhambra*.

Generalife Gardens

The *Generalife Gardens* (Gardens of the Architect), country estate of the Nasrid kings, were begun in the 13th century. They are serenely beautiful and composed of patios, terraces and fountains, mature trees and exquisite flowers. The Patio de la Acequia, an enclosed oriental garden, is built around a central pool. A more modern garden, Jardines Altos, reveals a stairway of cascading waterfalls.

The most representative of Moorish neighborhoods, the Albaycín occupies the hillside opposite the Alhambra. It personifies

Granada's Moorish ancestry, with whitewashed alleys and hidden gardens. The area was once home to nearly three dozen mosques. During the course of many years, however, Christian churches were built over the sites. Few experiences can surpass the view from the Albaycín's hillside setting across to the Alhambra, a dazzling sight at sunset when the towers of the fortress glow red against the backdrop of the snow-capped Sierra Nevada. Across the Darro River and facing the Alhambra is Sacromonte Hill, a place honeycombed with caves still occupied by Granada's gypsies. At the very top of the hill is the Abadía del Sacromonte, a Benedictine monastery.

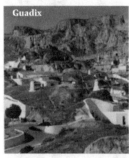
Guadix

Northeast of Granada are the towns of Guadix and Baza. Based on a high plateau between two mountain ranges, Guadix is one of the oldest settlements in Spain and is dominated by an 11th century Moorish castle. The landscape is marked by cave dwellings carved from the hills. In the Barrio de Santiago, many inhabitants still live in cave dwellings hewn from the local tufa. Outstanding monuments include the Mudéjar-inspired Iglesia de Santiago and the Gothic, Renaissance and Baroque cathedral. Built between the 16th and 18th centuries on the foundation of an earlier mosque, the structure is underscored by a massive tower.

Baza's Arab past is exemplified by its Alcázaba fortress, walls and baths. Traces of the old Jewish Quarter also remain. The town's *Dama de Baza* sculpture represents an example of Iberian culture during the 3rd and 4th centuries. Of particular interest: the Gothic church with a Plateresque façade by Diego de Siloé, the 16th century town hall and the Fountain of Caños Dorados.

Another nearby region is Las Alpujarras, a medley of atmospheric towns and villages in a wildly beautiful realm on the

Las Alpujarras

southern slopes of the Sierra Nevada. Alpujarras' dwellings were first introduced to the region by Berber settlers. Unique examples of North African architecture, they are compact clusters of irregularly shaped houses, generally two-story cubic structures covered by a flat roof with distinctive protruding chimney pots. The Moors inhabited these enclaves until the beginning of the 17th century and their cultural and traditional imprint is still apparent.

Costa del Sol

The Costa del Sol and the port town of Málaga are a short distance away. Prosperous since Phoenician times, Málaga is the second largest city in Andalucía. Although the town's cathedral was begun in the 16th century, construction continued for two hundred years, hence the hodgepodge of styles. The church is known as *La Manquita* (the one-armed) due to the fact that only the west tower was completed. The Museo de Bellas Artes exhibits paintings by Spanish artists such as Ribera, Murillo and Morales in addition to early sketches by Pablo Picasso. The Casa Natal de Picasso is headquarters for the Picasso Foundation and preserves a small sampling of his work.

Málaga's immense Alcázaba was built in the 11th century and is characterized by a double wall and several towers. Among its treasures are a partially excavated Roman amphitheater and a museum which shelters Phoenician, Roman and Muslim relics. Directly behind the Alcázaba are the ruins of the Castillo de Gibralfaro, a 14th century Moorish fortress.

Accommodations
20 beds in 1 triple, 1 quadruple, 3 single and 5 double rooms. There are 4 shared baths. Both men and women are welcome.

Amenities
Towels and linens are supplied on request.

Meals
Meals are not supplied with the lodging. Guests may use the kitchen and dining room.

Cost of lodging
Voluntary contribution.

Products of the institution
The nuns bake and sell a large variety of pastries to establishments outside the convent. On request, guests can also purchase them. Although the nuns live in seclusion, they pass the baked goods through a revolving door, a practice that allows them to talk to guests while maintaining their privacy.

Special rules
There is an 11:00 pm curfew. The convent is open year round.

Directions
By car: From Granada take route A329 west (becomes A92 west) to a left turn on route A335 south and then exit at Alhama.
By train: Get off at Granada and take the bus to Alhama.

Contact
Encargada de la Hospedería
Convento Inmaculada Concepción
San Diego, 24
18120 Alhama de Granada (Granada), Spain
Tel: 958/350207

MONASTERIO PURÍSIMA CONCEPCIÓN
Trinitarian Nuns

The monastery is in the center of Andújar, a small town thirty miles from Córdoba. Originally an Iberian settlement named Illiturgo, it was destroyed by Scipio during the Punic Wars. The monastery was founded in 1587 and has been inhabited by the Trinitarian sisters almost uninterruptedly since its inception. The only exception was a short period during the Civil War (1936) when the sisters were forced to leave.

A very important date in the history of the monastery is 1680. At that time, Andújar suffered from an epidemic of cholera. According to tradition, one of the sisters had a vision of Mary who told her that in order to stop the epidemic, the clergy had to redeem itself. The "licentious" comedies represented in town had to be stopped. They were and shortly afterwards, the epidemic passed. Every year since then there has been a solemn procession to celebrate the Virgin on the date of the immaculate conception.

"As the rules of our order dictate, the church and monastery are quite simple," said the Mother Superior. The exterior of the church is whitewashed and highlighted by yellowish stone decorations, typical colors of Andalucía. The interiors are adorned with a few images, the main one of the Virgin Mary by artist Duque Canedo. The monastery has undergone several renovations but has preserved its simplicity and peaceful atmosphere.

Thirteen sisters inhabit the monastery. They are actively involved in cultural and charitable activities and also work with the prison of Jaen where they meet with the prisoners.

Not far from the monastery is the Parque Natural de las Sierra Subbética. Composed of rugged limestone landscapes and karstic formations, the vegetation of the park includes evergreens on the south facing slopes and gall oaks on the northern flanks. The park encompasses the small towns of Priego, Rute and Zuheros. Priego is noted for its artistic and monumental heritage while Rute is known for anisettes and olive oils. A short distance from the village of Zuheros is the *Cueva de los Murciélagos* (Cave of Bats), an archaeological and speleological attraction. Group tours may be arranged.

Nearby Córdoba grew along the banks of the Guadalquivir River. The old quarter spreads out north of the river and is crossed by a Roman bridge. An important part of the walled enclosure still stands, delineated by medieval Arab towers known as *rondas*. In its

heyday, Córdoba was a city of more than half a million people. The long-time center of Moorish Spain, it once housed hundreds of mosques. The city's crowning jewel, however, is the Great Mosque or Mezquita. The focal point of historic Córdoba, it has been declared a World Heritage site by UNESCO. It was erected by emir al-Hakam II in

785 over a Visigoth basilica. In 848, a new minaret was added and in 961, the ground plan was extended. Artists from the orient decorated its *mihrab*, a niche that holds the *kiblah* or sacred stone. A sumptuously embellished hall, the mihrab features carved marble, stuccoes, mosaics and plaster walls dramatized by Moorish drawings and motifs.

Undoubtedly though, the mosque's most elaborate artwork is epitomized by more than eight hundred and fifty delicate marble, granite and jasper columns and interwoven, double-tiered striped arches. The floor plan consists of nineteen naves holding two levels of arches; the first level constitutes horseshoe arches, the second semicircular ones. The elements come together to create an almost magical, maze-like interior. The district surrounding the mosque embraces a famous little alley known as *Calljón de las Flores* (Street of the Flowers).

The *call*, one of the most evocative Jewish Quarters in Spain, begins at the northwestern section of the mosque on Calle Judíos. The district spreads out to the edge of the walls and to the Gate of Almodóvar. Once the heart of medieval Córdoba, it is a place of prodigious her-

The *call* (Jewish Quarter)

itage. The atmosphere conserves the very essence of Andalusia in its whitewashed alleys, small squares and gardens. Its neighborhoods are filled with memorable architecture, accented by wrought ironwork, flower-bedecked courtyards and delicate archways. Set back from the street in a tiny courtyard is the synagogue, one of the oldest Jewish monuments in Spain. The interior of the 14th century structure contains Alhambra-style arabesques and Hebrew inscriptions. The Córdoban Jews lived in the area until the Catholic monarchy ordered their expulsion in 1492. The Plaza of Juda Levi marks the beginning of Abucassis, a street featuring the Plaza de Maimónides. A statue of the namesake Jewish philosopher commemorates the site of the house where he lived. Between the Jewish Quarter and the mosque is an area called "Quiet Córdoba," in reference to the writing by poet Antonio Machado. Its silent streets are defined by noble houses that reveal patio's abloom with flowers.

The more modern part of the city and the essential heart of present-day Córdoba centers around the Plaza de las Tendillas and the 17th century Plaza de la Corredera, an arcaded square with a daily market.

Accommodations
8 beds in two rooms, a double room and a dorm with 4/6 beds. The bath is shared. Both men and women are welcome.

Amenities
Towels and linens are supplied. A living room and small kitchen are available for guest use.

Meals
Meals are not supplied with the lodging. Guests are welcome to use the kitchen.

Cost of lodging
Voluntary contribution.

Products of the institution
The nuns decorate liturgic ornaments with golden embroidery.

Special rules
Curfew at 10:30 pm. Open year round.

Directions
By car: Andújar is north of Cordoba on the Madrid-Córdoba-Cadiz highway (N IV / E5). Exit at Adujar and ask directions to the monastery.
By train: Get off in Madrid or Córdoba and take a bus to Andújar.

Contact
Call or write to Madre Superiora (preferably at the first phone number)
Monasterio Purísima Concepción
Granados, 1
23740 Andújar (Jaén), Spain
Tel: 953/501681 - 953/519105
Fax: 953/501681
Website: inicia.es/de/trinitarias
E-mail: monjas@teleline.es

MONASTERIO PURÍSIMA CONCEPCIÓN
Concepcionistas Franciscanas

The monastery was originally founded by a group of twelve women from Lebrija. They had formed a community although they did not belong to any specific order. In 1518 a group of nuns from San Juan de la Palma, a monastery in Seville, joined the group and established the Franciscan monastery. During the religious suppressions, the sisters remained in residence, however, a small part of the building was set on fire. "The damage was small and nothing serious happened," said one of the nuns. Since the order lives in seclusion, the monastery is not open to visitors. "But guests can visit our church," said the Madre Hospedera. "It is a beautiful Baroque building with a central and two lateral retablos," she added.

The sisters are renowned for their pastries and are particularly busy during the Christmas holidays. "Two months before Christmas, we have to stop taking orders, otherwise we would have too many to fill," said the madre. In addition to the hospitality offered to visitors throughout the year, the monastery is open to students and young women who work in Lebrija.

The monastery is next to the *Ayuntamiento* (town hall) in the very heart of Lebrija, a walled town. Its church, Santa María de la Oliva, is a former mosque dating to the 12th century. The surrounding landscape is typically Andalusian, composed of round hills of almond trees and vineyards which produce Manzanilla, a type of sherry.

Lebrija is well situated for touring the Pueblos Blancos, a route through fortified hilltop towns and villages amid a charming tangle of gorges, cork forests and vast rocky peaks. Framed by Moorish arches and draped in bougainvillea, these cliff-top towns are so named because they are whitewashed in the Moorish tradition. They retain an atmosphere reminiscent of the Muslim Middle Ages.

One itinerary travels from Arcos de la Frontera to Gaucín, Jimena de la Frontera, Zahara de la Sierra, Setenil and Ronda. Arcos de las Frontera stands on the banks of the Guadalete River. Inhabited since the Roman era, the old town contains the Condes de Aguila Palace, once home to Muslim rulers. Other highlights include a ruined Moorish castle in Jimena de la Frontera, the Rock of Gibraltar and from Gaucín, the Rif Mountains of North Africa. Founded by Arabs in the 8th century, Zahara de la Sierra has been declared a national monument. Its mountainside setting is overseen by a castle. In the unusual town of Setenil, some of the streets are covered by rock overhangs. The gorge was carved from volcanic tufa rock by the Río Trejo.

Ronda is considered one of the most dramatically sited cities in Spain. Enveloped by the Serranía de Ronda and perched on a rocky outcrop,

Ronda

Ronda exemplifies the quintessential mountain city. Straddling a steep limestone hollow, the old and new towns are divided by a precipitous gorge. The city's Moorish heritage is undeniable and distinguished by cobbled alleys, window grills and the whitewashed buildings. Although the Palacio Mondragón was rebuilt following the reconquest, its Islamic heritage is evident in the Moorish-inspired arcaded patio. Ronda is also the spiritual home of bullfighting. The Plaza de Toros was inaugurated in 1785 and continues its reputation as one of the most important bullrings in Spain.

Lebrija is very near the Doñana National Park. Declared a Biosphere Reserve by UNESCO, it is the largest aviary reserve in Europe. Its richness is the result of excellent climactic conditions and strategic geographic location along bird migration routes. The reserve constitutes three ecosystems: sand dunes, pastures and swamps.

Nearby Seville, capital of bullfighting in Spain, is on the plain of the Guadalquivir River. Although the Tartessians were the original founders of ancient Seville, it was the Moorish occupation of the Iberian peninsula from 711 to 1248 that left the most indelible mark. The monuments from that period represent the sum and substance of Andalusian culture.

Barrio Santa Cruz

Murillo Gardens, named for the famous painter and native son, border the walls of the Alcázar. Sevillian in style, the gardens brim with arcades foliage and ceramic work and lead to the Barrio Santa Cruz, once the old Jewish Quarter. Ensconced in the historic center and still protected by walls, the neighborhood is underscored by symbolic whitewashed buildings and iron filigreed balconies. It is also the locale of the Gothic cathedral, one of the world's largest. Built on what was once a mosque, only two parts of the original structure remain: the Court of Oranges and the Giralda, a mosque tower and the city's most prominent monument. Its foundation is comprised of Roman stones carried from Itálica. The structure was continued in brick by the Almohades who decorated the façades with *sebka* (brick façades only occasionally broken by a diamond pattern) and poly-lobed horseshoe windows.

Declared a World Heritage Site by UNESCO, the cathedral was designed by Alonso Martinez, Simón de Colonia and Juan Gil de Ontañón and shelters five aisles in Gothic style with a large transept. The interior is extraordinarily rich and sustains many precious works of art: the sepulcher of Christopher Columbus, a choir with Mudéjar stalls, Baroque organ boxes and paintings by Murillo, Goya and Zubarán. The main chapel is adorned with an altarpiece and Plateresque grill. The royal chapel is executed in Plateresque style.

Reales Alcázares

Adjoining the cathedral is the Reales Alcázares, one of the oldest royal residences in Europe. Built in Moorish style on order of Pedro I, it rivals the Alhambra in its exquisite embellishments and grand halls. The location has been occupied by a series of buildings including a Roman acropolis, Paleochristian basilica, Visigothic structures and the first Moorish fortress of the 9th century.

The neighborhood of San Bartolomé preserves the atmosphere of old Seville, an intricate network of narrow streets filled with well-preserved Arab and medieval buildings as well as palatial and religious constructions of the 17th, 18th and 19th centuries. The church of Santa María La Blanca was built over the remains of an old synagogue. The interior displays creative Baroque plaster work by the Borja brothers. Nearby is the home of Miguel de Mañara, model for Don Juan, famous character of world literature. An impressive Renaissance building, its façade is arrayed with fresco paintings imitating brick surfaces.

Just outside of Seville, in the town of Santiponce, stand the remains of the Roman city of Itálica. Founded by General Scipio, the city gave

Remains of the Roman city of Itálica

two emperors to Rome, Trajan and Hadrian. The area open to visitors includes the neighborhood built by Hadrian, a theater in the old center and a modern park surrounding the amphitheater. One of the largest of the Roman empire, the arena could hold 25,000 spectators.

Accommodations
13 beds in single rooms, 2 of which have private baths. The others share 3 baths. Only women are welcome and extended visits are preferred.

Amenities
Towels and linens are supplied on request. Reading room, kitchen and laundry room.

Meals
Meals are not supplied with the lodging. Guests may use the kitchen.

Cost of lodging
$108.00 per month. Guests staying shorter periods: $6.00 per night.

Products of the institution
Large variety of pastries. The most famous are *coronillas*, almond paste confections.

Special rules
Guests are given a key to the guest house. Open year round. If there are no confirmed bookings, the guest house might be closed during the summer months for ongoing restoration.

Directions
By car: From Seville (heading south) or Cadiz (heading north) take highway A4 to route 471 and go west following the signs to Lebrija.
By train: Get off at Lebrija. There are also buses from Seville and Cadiz.

Contact
Madre Hospedera
Monasterio Purísima Concepción
Antonio de Lebrija, 3
41740 Lebrija (Seville), Spain
Tel: 95/5972165

MONASTERIO DE LA PURÍSIMA CONCEPCIÓN

Clarisse Nuns

Monasterio de la Purísima Concepción

The monastery is housed in a 17th century palace just outside the town of Marchena. "It is away from crowds and noise and ideal for those who need to relax or meditate," said the madre. Built in a solitary spot in 1624 by Duke Don Rodrigo Ponce de León and his wife the Duchess Doña Ana de Aragón, it was later donated to the Clarisse nuns. The change of ownership took place in 1631 after many requests by Madre María de Antigua. The palace conserves some fine works of art: drawings bestowed by the Duchess Ponce de León, 17th century wooden statues and a treasured 16th century organ.

The church was erected in 1751 and is based on the design of Nicolas Carretero. It is enriched by 17th and 18th century paintings and a collection of engravings donated by Don Joaquin Ponce de León. There are minor retablos and a main one in traditional wooden form.

Marchena is an attractive town of unspoiled charm, a town of artists, monuments and folklore. Many wall defenses dating from Roman times remain as part of the landscape. Moorish and Christian influences added at a later date are also obvious. The town's interesting works of art include a retablo by Alejo Fernández and a sculpture by Pedro Roldán harbored within the Gothic church of San Juan Bautista.

Steeped in Moorish culture, the region of Andalucía stretches from the grand mountains of Sierra Morena in the north, west to the plains of the Guadalquivir Valley and south to the Costa del Sol. Considered by many to be the true heart of Spain, it was first occupied by the Moors in the 8th century. Its golden period occurred during the rule of the Nasrid Dynasty, from the early 13th century to the last part of the 16th.

A short distance from the monastery, El Arahal is notable for its bleached white appearance and is home to a number of Baroque buildings including the Mudéjar-inspired church of La Victoria.

At the center of Andalucía, Carmona was established by the Phoenicians. It later became an important Roman city as witnessed by the necropolis, a Roman burial ground discovered in 1881. The complex encompasses subterranean chambers and vestibules, pillars, domed ceilings and carved reliefs. Other noteworthy monuments include the Roman amphitheater and the ruins of the Alcázar Almohade. Towering above the town, the Moorish-inspired structure was once the residence of King don Pedro the Cruel.

Carmona exudes the ambience of an Arab medina, its winding, cobbled streets offset by religious buildings and palaces. The old quarter was built on a hill and protected by Mudéjar walls. Its most beautiful gateway, Puerta de Sevilla, leads to a cluster of mansions (many built of brick and stone, a combination typical of Carmona), Mudéjar churches and picturesque squares. Considered the finest church in the city, Iglesia de Santa María la Mayor was erected in the 15th century on the site of a mosque whose patio still exists.

At the border with the province of Córdoba stands Écija, city of sun and towers. Nicknamed the frying pan of Andalusia, it is known for very hot weather. Once a Phoenician and then a Roman settlement, the city maintains an assemblage of mosaics from Roman times. Its greatest glory was achieved during the 17th and 18th centuries when it acquired the name, "City of the Towers." Eleven Baroque towers remain, many lavishly ornamented with azulejos. Most were rebuilt after the earthquake of 1755.

The palace of the Marqueses of Peñaflor ranks among the finest works of Andalusian Baroque. Highlighted by a pink marble doorway topped by twisted columns, the sumptuous façade is delineated by a wrought iron balcony. It houses an assortment of archaeological remains and Roman mosaics. The palace's museum showcases 18th century art and sculpture along with contemporary art and local traditional costumes.

Once a key Roman garrison town, nearby Osuna is an appealing enclave of white houses with symbolic rejas over every window. A ducal village, it rose to prominence in the 16th century, the period in which its most important edifices were built. The Renaissance Colegiata de Santa María has Baroque reredos and paintings by José de Ribera; it contains the tombs of the Dukes of Osuna.

Accommodations
Hospedería Santa María has 1 single and 9 double rooms, all with private bath. Both men and women are welcome.

Monasterio de la Purísima Concepción

Amenities
Towels and linens are supplied.

Meals
Meals are offered only to guests on spiritual retreats.

Cost of lodging
To be determined when reservations are made.

Products of the institution
The nuns are renowned for their almond and honey pastries.

Special rules
Curfew at 11:30 pm.

Directions
By car: From Seville take A92 east to exit 49 (Marchena exit) and proceed north on A364 to Marchena (approximately 8 kms). Follow signs to the monastery.

By train: Get off in Seville and take the local bus to Marchena.

Contact
Sor Magdalena or Sor Inmaculada (they speak English)
Monasterio de la Purísima Concepción
Calle Palacio Ducal, 9
41620 Marchena (Seville), Spain
Tel/Fax: 95/4843983

ARAGÓN

MONASTERIO DE SAN ESTEBAN Y SAN BRUNO
Dominican Nuns

Monasterio de San Esteban y San Bruno

The monastery resides on the outskirts of Albarracín, considered one of the most beautiful villages of Spain. "The village, the landscape, the view... everything is so beautiful that it has been recognized as a UNESCO monument of worldwide interest," said one of the sisters.

Founded in 1621 by a group of nuns from Daroca, the order has inhabited the monastery without interruption despite the turbulence of the 19th century. Since the nuns live in seclusion, the monastery cannot be visited, however, the church is open to guests. A Baroque structure, it contains a single nave with five altars. The 17th century retablo of the main altar displays paintings representing Saints Bruno and Esteban, Teresa de Ávila, Dominque and Catherine from Siena. Four of the altars are: Virgen de la Saleta (1872), Santo Domingo en Soriano (1657), Virgen del Rosario (18th century) and Virgen del Pilar (17th century). A niche along the right-hand side houses the fifth, the altar of San José, as well as a mannerist retablo of the 17th century.

In Visigothic times, Albarracín was known as Santa María de Oriente. Founded in the first period of the Muslim conquest, it became the capital of a petty kingdom before falling to the Almoravids. It remained as such until the 14th century when it was incorporated into Aragón. Now protected as a national monument, the town is a jumble of cobbled lanes and walls that preserve a decidedly medieval atmosphere and style.

A dramatic cliff above the Río Guadalaviar provides the ideal setting for the town's cluster of red brick buildings, many enhanced by verdant gardens. A number of half-timbered buildings have projecting balconies that lean at precarious angles and create an altogether alluring sight. The 16th century Renaissance church has a fine collection of Flemish tapestries.

There is a legend with a romantic flavor concerning the town's Torre de Doña Blanca. The ghost of a beautiful princess is said to appear in the tower every full moon at midnight. The princess is dressed in white and comes to bathe in the Guadalaviar River. According to the tale, the young woman was in love with a Jewish man but their love was forbidden and she died from longing.

In the mountains above town is the small summer resort of Bronchales. A ceramics factory of *terra sigillata hispanica* dating from the second century before Christ was discovered in its vicinity.

Monasterio de San Esteban y San Bruno

Monasterio de San Esteban y San Bruno

Orihuela del Tremedal is another mountain village in a milieu of pine forests. It conserves an 18th century parish church and many homes embellished with Renaissance grills and wrought ironwork. The entire region is a landscape of meadows, canyons, woodlands, prehistoric caves and sparkling water oases.

Teruel, the provincial capital, is approximately thirty-six miles southeast of the monastery. Of Iberian origin, it later became a Moorish stronghold. Despite the reconquest, the Moors maintained a mosque until the early part of the 16th century. Teruel also had a large Jewish community which lived in peaceful coexistence with both the Christians and Moors.

Sprawled on a hill and beset by gorges, the silhouette of the city is clearly marked by its Mudéjar architecture and a gracefulness that reflects Hispano-Muslim style. The Teruel *Moriscos*, (baptized Moors), enriched the cityscape with beautiful Mudéjar buildings.

The old quarter is home to the wedge-shaped Plaza del Torico and is near the five remaining Mudéjar towers. The 12th century church of San Salvador is an ornate, striking Mudéjar monument, its tower adorned with intricately patterned brickwork, checkered tile insets and a crenelated top. Representing one of the most typical pictures of Teruel, the tower stands at the end of a narrow street and has an arch with cross vaulting through which one can walk. Another fine specimen of Mudéjar architecture, the church of San Martín dates to the 12th century and is accented by multi-patterned brickwork studded with blue and green ceramics. According to legend, the last two towers built in Teruel were constructed by rival builders who wanted to marry the same girl. Omar and Abdala built the towers in a very short time and took care to hide their work from Zoraida, the girl they were pursuing. When the scaffolding was removed, it was discovered that both were equally grand but Omar's, the tower of San Martín, was leaning.

The Plaza de Carlos Castell is the heart of town and home to the Fuente del Torico and the Catedral de Teruel, a landmark structure distinguished by a bell tower with glazed bricks and green and black azulejos. Its interior has a coffered ceiling with scenes of contemporary and court life. The carpentry and assembly of wooden coffered ceilings was a specialty of Mudéjar artists.

The cathedral shelters the tombs of the "Lovers of Teruel," star-crossed romantics immortalized by several Spanish poets. Legend holds that in the 13th century, Diego Garcia de Marchilla wanted to marry Isabella de Segura but could not because her father preferred to find a rich husband for his daughter. Although Diego eventually made his fortune, as fate would have it, when he returned to claim his beloved, it was on the very day she married another. Diego died of a broken heart;

"Lovers of Teruel"

Isabella died the very next day. The lovers lie in a chapel attached to the church. The site has become a popular place for newlyweds to visit. Every February 14th, a festival takes place in honor of the ill-fated pair.

Accommodations
12 beds in 1 apartment with 4 bedrooms, private bath and kitchen plus 3 double and 2 single rooms with shared bath (all rooms have private sink). Both men and women are welcome.

Amenities
Towels and linens are supplied.

Meals

Meals are not provided with the lodging. Guests staying in the apartment may use the kitchen or dine in nearby restaurants.

Cost of lodging

Provisional cost: $24.00 per room/per night. Price of the apartment will be arranged upon arrival.

Products of the institution

The nuns embroider upon request.

Directions

By car: From Teruel take route 234 North. After about 15 kms, turn left following the signs to Albarracín.

By train/bus: Get off at Teruel. There is a daily bus to Albarracín leaving at 3:30 pm.

Contact

Madre Hospedera
Monasterio de San Esteban y San Bruno
Camino del Cristo, 15
44100 Albarracín (Teruel), Spain
Tel/ Fax: 978/710007

Monastery detail

MONASTERIO DE SANTA MARÍA DE CASBAS
Cistercian Nuns

Monasterio de Santa María de Casbas

The monastery is in Casbas de Huesca, a small village at the foot of the Sierra de Guara. "The area of the Sierra is beautiful and many people come here for excursions. They especially enjoy the river which is an hour walk from us. The setting is particularly pretty and so peaceful," said one of the sisters. The complex encompasses a Romanesque church; the monastery houses a Gothic cloister.

Monasterio de Santa María de Casbas was founded in 1173 by Doña Oria who originally wanted to turn the place into a mausoleum for her family. When her husband died, she retreated into the monastery and became a nun. The surrounding area is called *Zona de Palacio* and marks the place where Doña Oria once lived.

"We host all kinds of guests, whether they seek a spiritual retreat, a yoga workshop or a pilgrimage. We prefer not to make distinctions since everyone who comes is searching for something special," the sister added. In addition to managing the guest houses, the nuns make and sell homemade pastries and jams.

Nearby Huesca, capital of Alto Aragón, is situated at the foot of the steepest part of the central Pyrenees. Delineated by fir, beech and hazel woodlands, glacial lakes, green meadows and evocative castle ruins, the scenery is backdropped by lofty mountains. Known to the Romans as Osca and to the Moors as Washka, the city was founded in the 1st century BC and was a Moorish stronghold until the 8th century. In 1096, it was captured by Peter of Aragón and remained the region's capital until 1118.

A typical Pyrenean town, it sprawls on the slopes of a hill above the Río Isuela and boasts a splendid Gothic cathedral highlighted by a Mudéjar-style wooden gallery and octagonal tower. Work on the cathedral began at the end of the 13th century during the reign of Jaime I. The door in the main façade is flanked by fourteen life-sized statues. The interior is almost square in design with three naves, a transept, five chapels in the shape of an apse and a rose window in the apex of the arch. The church has an alabaster retablo by Damián Forment, master sculptor.

The Renaissance *Ayuntamiento* (town hall) is an Aragónese gem offset by graceful gable ends. It displays *La Campana de Huesca*, a 19th century painting depicting the town's most memorable and grisly event. Known as the *Bell of Huesca*, it shows the beheading of a group of rebellious nobles in the 12th century by King Ramiro II.

Huesca's oldest church, Iglesia de San Pedro El Viejo, was built on the remains of a Benedictine abbey. King Ramiro II and his brother are buried within. An elegant 12th century Romanesque structure, it has a remarkable cloister with exquisitely carved capitals.

A short distance east of town is the village of Alquézar. Imbued with Moorish origins, it lays claim to a spectacular setting which includes a well-preserved 12th century castle and 16th century collegiate church. The church crowns a hill rising above the unusual rock formations of the canyon of the Río Vero. The ruined walls were part of the original alcázar and the root of the village's name.

The Castle at Monzón, 42 miles from Huesca, has an unmistakable appearance. The complex which dates from the 10th and the 12th centuries stands on a rugged base above the small village of Monzón. Several massive, bare walls follow each other in picturesque rows, encircling the ascending slope on the way to the fortress. The keep is of Arab provenance while the church is Romanesque. The large towers exhibit Arab and Gothic features. Portions of the interior were restored in simple Renaissance style. The chapel is a two-story design with a high vault; the ashlars are engraved with symbols.

Beginning in the 12th century, the castle became the property of the Knights Templars, a brotherhood of monks turned soldiers. The power of the group grew and in the 14th century, Spain outlawed the order. The nights refused to disband and a siege began. It took several months for the king's army to regain control.

Accommodations

There are 2 types:

1) Inside the monastery: 28 bedrooms including single, double and triple rooms (some rooms have up to 8 beds). Baths are shared.

2) Outside the monastery: There is a hostel for large groups with 28 beds in large dorms. Baths are shared.

Both men and women are welcome.

Amenities

Towels and linens supplied. Meeting room.

Meals

Breakfast, lunch and dinner are provided with the lodging.

Cost of lodging

Voluntary contribution.

Products of the institution

The nuns produce a large variety of pastries. The most typical are *suspiros*, a meringue-type confection cooked in the oven for five hours. The nuns also produce jam. All products are sold in a small shop on the monastery grounds.

Special rules

Guests are provided with keys. Maximum stay 8/10 days.

Directions

By car: From Huesca or Lérida take route 240 and exit heading north at Angues. Follow signs to Casbas de Huesca.

By train/bus: Get off at Huesca and take the local bus to Casbas. There is one in the morning and one late afternoon. Or take the bus to Angues; there are several during the day. Once in Angues, call the monastery and they'll arrange transportation.

Contact

Madre Hospedera Angelina
Monasterio de Santa María de Casbas
22142 Casbas de Huesca (Aragón), Spain
Tel: 974/260396
Fax: 974/260537
Email: casbas@ran.es

Monasterio de Nuestra Señora del Olivar
Padres Mercedarios

Surrounded by woodlands, the monastery occupies an elevated position in a valley near El Olivar River. Following the Miracle of the Virgin

Monasterio de Nuestra Señora del Olivar

of the Olive Grove, the first building was erected at the beginning of the 13th century. According to tradition, a shepherd named Pedro Nobés witnessed a burning olive tree with an image of Mary inside the fire. Upon hearing of the vision, Don Gil, the nobleman he worked for, built a small hermitage and invited the Order of Mercy to take up residence and become guardians of the image. By the 14th century, the first monastery was built to the west of the original hermitage. All that remains at the original site is the round well of the central patio.

The existing monastery was built between 1627 and 1632 under the direction of Father Juan Cebrián of the Order of Mercy. Almost square in shape, the cloister joins the south wall of the church. The two-story structure is enhanced with a small central patio. The lower cloister has four spacious wings formed by the four sides of the building. The tall ceilings are lavishly decorated with cannon vaults supported by Roman arches and twenty cross-shaped pillars. The inner vault of each wing is ornamented by single bands and plaster molding. The outer vault is embellished with rosettas and geometric figures. There is a cupola at each end of the four corners that seems to anchor the soaring vaults to the floor.

The lower cloister is a place of harmony, pure lines and aesthetic pleasure. It leads to various areas of the monastery: the doorway and entrance hall; a grand stairway to the upper cloister; the *Sala Capitular* (conference room) and the old library. The coat of arms of Archbishop Juan Cebrián is displayed over the main door of the Sala. The *De Profundis* room is on one side, so called because it was where the religious recited the 129th Psalm for their deceased brethren before entering the adjoining refectory.

Brilliant white plaster walls define the upper cloister where hallways lead to the guest rooms and to the rooms of the monastic order. The ceiling is a series of beautifully curved lines with multiple barrel vaults separated by wooden beams. The  uneven stone-floored patio is softly illuminated by an ochre-toned light that streams through twelve sets of windows. The west corridor leads to the private chapel; the north corridor is the old doorway to the choir of the church.

The old-world town of Alcañiz is not far from the monastery. Situated on the Río Guadalope, the town is enclosed by hills. Home to the 12th century Castel de los Calatravos, the cloister, chapel and keep are all that remain from the original construction. The chapel contains the tomb of master artist Damián Forment. The keep and great hall are ornamented with 14th century frescoes, most depicting scenes of chivalry. The castle has been restored and is now a parador.

The heart of town is the Plaza de España, site of the *Ayuntamiento* (town hall) whose Renaissance façade incorporates the town's coat of arms. The elaborate 15th century *Lonja* (commodities exchange) is characterized by lacy Gothic arches. Not far from the square is the 18th century Santa María la Mayor with a Baroque portal and Gothic tower. Its interior is spotlighted by a grand high altar and domed chapels.

The monastery is close to a region called El Maestrazgo, a milieu of high mountains, deep gorges and stark countryside. Villages and hamlets are tucked here and there throughout the landscape. Beceite is typically Aragónese. Peñarroya de Tastavins is known as the Albarracín of Lower Aragón because of its beauty. Rubie los de Mora is completely girdled by a wall, its stone and timber houses underscored by coats of arms. Medieval Mora de Rubielos claims a 12th century Gothic collegiate church, its chapels adorned with azulejos.

Accommodations
The guest quarters were built during the reconstruction of the monastery. There are 38 rooms with private baths. Women, men, families and groups are welcome. For those who prefer camping, there is a well-equipped campsite.

Amenities
Towels and linens are supplied. There is a swimming pool and soccer field.

Meals
All meals are included with the lodging.

Cost of lodging
$23.00 per person, includes full board.

Directions
By car: From Zaragoza take route N232 south towards Alcañiz to route N211 west to Gargallo. From there follow the directions to Estercuel (10 kms) and then to the monastery (less than 2 kms).
By train: Get off in Alcañiz and take the local bus to Estercuel. Phone the monastery from Estercuel to arrange transportation.

Contact
Padre Hospedero
Monasterio de Nuestra Señora del Olivar
44558 Estercuel (Teruel), Spain
Tel: 978/752300
Fax: 978/727009
e.mail: elolivar@arrakis.es
website: http://www.arrakis.es/~elolivar

MONASTERIO DE SANTA CRUZ

Benedictine Nuns

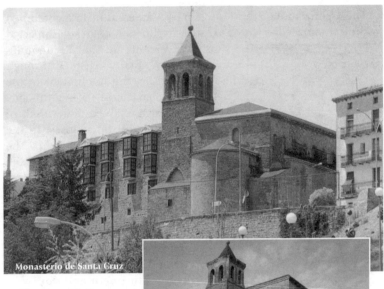

Monasterio de Santa Cruz

The Benedictine community inhabiting the monastery is among the oldest in Spain. It was established in Santa Cruz de la Seró in the 10th century and transferred to Jaca in 1555. The monastery is an active institution. The nuns manage a kindergarten and boarding school for girls during the winter; in summer, they provide a residence for women.

The structure of the monastery is an unusual one partly built on the walls of the city. The church is Romanesque in style and contains a sarcophagus of the Infanta, daughter of King Ramiro I.

Located approximately eighteen miles from France, the origins of Jaca date to the 2nd century AD. In the 8th century, the town withstood invasion by the Moors, an act of bravery honored every year in a popular festival. In 1035, Jaca became the first capital of the Kingdom of Aragón.

The architecture of the 11th century Cathedral of Jaca combined technical knowledge with a creative freshness that greatly impacted 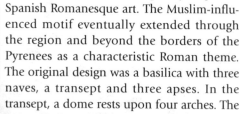 Spanish Romanesque art. The Muslim-influenced motif eventually extended through the region and beyond the borders of the Pyrenees as a characteristic Roman theme. The original design was a basilica with three naves, a transept and three apses. In the transept, a dome rests upon four arches. The rolled modillions and cornices in the dome exemplify the highly novel design elements that came to symbolize Spanish Romanesque style.

Although the structure has undergone many renovations, traces of its underlying majesty are visible on the restored south porch and doorway. They are represented by carvings depicting biblical scenes of Abraham's sacrifice and King David playing his harp. Romanesque and Gothic frescoes as well as sculptures rescued from abandoned churches are preserved within the cloisters.

The Parque Nacional de Ordesa lies just east of Jaca. A dramatically rugged landscape of woodlands, waterfalls, glacial canyons and limestone cliffs and gorges, it stretches over 37,000 acres in the very heart of the Pyrenees. The environs include the Pineta Cirque with its hanging glaciers and the deep karst gorges of Anisclo and Escuain. Torla, a small stone village at the gateway to the park, boasts an exceptional setting; its buildings are backdropped by the snow-covered slopes of Mondarruego.

Loarre Castle

South of Jaca, the Church of the Loarre Castle was clearly influenced by the Cathedral of Jaca. Constructed on a mountain slope, a crypt overcomes the difference in levels. The church has a single nave, its apse underscored by blocked arcading and seven windows. The structure forms part of the Loarre Castle-Abbey, the oldest and perhaps most remarkable citadel in Spain. It was erected on the site of an Iberian fortress and built in the purest Romanesque style combining military and religious concepts.

Sitting in the middle of the Sierra de Gratal, the castle was designed to blend with and be concealed by the rocky outcrop on which it was built. Depending on the time of day and the light, the complex can seemingly disappear from sight. From its lofty perch, views of the great plain of Aragón are visible in every direction.

Built by Sancho Ramírez, a noble king of Navarra, the fortress has been restored to its former glory. The civil halls, cells and soldiers' quarters blend into each other and provide insight into the way the monks, nobles and soldiers lived together at that time. The castle rooms are not large, excepting the famous *Torre de la Reina* (Queen's Tower). Rectangular in design, it has an interesting gallery of windows including one with Byzantine capitals and double arches. The tower is complemented by Mozarabic adornments and reliefs. The Romanesque chapel is reached by a monumental staircase ornamented with alabaster windows.

Pathways and steep stairs wind around the castle's towers, keep and dungeons. The walk that surrounds the keep is delineated by statues representing Spanish medieval sculpture including the Virgin and the Savior, symbols of the apostles and a group of angels.

Accommodations
The hospedería is open during July and August; exact opening and closing dates vary each year. Since lodging dates are limited, reservations must be made well in advance. Only women are permitted. 65 beds in single and double rooms, most with private bath.

Amenities
Towels and linens are provided.

Meals
All meals are included with the lodging.

Cost of lodging
Provisional cost only, $30.00 per person, all meals included.

Special Rules
Curfew at 10:30 pm.

Directions
By car: From Pamplona take route 240 to Jaca.
By train: Get off in Jaca and walk to the monastery.

Contact
Encargada de la hospedería
Monasterio de Santa Cruz
Mayor, 52
22700 Jaca (Huesca), Spain
Tel: 974/360592

MONASTERIO NUESTRA SEÑORA DE MONLORA
Hermandad de Nuestra Señora de Monlora

Enveloped by a verdant woodland, the monastery occupies a mountaintop location. Founded at the end of the 17th century by the Benedictine Order on the site of the Shrine of Nuestra Señora de Monlora, it is about two miles from the small village of Luna.

Monasterio Nuestra Señora de Monlora

A Gothic hermitage is all that endures of the very first settlement. The remainder of the complex is Baroque in style. The institution is presently in transition; the monks left in October 1999 and temporarily entrusted the monastery to the brotherhood of Our Lady of Monlora.

Between the monastery and Zaragoza is the Cartuja de Aula Dei, home to Goya murals. In 1774, thanks to his friendship with the then Prior Pedro Salcedo, Goya painted fourteen scenes of the Virgin Mary for a Spanish church used by sequestered Carthusian monks. Until recently only three women, one a Spanish princess, had seen the paintings. In November 1998, Queen Sofia led a contingent of fifty women on an unprece-dented visit to see the murals. To protect the priva-cy of the monks, they were able to enter the church through a tunnel underneath the monastery and emerged in a sin-gle-nave church where the Goyas are displayed.

Goya mural

Guided tours are available by prior appointment only. The demand is so enormous that arrangements for the tour must be made years in advance. Tel: (34) 976-714-934, Fax: (34) 976-714-808. Francisco de Goya served his apprenticeship and painted his first works in Zaragoza. His paintings are exhibited in the Basilica of Nuestra Señora del Pilar and the Provincial Museum of Fine Arts.

Many of the cities, towns and villages of Aragón lay claim to the most characteristic forms of Mudéjar art. Throughout the countryside, numerous Christian churches were built by the Mudéjars or Moriscos as they came to be known when they were forcibly converted to Christianity. Between the 12th and 16th centuries, extensive Mudéjar communities existed and bequeathed a legacy of bricklaying and deco-rative arts. The brick bell-towers, often festooned with glazed ceramic tiles, are peculiar to the region.

At one time, nearby Zaragoza claimed more than fifty brick towers. Positioned along the Ebro River, the town perpetuates a rich historical and artistic heritage, the result of more than two thousand years of existence. Iberians, Romans, Moors, Jews and Christians all left their mark. Zaragoza, the region's capital, is one of the great monumental cities of Spain and home to the Baroque Basilica of Nuestra Señora del Pilar, a place of pillars and spires sited on the Plaza del Pilar.

Basilica del Pilar

During the 11th century, at the time of the *taifas*, or petty kingdoms, La Aljafería was built. An extraordinary example of Moorish architecture, the palatial retreat was defended by twenty-seven battlemented keeps. Its capitals and decorative motifs are outstanding, particularly those of the mihrab and Hall of Marble. In the 15th century, the palace underwent repairs and enlargements which included coffered ceilings.

La Aljafería

Zaragoza is also home to the churches of San Pedro and San Pablo, distinguished by square-shaped bell towers with rhomboid adornments. Octagonal in shape and horizontally divided by decorative bands, the towers are classic representations of this type of construction.

Accommodations

15 single and 3 double rooms. All rooms have a sink; bathrooms are shared. Both men and women are welcome. The monastery is open year round.

Amenities
Towels and linens are supplied and a laundry service is available. There are two dining rooms that can be used as meeting rooms and a TV room.

Meals
Breakfast is included with the lodging. Other meals can be taken at a nearby restaurant.

Cost of lodging
To be determined.

Products of the institution
The monks prepare and sell assorted pastries.

Directions
By car: From Zaragoza or Huesca take route N330-E7 which connects the two cities. Get off at the exit to Monasterio de Monlora.
By train/bus: Get off at Zaragoza and take a bus to Luna. Once in Luna call the monastery and they will arrange transportation.

Contact
Anyone who answers the phone
Monasterio Nuestra Señora de Monlora
50610 Luna (Zaragoza), Spain
Tel: 976/689305

CONVENTO DE NUESTRA SEÑORA DE VALENTUNAÑA

Augustinian Friars

Convento de Nuestra Señora de Valentunaña

The monastery lies on the outskirts of Sos del Rey Católico, a medieval town and birthplace of Ferdinand of Aragón (hence the town's royal name). Also known as *el Rey Católico*, the Catholic King, Ferdinand unified Spain by marrying Isabel of Castilla.

According to legend, the story of the shrine began in the 13th century when the image of Mary appeared upon an oak tree. Since the belief of the local people was not strong enough, the Virgin left an additional sign of her presence by making a miraculous spring appear. The spring is still known as the *Fuente de la Virgen*, Spring of the Virgin. At that time, the shrine constituted only a hermitage, the Casa de la Virgin. The sanctuary and convent were added at a later date by Carmelite monks. The complex suffered during the uncertainty of the 19th century when the monks were forced to leave. After their second departure in 1835, they never returned. The convent was abandoned for decades. In 1902, it was sold to the Augustinian Order which has remained in residence ever since.

Convento de Nuestra Señora de Valentunaña

The stone exterior of the 18th century church and convent are sober affairs. The interior of the church is enriched with nine Baroque retablos. The most remarkable one is above the main altar. There are two lateral retablos attributed to Francisco Pejon, a famous local sculptor.

Solemn celebrations of the Virgin of Valentunaña take place on September 8th and on the Sunday and Monday of Pentecost. At that time, the entire village celebrates their patroness during the Fiesta del Convento.

Sos del Rey Católico is one of the *Cinco Villas* (five villages) recognized by Felipe V for their loyalty during the War of the Spanish Succession. The village is surrounded by imposing walls built with seven entryways; its houses are accented by Romanesque and Gothic windows. Palacio de Sada, the king's birthplace, is on a small square in the midst of narrow, cobbled lanes. An elegant stone mansion with a lovely inner courtyard, the palace harbors artwork and artifacts related to the king.

The plain of las Cinco Villas is crossed by the mountain ranges of Uncastillo, Sos, Luesia and Biel. In Roman times, it was considered the granary of the region because of the abun-

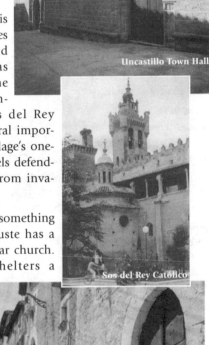

Uncastillo Town Hall

Sos del Rey Católico

dance of cereal crops. Sos del Rey Católico was its capital. Several important fortresses attest to the village's one-time prominence. These citadels defended the Kingdom of Aragón from invasions of the Navarrese.

Each of the Cinco Villas has something special to recommend it. Tauste has a splendid 13th century Mudéjar church. Ejea de los Caballeros shelters a Romanesque church. In Sádaba, there is a 16th century church built in Aragónese-Gothic style. Uncastillo is a picturesque hodge-podge of steep streets and alleys, its homes marked with shield-shaped

Sos del Rey Católico

surfaces containing coats of arms. The arcaded Plaza del Campo is the heart of town and home to the Romanesque Santa María la Mayor.

Accommodations

34 single and double rooms with private bath. Both men and women are welcome. Closed at Christmas. During the month of July, the hospedería is usually booked.

Amenities

Towels and linens are supplied.

Meals

All meals can be supplied on request.

Cost of lodging

Provisional: $24.00 per person with full pension.

Special rules

Punctuality at meals.

Directions

By car: From Pamplona take N240 south and exit at A127 following the signs to Sanguesa and then to Sos del Rey Católico. Once in Sos, follow the signs to the Sanctuary of Nuestra Señora de Valentunaña.

By train: Getting to Sos by public transportation is not easy. There is only one bus from Zaragoza, leaving at 7:00 am. It is best to get off at Pamplona and take a bus to Sanguesa and a taxi to Sos.

Contact

Padre Prior
Convento de Nuestra Señora de Valentunaña
50680 Sos del Rey Católico (Zaragoza), Spain
Tel/Fax: 948/888072
Email: oarsos@teleline.es

ASTURIAS

SANTUARIO DEL ACEBO
Order Property of the Parish of Cangas de Narcea

Santuario del Acebo

In a milieu of mountains near the Parque Natural de Somiedo, the Santuario of Acebo occupies a lofty position in Cangas del Narcea, the largest town in southwest Asturias. The history of the shrine began in medieval times when a small chapel dedicated to the Virgin was erected. According to legend, a paralytic woman suddenly started to walk. The miraculous event led to the construction of a larger church completed in 1590. The church remains visible today. "It is one of the most important sites of devotion in the entire region," said the priest in charge of the shrine.

The church and main retablo are Baroque. The venerated image of Mary in the first chapel is Romanesque in design. The hospedería is now managed by lay personnel.

Nearby Luarca is a little village along Spain's northern coast. It lies on both banks of the Río Negro and is spanned by several bridges. The core of the town is filled with 18th and 19th century houses separated from the sea by a hill. A quaint cemetery and church are quartered on a clifftop headland overlooking the town. East of Luarca is Cabo Vidio and wonderful views of the sea and Cabo de Peñas.

Luarca

This part of Asturias is near the land of the cowherders, a group of people who centuries ago immigrated from northern Italy. Once each year a cowherder wedding is held according to the rituals of the past. Centuries-old dances are performed to the beat of a square tambourine and *payetchas* (a pan with a long handle that is hit with a key).

Tineo, another nearby town, boasts a number of medieval churches and a 13th century parish church. A short distance from Tineo is the hamlet of Llamas del Mouro, home to potters of Celto-Iberian ancestry. The artisans are known for their shiny black ceramic jugs and bowls. As they have for centuries, the potters fire the pieces in circular ovens buried in the earth.

Accommodations
A total of 14 single, double and triple rooms, each with private bath. Both men and women are welcome.

Amenities
Towels and linens are supplied.

Meals
All meals can be supplied with the lodging in the restaurant annexed to the hospedería.

Cost of lodging
Provisional cost per double room: $22.00, meals excluded. Open year round. During the winter, the hospedería hosts only groups of 10 or more.

Directions

By car: From Oviedo take N634 west until La Espina and turn left on AS15 (also marked as C630). Follow the signs to Cangas del Narcea. Once there follow the signs to the Santuario del Acebo.

By train: Get off at Oviedo and take a bus to Cangas de Narcea. From there take a taxi to the santuario (there is no public transportation).

Contact

Anyone who answers the phone
Santuario del Acebo
33800 Cangas de Narcea (Asturias), Spain
Tel: 98/5810466

CASA DE EJERCICIOS DIOCESANA
Esclavas del Corazón de María

Sanctuary of Covadonga

Built in 1954 and operated by a community of nuns, the casa is annexed to the legendary Sanctuary of Covadonga, one of the most revered shrines in Spain. "The casa is a beautiful building; people say it looks like a parador," said one of the sisters. Reached via a beautiful road through a mountain valley, Covadonga is regarded as the birthplace of Spain. It is known for its glacial lakes and the Virgin's Cave.

The sanctuary was built after a miracle which helped King Pelayo defeat the Arabs in 722. According to legend, a small group of soldiers led by Pelayo, a Visigothic nobleman, faced the Arabs armed only with stones. The Moorish army shot arrows at the Christian soldiers but the arrows turned back towards the Moors and in doing so, allowed Pelayo to win. The Christian armies, strengthened by the victory, officially began the reconquest of the Spanish peninsula and Pelayo became king of Asturias. A statue of the warrior with the Asturian cross above his head stands before the classically beautiful Neo-Romanesque basilica on the site of his victory.

Cave of the Virgin

Not far from the casa is Santa Cueva. An ancient cave, the *Santina*, (statue of the Virgin), was worshipped here before construction of the shrine. Reached through a tunnel, the 8th century cave lies high up on the rock face and overlooks a pool and waterfall. The remains of King Pelayo, his wife and sister are believed to reside in the tiny chapel.

Picos de Europa

The casa and shrine are situated in a spectacularly beautiful region of Spain, the Parque Nacional of the Picos de Europa. Tradition holds that this mountain chain was named by sailors who, when seeing the peaks from a distance, knew they were close to home.

The park straddles three regions: Asturias, Cantabria and Castilla - León and is the largest national park in Europe. The Picos is a wild and impressive range of lofty mountains, perpetual snow, lakes and narrow passes. One of the highest summits is Naranjo de Bulnes; the heart of the massif soars to over 8,000'. Within the parkland, Fuente Dé Cable Car whisks visitors to a rocky plateau and outstanding views of the pinnacles and valleys. The Cares River has cut a deep gorge in the heart of the Picos. A footpath follows the gorge on a scenic journey through tunnels and over high bridges offering vistas of gorges and precipices, green valleys and lush meadows. Stark, limestone cliffs rise abruptly over dense woodlands of beech, oak and birch. The cows and goats that graze in the pasturelands produce the famous Cabrales blue cheese. It is the chamois, however, that is the park's most representative animal.

Heading to the coast is the harbor town of Llanes, where traces of the ancient walls can still be seen. The old part of town is occupied by the Plaza del Cristo Rey, locale of the 13th century Iglesia de Santa María. Of architectural interest, the portal is defined by interlaced arcading and offset by a 16th century Flemish altarpiece. The town also shelters a pretty little beach popular with vacationers.

The small town of Cangas de Onís is close to Covadonga. More than 2,000 years ago Celts inhabited the area. A gateway to the Picos de

Europa, Cangas de Onís became the first capital of the Asturian kings. At the beginning of the reconquest, it served as the first Spanish court. An elegant medieval arched bridge and the 15th century Ermita de la Santa Cruz are monumental highlights. The church's tiny chapel displays an engraved Bronze Age dolmen - a Neolithic tomb con-

Medieval arched bridge

sisting of a large, flat stone laid across upright stones with carved drawings. About three miles east of town is the Cueva del Buxu, a cave containing rare Paleolithic paintings and engravings.

Situated in the Valle de Liébana, riverside Potes is underscored by balconied houses. Its main square reveals the 15th century Torre del Infatado, now the Town Hall.

Accommodations
50 beds in 30 single and double rooms with private bath (rooms have been recently renovated). Both men and women are welcome.

Amenities
Towels and linens are supplied. Meeting rooms are available for guest use.

Meals
All meals can be supplied on request (full pension, half pension or breakfast only).

Cost of lodging
$30.00 per night, full pension.

Special rules
Curfew at 11:00 pm. Open year round.

Directions
By car: From Oviedo take route E70 to Arriondas, exit and follow the signs to Covadonga.
By train: Get off at Oviedo and take a bus to Covadonga.

Contact
Anyone who answers the phone
Casa De Ejercicios Diocesana
33589 Covadonga (Asturias), Spain
Tel: 98/5846030

CASA DE ESPIRITUALIDAD SANTA MARÍA DEL ARAMO

Esclavas del Sagrado Corazón

In a tranquil site just outside the town of Oviedo, the Casa de Espiritualidad possesses a beautiful panorama of the Sierra del Aramo Mountains. "It is an enchanting spot. At this very moment, for example, I can see the mountains backdropped by a stunning blue sky dotted with white clouds," said the sister in charge of hospitality. "The truth is that people are always contented with their stay at our casa. The mountains near the house are laced with hiking trails and pleasant walks," she continued.

The casa was founded in 1984 by a group of nuns from Oviedo. It was built with the precise mission of hosting groups seeking spiritual retreats. When the house is not so occupied, the nuns are happy to host guests merely seeking a peaceful sojourn. "The casa has been recently enlarged and renovated and is particularly comfortable," she added.

Asturias stretches along a small section of the Cantabrian coastline between the Eo and Deva rivers. The inland ridges of the Cantabrian Mountains comprise its southernmost boundaries. These geographical characteristics and the rainy coastal climate have made Asturias a natural paradise filled with flora and fauna.

Basilica del Salvador

Enclosed by the foothills of the Cantabrian Mountains, Oviedo is the region's capital and is located more or less at its geographical center. The city is noted for its pre-Romanesque monuments and great cathedral, the Basilica del Salvador. Situated on the Plaza de Alfonso II, the cathedral dates to the 14th century and is considered one of the finest examples of Spanish Flamboyant Gothic, a design characterized by ornate tracery forms. The church is home to the tombs of Asturian kings and is distinguished by a high square tower with delicate stone lattice work. The oldest part of the church is the east end; the chapter house and cloister were begun in the 13th century. Worthy of special mention is the main retablo in the Capilla Mayor. Dating from 1511, it was produced by Giraldo de Bruselas and Juan de Balmeseda.

Visigothic culture and Asturian or Ramirense art (after King Ramiro) constitute a prelude to Romanesque style. In 1985, UNESCO declared several of the city's post-Visigothic, pre-Romanesque churches among the finest architecture produced in 9th century Christian Europe. Now protected as part of the "Patrimony of Humanity," the oldest and largest, San Julián de Los Prados, was built by Alfonso el Castro. A simple, solid design with three square apses, it is noted for frescoes that once covered the interior.

Many churches are scattered in the hills of Asturias including the picturesque Santa María de Naranco and San Miguel de Lillo. Halfway up the mountain on the slopes of the Sierra de Naranco, these pre-Romanesque structures offer excellent views. Both were built by Alfonso el Castro's successor, Ramiro I. Santa María's golden stone structure is supported by unusual flat buttresses and flanked by two porches. It has a barrel-vaulted hall on the main floor and arcaded galleries at either end. San Miguel was built on a more traditional cruciform design. Its interior is highlighted by typical Asturian twisted columns.

Santa María de Naranco

Throughout the region surrounding Oviedo, many noble palaces were built by the so-called *indianos* - people who made their fortunes in the New World.

Not far from Oviedo is Avilés, a large industrial town with a well-preserved historic center and two plazas: the arcaded Plaza España and the diminutive Plaza San Nicolás. The Iglesia of San Nicolás de Bari contains a 14th century chapel. The Iglesia de San Francisco is decorated with frescoes and marked by a Renaissance cloister. Two interesting sites are just north of town: a lovely beach at Salinas and an old lighthouse at the entrance to the river at San Juan de Nieva.

Casa de Espiritualidad Santa María del Aramo

Accommodations
48 beds in single and double rooms, each with private bath. Both men and women are welcome. Make reservations well in advance. The house is open from 8:00 am until 11:00 pm. Closed in September.

Amenities
Towels and linens are supplied.

Meals
All meals are supplied with the lodging.

Cost of lodging
To be arranged when reservations are made.

Directions
By car: Reach Oviedo and then ask for Santa María del Aramo (about 4 kms from town).
By train: Get off in Oviedo and take a taxi to the casa.

Contact
Engargada de la Casa or anyone who answers the phone
Casa de Espiritualidad Santa María del Aramo
Ctra. De Latores, 11
33193 Oviedo (Asturias), Spain
Tel: 985/254763 / Fax: 985/231796

Monasterio Santa María La Real de Valdediós
Cistercian Monks

Monasterio Santa María La Real de Valdediós

Lying in a secluded valley of Asturias, the monastery is a few miles from Villaviciosa and close to some of the most important sites of the province. "We have guests year round because the monastery is in a 'strategic' position for those who want to see places like Oviedo, Covadonga, Picos de Europa, Gijón and Cangas de Onís. In spite of our popularity, we still preserve a peaceful and remote atmosphere," the Padre Hospedero added.

The monastery has a royal foundation (hence the name Santa María La Real). Dating to the 13th century, it was inhabited by the Cistercian Order until 1836 when the monks were forced to leave by the laws of the *Desamortización*, the suppression of all monastic orders.

Following the arrival of the Cistercian and Benedictine orders and the increased importance of the Pilgrim's Way to Santiago de Compostela, the somewhat late Asturian Romanesque style began its development. The monastery is a fine example of that singular architecture. Other similar structures include the Monastery of San Salvador de Cornellana and the churches of San Antolín de Bedón and San Pedro de Villanueva.

Monasterio Santa María La Real de Valdediós

The monastery was remodeled many times during the 16th and 18th centuries. Only the church has preserved its original Cistercian simplicity. The cloisters, sacristy and the remainder of the rooms are Renaissance and Baroque in style. Except for a short period when it was occupied by the Seminary of the Diocesis of Oviedo, the monastery remained abandoned until 1992 when the Cistercian monks returned. In 1986, the complex was completely renovated thanks to the funds of the European Union and the Principality of Asturias.

Occupying a bucolic setting a few miles from the monastery is the pre-Romanesque church of San Salvador (9th century). Built as part of a palace complex for Alfonso III, its ceiling is adorned with vivid Asturian frescoes. The church, which adjoins the monastery, is 13th century Cistercian.

Monasterio Santa María La Real de Valdediós

The eastern section of the coast of Asturias is a place of beaches and isolated coves. Villaviciosa, considered the cider capital of Asturias, is an old-world port and fishing town amid a landscape of apple orchards and rolling hills. A graceful resort town, it is made all the more engaging by glass-fronted mansions. The Gothic Church of Santa María de la Oliva has a lavishly embellished doorway while the Romanesque San Juan de Amandi is renowned for its carved portal and capitals. Neighboring Mirador del Fito provides an incredible view of the Picos de Europa.

Nearby Gijón, or Xixón in Asturian dialect, is an historic city of pre-Roman origin. A busy port, industrial hub and the largest city in Asturias, it possesses one of the best harbors on the north coast. The original core of Gijón is the old fishing quarter of Cimadevilla, a warren of narrow lanes and houses overlooked by Monte Santa Catalina. From the top of the mountain, far-reaching views encompass Picos de Europa, Cabo de Peñas and Cabo de San Lorenzo.

The Plaza Mayor in the old town is porticoed on three sides and is the site of the Ayuntamiento and the Palacio de los Valdés. Relics of Roman baths dating from the 1st century AD were found in the cellars of the palace. Pueblo de Asturias, an open-air museum complete with a factory producing the popular *giatas* (Asturian bagpipes) is located in the new part of town. The museum also features typical Asturian buildings including farmhouses and *hórreos* (raised granaries). Unlike the hórreos in Galicia, these structures are built of wood and set on stone pillars.

When Rome came to Spain, a roadway was built, which after a time came to be called the *Vía de la Plata* (Silver Way). The route runs for hundreds of miles from Gijón to Seville. Rich in contrast and history, this scenic and cultural venue was used for the transportation of goods and troops. The Cantabric Sea is the starting point of the itinerary in Gijón. Known to the Romans as Gigia, Gijón is considered the capital of the Green Coast.

Ribadesella is a fishing town and seaside resort at the mouth of the Río Sella. Divided by a wide bridge which separates the old town from the new, it is composed of a quaint section of old streets and a long, protected beach. A short distance from the new town is Cueva de Tito Bustillo, a cave system with animal paintings between 15,000 and 20,000 years old. In addition to the paintings and engravings of horses and stags, there is a series of vast chambers with otherworldly stalactitic formations.

Accommodations

There are two types:

1) Hospedería: 8 doubles and 1 single with private bath. Both men and women are welcome. Open year round.

2) Inside the monastery: 12 singles with private bath. Only men seeking spiritual retreats are allowed. They are expected to participate in the daily life of the monastery.

Make arrangements well in advance. Busiest periods are Easter, Christmas and the summer months.

Amenities

Towels and linens are supplied. In the external hospedería, there are living areas that guests may use.

Meals

All meals are supplied.

Cost of lodging

Voluntary contribution.

Special rules

1) Outside the monastery: guests must be punctual at meals. Those not dining at the monastery are asked to communicate their dining requirements in advance. Curfew at 10:00 pm. Maximum stay 15 days.

2) Inside the monastery: guests must conform to the rules of the monks. Maximum stay 8 days.

Directions

By car: From Gijón take N632 to Villaviciosa. From there turn right following the signs to the monastery.

By train: Get off at Oviedo and take the Oviedo-Villaviciosa bus. There is a bus every 2 hours.

Contact

Padre Hospedero
Monasterio Santa María La Real de Valdediós
33312 Valdediós - Villaviciosa (Asturias), Spain
Tel/Fax: 98/5892324

BALEARIC ISLANDS
(BALEARES)

CASTILLO DE ALARÓ
Property of the Parish of Alaró

Castillo de Alaró

The Hermitage and Refugio of the Castillo de Alaró are quartered in a relatively inaccessible spot on the mountains above Alaró. "It is a natural terrace with the most spectacular view of all Mallorca, absolutely the best," said the man in charge of the refugio. Built in the 17th century, the interior preserves interesting reliefs and a reredos recounting the martyrdom of Cabrit y Bassa, two popular heroes who defended the kingdom of Mallorca from Aragónese incursions in the 18th century.

"It was like a natural fortress, with only one access," the innkeeper continued. The fortress is on a sheer promontory and provides a panoramic view as far as Palma to the south and a large part of the central plain to the east. The site was originally an Arab castle dating to the 8th century but only the walls remain. According to legend, the Moors who had conquered the islands in 798 sought shelter at the castle during the Christian reconquest in 1285, long after their compadres in the lowlands had surrendered. After a two-year siege, the defenders were driven out and their leaders slain.

The small church dedicated to Nuestra Madre de Deu is four hundred years old. The hospedería annexed to the hermitage was specifically conceived for mountaineers. In fact, the only way to reach the place is by walking three miles from the village of Alaró, a tiny town of sloping streets.

"We have visitors year round. From Monday through Friday, our guests are mainly foreigners. On the weekends, most visitors are Spaniards. Winter is our high season. During the summer, people prefer to stay near the beach," the innkeeper added.

The convents of Santo Domingo and San Francisco are Alaró's most notable buildings. The church of Santa María la Mayor is Gothic in origin although Baroque additions have altered its appearance.

Palma de Mallorca

The town of Palma de Mallorca is approximately 15 miles from Alaró. A picturesque, lively city, it is an important port and the cultural center of the islands. The Palma Cathedral or *Seo* as it is called by Mallorcans, is one of the most impressive buildings in Spain. A massive golden sandstone structure, it is poised high on the sea wall and offers stunning views of the bay. It appears to dominate the city, particularly at night when an incandescent light streams through its stained glass windows. Begun in the 13th century, the church has been reconstructed many times. Its interior is embellished with stained glass and rose windows. The largest rose window is in the apse and dates from the late 14th century. In the early 20th century, Antoni Gaudí remodeled the interior. The royal chapel contains the high altar over which Gaudí suspended a gigantic baldachin (a structure resembling a canopy) in the form of a crown of thorns. Beside the Seo stands Almudaina, the royal palace where the king and queen of Mallorca lived. The elaborate edifice was built on the remains of the Muslim alcázar.

Palma's medieval old town is a labyrinth of cool, cobbled lanes and shady boulevards. Possessing a noble aura, it is filled with sumptuous Gothic churches and grand Baroque palaces, most built in the 17th and 18th centuries.

The Moors once dominated the islands and their heritage is evident in the layout of the old town (the Muslim medina), the Almudaina Arch and the Baños Arabes. The 10th century baths feature elaborate arches, each topped by a different capital.

Almudaina Palace

Miró studio

The Parque del Mar displays a tile panel with a picture by Joan Miró. Palma is also home to the Fundació Pilar i Joan Miró. After 1941, Miró lived mainly in Mallorca. When he died, his wife converted his former studio and home into an art center. Designed by architect Rafael Moneo, it is known as the Alabaster Fortress and regarded as a unique example of modern architecture.

The Pueblo Español is a copy of the village of the same name in Barcelona. It replicates old buildings and famous monuments from throughout Spain. Many of the structures house artists' workshops.

Just outside the city center and overlooking the Bay of Palma is the Gothic Gallorgan Castell de Bellver. On a hill surrounded by pine trees, the castle dates to the 13th century and was once a royal stronghold. Built in a circular design, three towers form part of the main castle wall. The fourth, the keep, stands apart from the castle, isolated by a deep moat and linked by a high walkway. The tower is round and consists of five rooms reached via a winding staircase. Characterized by

Castell de Bellver

thick walls and tall, narrow windows, the fortress gates are protected by strong thresholds. The castle was built by Pere Salvá, the same master craftsman who designed the Almudaina, a superlative specimen of defensive architecture of the Gothic period.

Somewhat further afield, the town of Muro sits in a landscape of orchards. It retains graceful façades from old *payesas* (peasant farmers' houses) and a Gothic church. Muro is home to the Ethnological Museum of Mallorca which exhibits utensils from crafts that disappeared many years ago.

Close to the hermitage, Valldemossa is a mountain town built on the slopes of the Sierra de Tramuntana. A place of tree-lined streets and old stone buildings, it harbors the Cartuja de Valldemossa, an ancient Carthusian monastery. Originally established in 1399 on the site of a Moorish alcázar, the monastery was rebuilt in the 17th and 18th centuries. It is particularly well known because it is where Frederic Chopin and George Sand spent the winter of 1838-39 and where Chopin's piano, manuscripts and letters remain. Their rooms, the monastic church and former monks' cells are open to the public. The Church of la Cartuja contains a pharmacy offset by beautiful Mallorcan drug jars and tiled walls. The atmospheric and lavish Palace of King Sancho adjoins the monastery.

Nearby Alfábia was once the country residence of the Moorish Viziers. The elaborate 19th century gardens and late Baroque house represent a typical Mallorcan aristocratic estate and exude a distinctive Moorish sensibility. The gardens shelter date palms, bamboos and citrus trees. Although little remains of the original architecture, there is a Mudéjar inscription on the ceiling of the entrance hall and Hispano-Arabic fountains and pergola.

Accommodations
14 rooms containing from 2 to 10 beds. Baths are shared. Both men and women are welcome.

Amenities
Although linens can be supplied on request, it is recommended that guests provide their own sleeping bags. Towels are not supplied.

Meals
All meals are available in the restaurant.

Cost of lodging
$6.00 per person/per night with sleeping bag.
$8.00 per person/per night with linens.

Special rules
The restaurant closes at 11:00 pm. Open year round.

Directions
By car: From Palma de Mallorca take C713 north about 15 kms to the turnoff for Consell and then follow the signs to Consell and Alaró.
By train: From From Palma de Mallorca take the train to Consell and walk to Alaró.
Note: It is a 5 km walk to Castillo de Alaró from the town of Alaró.

Contact
Anyone who answers the phone
Castillo de Alaró
07340 Alaró (Mallorca, Baleares), Spain
Tel: 971/182112

SANTUARIO DE SAN SALVADOR
Property of the Bishopric of Mallorca

Santuario de San Salvador

The monastery sprawls atop a mountain above Felanitx, a small, rural town renowned for its church, Esglesia de Sant Miquel. Begun in the 13th century, it was rebuilt in the 16th and 17th centuries by the kings of Aragón. The town of Felanitx is also noted for its *Sobrasada de Porc negre*, (an exquisite sausage of black pork) and for Sant Joan Pelós, a fiesta held on June 24th. As part of the festivities, a man is dressed in sheepskins to represent John the Baptist.

Santuario de San Salvador

The sanctuary is reached via a road of incredible natural beauty. Its lofty position offers far-reaching views of the coast. An important pilgrimage center, the sanctuary was founded in 1348 on the site of a miracle. According to tradition, while attending his herd, a local shepherd had a vision of the Virgin. At first, only a small chapel was built. At a later date, a larger church and hermitage were erected and inhabited by hermits of Saint Paul and Saint Anthony, an order found only on Mallorca. The hermits lived in the sanctuary until December 1992 when advancing age caused them to leave. Two families now care for the church, guest house and restaurant.

The church is the third one erected on the site. It conserves the original statue of the Virgin, various statues of saints and a valuable retablo. The remaining buildings of the complex do not contain works of art but according to the caretaker, "Everyone likes the view and the site, both foreigners and Spaniards. Our area is not too touristy and has fine views of almost the entire island." Approximately 4 miles from Felanitx is the Castell de Santueri. Founded by the Moors, it was rebuilt in the 14th century by the kings of Aragón.

The monastery is a short distance from the east coast of Mallorca. This section of the island has experienced a tremendous amount of tourism thereby sacrificing some of its pristine beauty. However, many fine stretches of beach and several towns are still worth visiting.

An interesting route along the coast begins in Cala Figuera, a fishing village approximately 12 miles southeast of Felanitx. Heading north along the coast is Cala Mondragó, home to one of the area's prettiest beaches. Set in a milieu of rocky outcrops, the town is fringed with pine trees.

Portocristo, another coastal town, possesses a small sandy beach and boat harbor and is close to *Coves del Drac* (Caves of the Dragon). The caves consist of four vast chambers that shelter an amazing assortment of unusually shaped stalactites and stalagmites. Lago Martel, an enormous underground lake of crystalline water (which causes an amazing optical effect), is part of the cave system. Tours of the cave and a boat trip on the lake are available.

Portocristo

Further north, the Coves d'Artá contain impressive mineral deposits. Inland, the town of Artá is overseen by a 14th century hilltop fortress. The town's museum harbors a small but worthwhile archaeological collection. Just south of town are the remains of Ses Paisses, a megalithic settlement encircled by a double ring of walls. The monuments date to prehistoric times and represent only a small fraction of the megalithic sites found on the island.

Accommodations

There are two types:

1) Inside the old hermitage: 7 double, triple and quadruple rooms, some with private bath.

2) Outside the monastery: 6 single and double rooms, some with private bath.

Both men and women are welcome.

Amenities

Towels and linens are supplied.

Meals

On request, all meals can be supplied in the sanctuary's restaurant.

Cost of lodging

$7.00 per person/per night (shared bath).

$9.00 per person/per night (private bath).

Special rules

1) Inside the old hermitage: guests must respect the curfew arranged with the family managing the guest house.

2) Outside guests are provided with a key to the guest house.

Both are open year round. Men and women are welcome.

Directions

By car: From Palma de Mallorca take Route C715 east to Manacor making a right on Route C714 south to Felanitx. From Felantix take the road to Portcolon and then turn right following the signs to the shrine (the road is steep).

By train: There is no public transportation to the shrine. Taxis are available in Felanitx.

Contact

Anyone who answers the phone

Call or write in advance of your stay

Santuario de San Salvador

07200 Felanitx (Mallorca, Baleares), Spain

Tel: 971/827282

Monasterio - Santuario de Nuestra Señora de Lluc

Missionares del Sagrado Corazón

Monasterio - Santuario de Nuestra Señora de Lluc

High in the mountains of the Sierra de Tramuntana lies the remote village of Lluc and the Monasterio de Lluc, considered by many the spiritual heart of Mallorca. The vast and austere monastery was built during the 17th and 18th centuries on the site of a 13th century shrine. Every year hundreds come to the church to pay homage to the original statue of the Virgin of Lluc, known as *La Moreneta* because of her dark-colored skin .

According to tradition, an Arab shepherd (recently converted to Christianity) and a Cistercian monk from the hamlet of Escorca found the statue of Mary in Lluc and took it to Escorca. The next day it disappeared from the church and reappeared where it was originally discovered. This happened on two more occasions. It was then understood that a superior power wanted a chapel to be built on the site of the apparition. Over the ensuing centuries, veneration of the statue increased and the chapel was enlarged and renovated numerous times.

In 1891, the direction of the sanctuary was entrusted to the Missionaries of the Sacred Heart.

The Baroque complex is an imposing structure. The church and monastery contain precious works of art which can be seen in the museum. The collection includes Mallorcan paintings and medieval manuscripts.

Along the *Camí dels Misteris* (Walk of the Mysteries), a paved walkway leading to the hilltop setting, is a series of bronze bas-reliefs. They were designed by noted Catalan architect and designer Antoni Gaudí who also contributed to the decoration of the church interiors.

Lluc is in the area of La Marina, a district studded with old windmills. The shore of La Marina consists of very high cliffs which drop precipitously to the sea. Heading south from Lluc to Cabo Blanco, a coast road passes near Capocorb Vell, a talayotic village of massive, tower-like stone monuments.

Each of the Balearic Islands has maintained an enduring sense of identity and strong links to the past. Gothic cathedrals, fishing villages, Stone Age ruins and scenic drives are found throughout the islands. One such drive begins in Palma, loops beside the coastline and heads into the interior before returning to Palma.

Estellencs is one of the towns along the eastern seacoast route from Palma. A village of stone buildings, it sits in a milieu of rolling hills. Continuing north, Banyalbufar is set above the coastline. The town is enveloped by stone-walled terraces carved into the hillsides, legacies of its Moorish heritage.

A popular artists' retreat, Deiá is an atmospheric place of stone houses and trees crowded together beneath a dramatic backdrop of mountains. The Deiá Coastal Path and Route of the Olive Trees offer excellent hiking opportunities.

Sóller and Port de Sóller are next en route. The former stretches across a flat valley of olive groves and orchards beneath the rugged outcrop of the Sierra de Tramuntana. The town is filled with grand manors, verdant gardens, inviting plazas and restaurants. Popular with hiking and boating enthusiasts, the two towns are linked by an old-world tram.

Slightly off the loop and a short drive from Sóller, the hamlet of Fornalutx sits in a region of orange and lemon groves. The village is composed of attractive stone houses accented by green shutters and colorful flower boxes.

Accommodations
121 beds in rooms with 1, 2 and 3 beds. All rooms have private bath and heating. Both men and women are welcome.

Amenities
Towels and linens are supplied. There are 3 restaurants (1 inside, 2 outside the santuario) and 1 café. The facility includes a football field, children's area, picnic area, pharmacy and shops.

Meals
All meals can be supplied by the restaurants for an additional cost.

Cost of lodging
Single room: 1 night $23.00; 2 nights $21.00 per night; 3 nights or more $20.00 per night.
Double room: 1 night $28.00; 2 nights $26.00 per night; 3 nights or more $25.00 per night.
Triple room: 1 night $31.00; 2 nights $29.00 per night; 3 nights or more $28.00 per night.

Special rules
Curfew at 11:00 pm. The guest house opens at 6:30 am; check-in is 8:00 am. Open year round.

Directions
By car: From Palma de Mallorca take route C711 north to C710 and make a right. Take C710 approximately 30 kms to the monastery.
By ferry or plane to Palma: From Palma de Mallorca take a bus to the monastery. From the airport take a bus to Palma and change to a bus to the monastery.

Contact
Anyone who answers the phone
Monasterio - Santuario de Nuestra Señora de Lluc
07315 Lluc - Escorca (Mallorca, Baleares), Spain
Tel: 971/871525 / Fax: 971/517096
Email: info@lluc.net
Website: www.lluc.net

ERMITA DE SANT MIQUEL
Property of the Bishopric of Mallorca

Less than a mile from Montuiri, the convent, church and hotel are positioned atop Sant Miquel. The complex is surrounded by trees and enjoys a vista of the island of Mallorca. The Romanesque stone church is very pretty and dates to the 13th century. The ensemble is divided into three sections: church, convent (inhabited by Trinitarian nuns), hotel and restaurant. The hotel and restaurant were restored at the end of 2001 and are managed by lay personnel.

Montuiri is a small, picturesque town somewhat off the beaten path. It is close to Algaida, home of the Gordiola glass works; visitors can watch glass blowers at work. A small museum highlights the history of glassware. About ten miles from Montuiri stands the agricultural village of Campos. It preserves a 15th century hospital and 16th century town hall. The nearby salt mine of Es Salobrar is separated from the sea by a strip of sand dune. This interesting ecological habitat is a nesting site for migratory birds.

Located opposite the Levante coast of the peninsula, Mallorca is the largest of the Balearic Islands. More than 300 miles of shoreline and a temperate year-round climate account for its popularity as a Mediterranean tourist destination. The island is renowned for its dramatic scenery including the steep Tramuntana Mountains, a vast central plain, the gentle heights of the Sierra de Levante and a stunning collection of cliffs, bays, creeks and sandy beaches.

Interesting remains of megalithic monuments dating to prehistoric times are scattered about the island. Examples include the *talayot* (tower-like monument) of Sa Canova, the settlements of Ses Paisses, Capicorb Vell and Claper dels Gegants. The pretty port of Alcúdia is also home to ruins of a Roman theater.

Catalan is the main language spoken on all the islands save Ibiza. Archaeologists date the first human settlements to around 5000 BC. The islands have been occupied by Phoenicians, Carthaginians, Greeks, Romans and Visigoths, but it was the Moors who left behind a lingering legacy of elegant mosques, palaces and orchards terraced in the Moorish style.

Accommodations

5 double rooms, each with private bath, TV and heating. Both men and women are welcome. Open year round. From October until May, the hotel and restaurant are closed on Mondays.

Amenities

Towels and linens are supplied.

Meals

Lodging includes breakfast; other meals can be supplied by the restaurant.

Cost of lodging

To be determined.

Directions

By car: From Palma de Mallorca take route C715 towards Manacor exiting at km 31. Travel north following the signs to Montuiri.

By ferry or plane to Palma: Take the bus to Montuiri. The convent and the hotel are a short walk from the main road.

Contact

Anyone who answers the phone
Ermita de Sant Miquel
07230 Montuiri - Puig de Sant Miquel (Mallorca, Baleares), Spain
Tel/Fax: 971/646314

ERMITA DE BONANY

Property of the Bishopric of Mallorca

Ermita de Bonany

The hermitage and its hospedería are on a mountain in the center of the island, a couple of miles from Petra. "You can see all of Mallorca from our institution," said the person in charge of hospitality.

The hermitage was originally a shrine dedicated to the Virgin Mary who appeared in the 16th century. At the onset, the temple consisted only of a roof and altar. Over the years, devotion by the local populace made it possible to build a church. A century ago, a group of nine hermits of the order of San Pablo and San Antonio settled in the complex and assumed responsibility for the shrine. Although they had to leave their voluntary seclusion to obey the order of the Bishop, the hermits inhabited the Ermita de Bonany until 1989, at which time their advancing age and scarce numbers forced them to leave.

Since 1989, the church and hospedería have been managed by a private family. "When people ask me when the church was built, I always answer that it is not yet finished," said the man in charge. The façade and altar are from the original building. The remainder of the complex has been renovated on numerous occasions.

"The hospedería is a very simple structure. It is all very unpretentious. Most of our guests arrive with backpacks and whatever they need for a few days. Many of our visitors are nature enthusiasts and come to be outdoors amidst the lovely surroundings. The walk from Petra to the Ermita is quite beautiful. I wish I could do it more often but I have three children to take to school every morning... maybe when they are older, they will walk it."

Ermita de Bonany

Mallorca is the largest of the Balearic Islands and Palma is its main city. The people of the island speak their own dialect of Catalan. It is believed that the first human settlements date from around 5000 BC. Prehistoric relics and monuments document that houses were made of stone and that the people farmed the land, raised domesticated animals and made pottery, tools and jewelry. The island is blessed with a mild climate and beautiful scenery and is known for its stalagmite caves, architectural treasures and vineyards.

Items from
Majorca Museum,
Palma de Mallorca

The Balearic Islands maintain a rich and flourishing tradition in local crafts including olive wood carvings, wrought iron, pottery, cut glass, fine embroidery and objects made from palm leaves and raffia.

The town of Petra is in the central region. It was the birthplace of Franciscan friar, Junipero Serra, an active missionary in the Mexican peninsula of Baja California and founder of the missions that gave rise to several California cities, headed by Los Angeles. For fifteen years, the friar taught philosophy in the college at Palma and is remembered in a series of Majolica panels sheltered in a street beside the church of San Bernardino. There are other commemorative panels in the house where the friar was born.

Accommodations

5 double rooms with shared bath. Both men and women are welcome.

Amenities

Towels and linens are not supplied; only the covers of the mattress are changed for each new guest. Linens are only available for a limited number of guests. It is recommended that guests provide their own.

Meals

Meals are not supplied. Guests are welcome to use the shared kitchen facilities.

Cost of lodging

$9.00 per person/per night.

Directions

By car: From Palma de Mallorca take C715 towards Manacor. Go north at Vilafranca de Bonany (PM331) following the signs to Petra. From Petra follow the signs or ask for the Ermita de Bonany.

By ferry or plane to Palma: From Palma de Mallorca take the bus to Petra. From there it is about 2 kms to the hermitage. Taxis are available in Petra.

Contact

Anyone who answers the phone
Ermita de Bonany
07520 Petra - Puig de Bonany (Mallorca, Baleares), Spain
Tel: 971/561101

ERMITA DE NUESTRA SEÑORA DEL PUIG

Property of the Bishopric of Mallorca
and Missionaries of the Sacred Heart

The monastery's position on the summit of the Puig de Randa offers views over the village and Bay of Pollença and the Sierra Tramuntana. The region is a scenic landscape of olive groves, pine forests, quaint villages and jagged, rocky coastline. "When it is clear, you can even see Menorca," said one of the sisters.

The first monastery built on the site belonged to the Augustinian nuns who settled here around 1350. "They say it was a very rich monastery since the nuns belonged to the upper bourgeois class. When the Black Death hit the island, people donated their possessions to the monastery which had a large and rich library and many works of art," recalled the lady at reception. After the Council of Trento established that female orders could not remain in isolated locations, the first community was forced to leave the complex. The nuns left and resettled in the monastery of Purisíma Concepción in Palma de Mallorca where the order still resides. "Of course, the sisters took all their possessions with them," the woman at reception added.

The monastery was abandoned for some one hundred years until a community of Missionaries of the Sacred Heart took up residence. They lived in the monastery until a few years ago when they left due to their advancing age and small numbers. The nuns had always run a hostelry and that tradition continues today under the management of the Bishopric of Mallorca.

Very little remains of the original 13th century structure. "The oldest parts are a refectory, the kitchen and a tower. The monastery's most interesting works of art and objects are on display in La Palma at the monastery of Purisíma Concepción," she continued.

Situated on the edge of fertile farmland, Pollença remains rooted in old traditions. The imposing gates add to the town's noble appearance. Its overall good looks are enriched by ocher-colored stone houses and winding lanes. The town has many monuments: a Gothic chapel, a parish church from the 18th century, a museum of local archaeology and the Baroque convent of Santo Domingo. There is also a Roman bridge on the outskirts of town.

Pollença is on the Mallorcan pilgrimage route. Many pilgrims come to climb *El Cavari*, 356 stone steps along a path fringed by cypress that leads from town to a hilltop chapel and small shrine. At the top, an 18th century hermitage sustains an old crucifix which, according to legend, arrived miraculously. The Puig de Pollença is crowned by a chapel and watchtower that once guarded the city.

Pollença is not far from the northeastern coast where the juxtaposition of cliffs and long, sandy beaches are characteristic of the region. The mountainous landscape is one of wild beauty and encompasses the Sierra de San Vicente and the Puig de Ternelles. The ruined Castillo del Rey dates from the Muslim period and offers views over the sheer cliffs to the sea. Puerto de Pollença is an ancient fishing district surrounded by grand estates.

Nearby is the archaeological site of Pollentia, a city founded by the Romans in the 7th century BC. The remains of a theater, fragments of the wall and an outline of the road can still be seen.

Roman theatre ruins, Alcúdia

The Badia D'Alcúdia dominates this section of the coast. Broad sandy beaches stretch around the resorts of Port d'Alcúdia and Can Picafort. The former is partly surrounded by 14th century walls and sandwiched between two bays. Alcúdia traces its origins to the Romans and ruins of the Roman theater still exist. Can Picafort is smaller in size and dotted with pine groves. This area is not far from the Parc Natural de S'Albufera Nature Reserve, a refuge of reed beds and lagoons populated by wading birds.

Southwest of Pollença, the bay of Sa Calobra is reached through a breathtaking, albeit serpentine, road through the hills that ends at a rocky cove enclosed by steep palisades. A quick walk up the coast leads to Torrent de Pareis, a deep gorge opening into the sea.

Accommodations
There are two types:
1) 10 rooms with 2, 4 and 5 beds with shared baths.
2) Two large dormitories with shared baths (for groups). Both men and women are welcome.

Amenities
Linens are supplied, towels can be supplied on request, but it is recommended that guests bring their own. There is a kitchen guests may use.

Meals
All meals are available on request.

Cost of lodging
To be determined upon arrival.

Special rules
Closed Christmas Eve, Christmas Day, December 31st and January 1st.

Directions
By car: From Palma de Mallorca take route C711 north to C710. Continue north to Pollença. Before entering the town there are signs to the ermita. Since the upper parking lot is often full, the monastery suggests that guests park cars below and walk to the monastery.
By ferry or plane to Palma: From Palma de Mallorca take a bus to Pollença and then a taxi to the monastery.

Contact
Anyone who answers the phone
Ermita de Nuestra Señora del Puig
Apartado de Correo 223
07460 Pollença (Mallorca. Baleares), Spain
Tel: 971/184132

MONASTERIO - SANTUARI DE MONTI-SION

Bishphoric of Mallorca

Monasterio - Santuari de Monti-Sion

The monastery is situated on a small mountain about a mile above Porreres, a small interior town on the island of Mallorca. Porreres is not far from two noteworthy religious sites: the Ermita de Nuestra Señora de Cura and the Sanctuary of San Salvador. Until recently, the monastery was inhabited by monks. Upon their departure, the institution was turned into a guest house/hotel. The church was built between the 16th and 17th centuries. "Although no legend is tied to the presence of the shrine", according to Padre Juan, "nonetheless, the locals are very devoted to the Virgin of Monti Sion."

The Balearic Islands lie in the western Mediterranean and have become popular vacation destinations, particularly in the summer months when visitors are drawn to the mild climate and sandy beaches.

Mallorca is the largest and most visited of the Balearics. No other European island has a broader scope of scenery. It is comprised of three distinctly different areas: the Sierra del Norte, a range of wooded hills; the Sierra de Levante, an area with stalactite caves; and the Llanura del Centro, the island's fertile plain.

Manacor, the island's second largest city and its most industrial, is approximately 20 miles east of the monastery. Known for making artificial pearls, Firma Mallorca was founded in 1890 and offers a factory tour along with insight into the century-old manufacturing process. Manacor's inner city preserves three towers from its ancient fortress. The town's parish church features a Gothic apse.

Accommodations
25 beds in 3 large dormitories with shared baths. The accommodations are similar to a youth hostel. Both men and women are welcome, preferably in groups. Open year round (except August 15th).

Amenities
Towels and linens are not supplied; guests must also provide their own sleeping bags.

Meals
Meals are not supplied. There is a restaurant on the premises where guests can dine.

Cost of lodging
$5.00 per person/per night.

Directions
By car: From Palma de Mallorca take route C715 east to route PM503 south and follow the signs to Porreres and the sanctuary.
By ferry or plane to Palma: There is no public transportation to the monastery. Buses stop in Porreres. Take a taxi from there.

Contact
Anyone who answers the phone
Monasterio - Santuari de Monti-Sion
07260 Porreres (Mallorca, Baleares), Spain
Tel: 971/647185

CONVENTO - SANTUARIO DE NUESTRA SEÑORA DE CURA

Franciscan Friars

Convento - Santuario de Nuestra Señora de Cura

The Santuari de Cura occupies a singular hilltop position. Its central courtyard highlights the typical beige stone of Mallorca. The loggia to the right of the church harbors a series of fine majolica panels while the church houses one of the Bethlehem Grottoes, typical of Mallorcan churches. The views from the sanctuary include the sea and many of the fifty-eight villages scattered throughout the island. The first community to inhabit the locale was a group of hermits who lived in caves. Once a day, they met to pray in a small chapel.

There are two small monasteries on the way to the tiny hamlet of Randa: 14th century Santuari de Sant Honorat and Santuari de Nostra Senyora de Grácia. The former was built on a ledge under an overhanging cliff and contains a 15th century chapel with Valencian tiles. The sanctuary has an open view of the *Pla*, a fertile plain composed of orchards and vineyards.

At the time of his conversion, Ramón Llull (1233-1315), theologian and mystic, inhabited the hermitage. He wrote his religious treatise, *Ars Magna*, while in residence. During that time, the sanctuary became an important center of intellectual and spiritual life. Over the years, Llull's celebrity impacted the importance of the convent. In 1510, it was established as the first university of the islands and became a place where many came to study philosophy, grammar and theology. Although the convent is no longer a center of international studies, its old classroom has been turned into a museum; its library conserves original copies of the handwritten works of Llull's followers.

Sierra de Tramuntana

Randa is just one of many quaint places on the beautiful island of Mallorca, largest in the Balearic chain. It is an island of remarkable diversity, from the rocky coastline of azure blue waters and hidden coves to the alpine-like peaks of the Tramuntana and the enduring charm of its whitewashed villages.

Accommodations
There are 25 rooms/mini apartments. Rooms have from 2 to 6 beds. The largest rooms include a kitchen. All the rooms have private toilets, showers are shared. Both men and women are welcome.

Amenities
Only linens are provided, towels are not.

Meals
Meals are not provided with lodging but guests may use the kitchen facilities. There is also a restaurant outside of the monastery.

Cost of lodging
$12.00 per person, per night.

Special rules
After midnight, guests are required to be quiet.

Directions
By car: From Palma de Mallorca take route C717 south. At the village of Llucmajor take route PM501 north and follow the signs towards Algaida and the convent.

By ferry or plane to Palma: The monastery is in an isolated place. There is no public transportation. Take a taxi.

Contact
Padre Hospedero
Convento - Santuario de Nuestra Señora de Cura
07629 Randa (Mallorca, Baleares), Spain
Tel: 971/660994 / Fax: 971/662052

BASQUE COUNTRY
(PAIS VASCO)

NUESTRA SEÑORA DE LOS REMEDIOS
Canon Regular Nuns

On the outskirts of the town of Artziniega, the monastery enjoys a picturesque view of the Basque Mountains. It was founded in 1606 by a group of Canon nuns when the territory was under the archidiocese of Burgos. (One of the nuns was the sister of the archbishop). They joined another group of nuns who lived in the Sanctuary of Nuestra Señora de Encino, close to the town of Artziniega.

The community bought and settled in a towered palace. Years later, in order to enlarge the complex, the nuns bought two adjacent palaces, one of which belonged to Carlo V. It was in this palace that they built a chapel. During the Civil War, the monastery was invaded by left wing troops. "But they were very respectful to the nuns and nothing happened," related one of the sisters. Although the order lives in seclusion, the original palace (now the guest house) and the chapel are open to visitors. "The interior of the chapel is simple... but the monastery itself is a work of art," she added.

One of the main cities of the Basque country, Bilbao is 18 miles from the monastery. A major banking and industrial center, the city has strong international ties. It has also become known for its art, particularly distinguished by the Frank Gehry-designed Guggenheim Museum, a dizzying design of silvery curves thought to resemble a metallic flower. The museum is akin to a large sculpture in metal, glass and stone and offers views of the city and the Nervión River. Quite interestingly, Bilbao's big city atmosphere is softened by the farmhouse dappled Basque mountains that seem to appear at the end of every street.

Known for its wonderful Basque food and tapa bars, the well-preserved medieval quarter, Casco Viejo, is the heart of the city. It boasts a graceful gray stone Gothic church and the arcaded Plaza Nueva. Nearby is the riverfront Mercado de la Ribera, largest covered market in Spain. The newer part of town is home to the Museo de Bellas Artes, considered one of Spain's finest art museums. Sited on the edge of the

Bilbao, City Hall

Bilbao, Arriaga Theatre

spacious Parque de Doña Casilda Iturriza, the museum's collection includes Spanish masters like El Greco and Goya and modern art by Picasso and Gauguin.

Between Bilbao and San Sebastián is a beautiful forty-mile drive along the Costa Vasca. A misty, verdant area with steep slopes and rugged cliffs, it is dotted by red-trimmed farmhouses. The narrow, twisting road, called the *Balcony of Cantabria*, maneuvers through fishing villages and climbs over cliffs to fishing ports and isolated sandy beaches. Clinging precariously to the hillside, Euzkadi is one of the most appealing villages en route. The village of Zugarramurdi is noted for its limestone caves and a legendary witch hunt of the 17th century.

The environs of the monastery are marked by small towns and villages, each possessing monuments of architectural interest. Amurrio's parish church has a 13th century portal and reredos dating from the 17th century. A short distance away, Quejana is the historic center of the Arala Valley. Its Chapel of the Virgin of El Cabello was founded in 1399 and preserves the alabaster tombs of Chancellor Don Pedro López de Ayala, his wife and parents.

Arciniega is defined by the vestiges of its walls and by Llodio, a 16th century tower. An industrial town on the border with the province of Biscay, Arciniega is enveloped by a pine woodland and preserves three churches: San Pedro de la Muza, San Bartolomé and Nuestra Señora del Yelmo.

Accommodations
Three-story guest house with 25 beds in single and double rooms, each with private bath. Both men and women are welcome. The nuns also offer hospitality to groups of scholars or students for organized courses.

Amenities
Towels and linens are supplied. There is a kitchen and dining room available to guests and meeting rooms on each floor.

Meals
Meals are supplied only on request, preferably to groups on spiritual retreats.

Cost of lodging
To be arranged upon arrival depending on the size of the group, number of meals, etc.

Products of the institution
Upon request, the nuns can prepare *rosquillas caseras*, homemade fried sweets typical of the area.

Special rules
Curfew 11:00 pm. During the winter, hospitality is offered only to groups large enough to occupy at least one of the three floors of the guest house. Open year round.

Directions
By car: From Bilbao go south on route 636 to Sodupe and then turn left onto route 2604 to Artziniega.

By train: Get off at Bilbao and take the bus to Artziniega. Buses from Bilbao leave every 2 hours (even hours); buses from Artziniega to Bilbao leave every hour (odd hours).

Contact
Madre Hospedera
Nuestra Señora de los Remedios
Calle Arriba, 2
01474 Artziniega (Álava), Spain
Tel/Fax: 945/396016

CASA VICENTE PALLOTTI

Pallottinos Monks

Casa Vicente Pallotti

The casa lies in a tiny town in the Valley of Carrenza, a tableau of woodlands, meadows and mountains close to Bilbao and the Basque coast. Built between 1895 and 1897, the casa was originally a private spa which achieved international fame. During the Civil War years, the spa was turned into a hospital, then a barracks and eventually an internment camp. The economic crisis that followed the war persuaded the families that owned the complex to sell it to the Pallottinos who later built a boarding house for their seminarists. The casa then became a school for the children of Carrenza. In 1976, it

Casa Vicente Pallotti

hosted its first visitors. Restored in 1985, guests can take advantage of the peaceful atmosphere as well as the beneficial waters of the hot spring.

Although Basque Country (known as Euskal Herria in the Basque language) is one of the most industrialized regions of Spain, there are many areas of pristine natural beauty including the parks of Valderejo, Urkiola, Urdaibai and the atmospheric landscapes along the Guernica River. The cliffs of Basque Country are broken by rocky coves, rías and bays with beaches of fine, yellow sand. Fishing villages are scattered all along the coast. Inland, small roads twist through wooded hills, valleys and gorges; isolated castles appear here and there as lonely sentinels guarding the countryside.

Occupying an area smaller than New Hampshire, Basque is comprised of seven provinces, three in France and four in Spain. They are a crescent-shaped mosaic of seashore cities, mountain villages, pastoral settings and country towns with timbered houses.

Called "the land of Basque speakers," the region is defined by its ancient language and cultural heritage. Even the local cuisine, *nueva cocina vasca* (new Basque cuisine), is quite different from the rest of Spain. It is a unique area, a place where men wear berets and every village centers on a church and a court for pelota. Pelota (jai alai), was created by the Basques in the 16th century and is played with paddles, rackets and baskets.

Casa Vicente Pallotti

Accommodations

8 single and double rooms each with private bath. 3 family accommodations consisting of a double room plus a room for children (each with private bath). 15 double rooms with sinks and shared baths. Men and women are welcome.

Amenities

Towels and linens are supplied. The entrance to the hot spring is independent from the lodging. There is a swimming pool and 16 single bathtubs with water supplied directly from the spring (86° to 88°F). A conference room, TV room, various meeting rooms and a small gym may be used by guests.

Meals

All meals are available.

Cost of lodging

$30.00 per person, excluding meals.

Special rules

Closed in November and February.

Directions

By car: From Bilbao or Santander take A8 and exit at Colindres taking N629 south to Gibaja. From there go east on Bl 630 to Carrenza, exit at Molinar and ask directions or follow signs to the Casa Vicente Pallotti.

By train: From Bilbao or Santander take the special train Feve (a train that runs on smaller tracks). Get off at Ambas Aguas/Carrenza. The casa is less than a mile from the station. Taxis are available.

Contact

Anyone who answers the phone
Reservations are accepted from 9:00 am until 1:00 pm
and from 5:00 pm until 8:00 pm
Casa Vicente Pallotti
Barrio de Molinar, 17
48891 Carrenza (Vizcaya), Spain
Tel: 94/6806002
Fax: 94/6806400

Monasterio Santuario de Santa María de Estíbaliz

Benedictine Monks

Monasterio Santuario de Santa María de Estíbaliz

The monastery, a fine Romanesque structure, sits in a woodland at the top of a hill in the small town of Estíbaliz. It was a stop along the northern route to Santiago de Compostela, one that passes from Irun and joins the main or French one at the Monastery of Santo Domingo de la Calzada. The church was founded in 1138 to host the sacred image of Santa María de

Estíbaliz who has always been the patron saint of the Álava province. In medieval times, the highly venerated image was carried to meetings of the local government to bless the council.

For reasons unknown at this time, the church was closed and donated or sold to the government of Nájera. In 1923, the institution was regained by the local government and reopened. The Benedictine Order was invited to take up residence. Of the original buildings that once stood on the grounds, only the Romanesque church remains. The capitals are quite remarkable as is the 12th century christening font. On a shelf at the bottom of the main apse is the statue of the Virgin, visited by thousands of pilgrims each year. The official Feast of Santa María de Estíbaliz is a special event celebrated by the monastery. It takes place every year on the second Sunday of September.

According to legend, the sacred image often intervened in the so-called *Juicios de Dios* (God's judgements). At the end of mass, the priest would address the litigants and ask them to forget their hate and become reconciled at the foot of the Virgen de Estíbaliz.

Estíbaliz is situated in the plains of Álava, close to the small town of Salvatierra. Founded in 1256, three of Salvatierra's main streets still preserve their medieval layout. In addition, there are relics of walls, several palaces and a number of secluded squares. The town also has two fortified Gothic churches: San Juan and Santa María. In the Iturrieta hills outside of town stands the Arrizala and Equilaz dolmens. Upright stone slabs of great size, they support a capstone or table and are typical of the Neolithic period in Europe.

Plaza de la Virgen Blanca

A few miles from Estíbaliz, the town of Vitoria is the seat of the Basque government. Most likely founded in the 6th century by Visigoths, in 1181, Sancho the Wise of Navarra named it Vitoria to commemorate a victory over the Moors. The entire town is an ensemble of well-preserved constructions. The oldest section, El Campo Suso was rebuilt after the victory. At its heart is the Plaza de la Virgen Blanca, encircled by houses with *miradores* (glazed balconies or turrets with fine views). Overlooking the plaza from its lofty position is the Gothic Iglesia de San Miguel, home to a statue of the Virgen Blanca, Vitoria's patron saint. A festival in her honor is held each year on August 4th. A six-day extravaganza, parties and champagne continue non-stop and elaborate fireworks light the sky each evening.

The street behind the church leads into the medieval section, once the wealthy part of town and the locale of two 18th century Plateresque palaces: Palacio Episcopal and Palacio de Escoriaza-Esquibel. The latter is distinguished by a Plateresque patio and Renaissance courtyard with a marble loggia. The old town is a patchwork of alleys linked by steep steps in a concentric pattern. Los Arquillos and Plaza de España are arcaded streets built in the late 18th century to join the old quarters with the new. The simplicity of the arcaded design of the plaza adds a note of tranquility to the setting. Heading away from the old town is the Church of Santa María. Dating to the 12th century, it preserves works by Van Dyck, Rubens, Caravaggio, Benvenuto Cellini as well as paintings of the Ribera school.

El Portalón is a 15th century merchant's house. A half-timbered structure, it is filled with Basque country furniture and art. The town's archaeological museum is also set in a half-timbered house. Among its treasures are dolmens and Neolithic tombs. The Museo de Naipes has an interesting collection of cards. Founded by a playing card factory, the oldest exhibits are 14th century Italian cards. Some of the tarot cards on exhibit were designed by Salvador Dalí.

Accommodations
There are two kinds:
1) Outside the monastery: 10 single rooms with shared baths; some can be turned into doubles. Both men and women are welcome.
2) Inside the monastery: 10 beds in single rooms with private bath; only men seeking retreat are allowed.

Amenities
Towels and linens are provided in all accommodations.

Meals
On request, all meals can be provided with the lodging. There is also a restaurant very close to the monastery.

Cost of lodging
To be arranged upon arrival.

Special rules
Curfew is flexible and arranged upon arrival. Maximum stay 2 weeks.

Directions
By car: From Vitoria/Gasteiz take N1 east towards San Sebastián. At an intersection going towards San Sebastián or Estella, go right on route 520 and follow the signs to Estella for approximately 7 kms.
By train: Get off at Vitoria/Gasteiz and take a bus to Estíbaliz.

Contact
Padre Hospedero (specify inside or outside accommodations)
Monasterio Santuario de Santa María de Estíbaliz
01193 Estíbaliz (Álava), Spain
Tel/Fax: 945/293088 (call before sending fax)
Email: santuario.de.estibaliz@euskalnet.net
        or santuario.de.estibaliz@euskaltel.es

MONASTERIO DE SANTA ANA
Cistercian Nuns

Monasterio de Santa Ana

The monastery was founded in 1646 by Doña María de Lazkano, a wealthy noblewoman who owned much of the land and buildings in the area. The first stone of the structure was set in 1650 and construction was completed in 1716. Doña María's son and daughter had died at a very young age; she founded the monastery in their memory and dedicated it to her son. The Carmelite monastery of Santa Teresa de

Ávila (today a Benedictine institution) was dedicated to her daughter. In the last years of her life, Doña María De Lazkano joined the sisters and lived as a nun until her death in 1658. The church contains the tombs of Doña María, her husband and son.

During the ensuing centuries, the monastery flourished. "It was considered a very 'rich' monastery," according to one of the sisters. "But we lost almost everything during the 1835 suppression of the religious orders. The monastery preserves a pretty stone cloister and some personal objects that belonged to Doña María. Our church is Baroque and quite charming," she added.

The monastery is part of the monumental area, *conjunto monumental* of Lazkao. "If you have never been here, I can assure you that it is very green and very beautiful," the sister continued. Situated in a landscape of russet and green rolling hills in the Guipúzcoa province of Basque Country, the terrain is dotted with inviting mountain towns.

Monasterio de Santa Ana

A narrow road leads from the shrine to Oñate, a town ensconced in a verdant valley backdropped by the dramatic peaks of mounts Amboto and Udalaitz. For many years, it was the site of the only Basque university. Oñate harbors a number of medieval palaces and monuments including the *Ayuntamiento* (Town Hall) and the Franciscan Convento de Bidaurreta. Gothic Iglesia de San Miguel is the resting place of the university's founder, Bishop Zuazola de Ávila; it features a pretty stone cloister in Plateresque style.

Azpeitia is an industrial town with grand patrician houses. St. Ignatius of Loyola, founder of the Jesuits, was baptized in the Gothic church of San Sebastián which sustains a portico by Ventura Rodriguez. The Sanctuary of Saint Ignacio is a Baroque affair in a simple rural setting. The complex was built over the course of two hundred years, beginning in the late 1600s. The church was completed in the mid-18th century and is defined by a high dome executed by Joaquin de Churriguera. Characterized by a circular nave, the interior is offset by marble, semi-precious stones and a Baroque high altar. Santa Casa, the house where the saint was born, has a Mudéjar-inspired façade.

Accommodations

There are two types:
1) 8 double rooms with shared baths.
2) 15 beds in a large dorm with 3 toilets, 3 showers and 3 sinks. Both men and women are welcome.

Amenities

Towels and linens are supplied, There is a well-equipped kitchen and private garden.

Meals

Meals are supplied only to groups seeking spiritual retreats. Other guests may use the kitchen at their disposal.

Cost of lodging

Voluntary contribution.

Special rules

Guests are provided with a key to their quarters. Maximum stay is 10 days.

Directions

By car: From Vitoria-Gasteiz take route N1 east to Beasain, approximately 63 kms. (Note that N1 turns north at Olatzi.) From there follow the directions to Lazkao, approximately 2 kms.

By train/bus: Get off at Beasain and take the bus to Lazkao. The bus stop is very close to the monastery.

Contact

Madre Hospedera
Monasterio de Santa Ana
Elósegui, 44
20210 Lazkao (Guipúzcoa), Spain
Tel: 943/880552

COLEGIO PADRES PAULES
Paules Fathers

The institution is in a beautiful and convenient location between Vitoria and Bilbao. "Try to envision verdant hills at the foot of a national park, close to interesting cities, an enchanting coast and a variety of ski resorts," said the man in charge of the hospedería.

The Colegio of the Paules Fathers was founded in 1888 as a seminary of the Paules Order. It suffered the vicissitudes of the Spanish Civil War but the fathers succeeded in reopening shortly thereafter. Since the number of seminarists has declined in recent years, the large building has been divided into several sections. One is still occupied by the seminary, one by an agricultural school and another by a large guest house which can accommodate up to two hundred guests.

The hospedería is currently managed by FEYDA, an international Catholic organization which operates in many countries including the United States. In addition to handling reservations, it organizes courses and outdoor activities. "We offer many recreational and learning opportunities. When guests call or write, they can inform us of their interests and we'll work with them to schedule a personalized program," he continued.

To the south of Murguía in an area considered the Upper Ebro, there are a number of interesting small towns and villages within the Cuartango Valley. Many are highlighted by Romanesque churches with capitals and archivolts common to that architectural period.

The southern section of the province is a mountainous tableau of oak and beech woodlands. In the area of Ventas de Armentia, a local road (C-122) leads to the villages of Urarte, Marquínez and Arlucea where Romanesque and pre-Gothic remains can be seen. At Peñacerrada Pass, there is a viewpoint known as *El Balcón de la Rioja*, with panoramas of La Rioja. Following the course of the River Ega, the village of Lagran reveals vestiges of medieval fortifications.

Numerous nearby towns are enveloped by olive groves, vineyards and vegetable farmlands. Labastida has a Baroque town hall and parish church dating from the 17th century. Laguardia preserves the medieval layout of its old town and two churches, San Juan and Santa María de los Reyes. Renowned for its Rioja-Alavesa wines, the Rioja area is also home to many prehistoric relics and settlements such as the dolmens of El Sotillo, San Martin, La Choza de la Hechicera and the proto-historic settlement of La Hoya.

Southwest of the monastery, one of the finest 13th century churches in the province can be seen in the town of Tuesta. Valdegovía shelters the Shrine of Angosto. Nearby are the salt pans at Salinas de Añana, still in use today.

Parish church, Tuesta

Accommodations

200 beds in 7 single and 7 double rooms with private bath and 4 large dorms with 30-45 beds each. Both men and women are welcome, but only as a group (preferably 20 and up).

Amenities

Towels and linens are supplied in the single and double rooms. Guests staying in the dorms must provide their own sleeping bags. The complex includes meeting rooms, dining room, theatre (approximately 100 seats), basketball court, soccer field, garden and a nearby municipal swimming pool.

Meals

All meals can be supplied on request. The lodging fee includes the use of a kitchen and dining room.

Cost of lodging
Basic prices (different combinations can be arranged when reservations are made):
Per person/per night in the dorms: $6.00 (no meals included).
Per room/per night: single: $12.00; double $16.00.
Full pension: groups up to 20 - $11.00 per day; groups from 20 to 50 - $9.00; more than 50 - $8.00.
Half pension: $6.00 for all groups.
Proceeds of the hospedería are donated to charity missions in Latin America.

Special rules
Arrangements can be made according to group needs. Open year round. Make reservations well in advance.

Directions
By car: From Vitoria take 622 north to Murguía and follow the signs to the Colegio. From Bilbao take highway A68 south and exit following the signs to Murguía on route 622.
By train: Get off at Vitoria and take the bus to Murguía. The hospedería suggests calling in advance for more detailed info about bus schedules.

Contact
Colegio Padres Paules
Domingo Sautu, 65
01130 Murguía (Álava), Spain
Tel: 945/430110 - 945/430710
Email: mariaivana@eresmas.com
Website: (only for Feyda) www.welcome.to/feyda

Note: Information Office in the US:
FEYDA Inc - 1300 S. Steele St - Denver, CO 80210-2599, Phone 303/715-3227, Fax 303/715-2045 e.mail feyda@earthlink.net

Santuario de Nuestra Señora de Arantzazu

Franciscan Friars

Dominated by the pointed peaks of mounts Amboto and Udalaitz, the historic town of Oñate lies in the Udana Valley between Vitoria and San Sebastián. It was a seat of the court of Don Carlos, brother of King Fernando VII, pretender to the throne. For centuries, its former university (ca. 1540) was the only one in Basque Country. The structure has a Renaissance façade and statues of saints. It contains objects of historical and artistic interest. Gothic Iglesia de San Miguel has a stone Plateresque cloister and contains the alabaster tomb of the university's founder, Bishop Zuázola of Ávila.

The Santuario of Arantzazu sits in the shadow of Mount Aitzgorri, highest mountain in the province. Far-reaching views encompass six Spanish and one French province. The shrine occupies a rugged setting reached via a mountain road from Oñate. The first building dedicated to the Virgin Mary of Arantzazu was a hermitage built around the 15th century. In 1469, a shepherd declared he had had a vision of the Virgin in a bush of thorns. "That was a time of internal conflicts in the area and legend holds that the apparition contributed to the return of peace," related one of the friars.

As the importance of the site grew, a new shrine was built. Shortly afterwards, the Franciscan friars settled in. The church was destroyed in a fire and then completely rebuilt by Jorge Oteiza in 1950-60. It is considered the most significant modern church of Spain and has won several awards. Its apse obtained the prize of the Biennal of

Basque modernism

Christian Art of Salzburg in 1964. An intriguing temple of Basque modernism, it perfectly matches the surrounding environment. "The artists who worked on the sanctuary were unknown at the time. Years later, they became famous and now the sanctuary is visited by many students of architecture," noted one of the friars. The architects involved included Sainz de Oiza and Laorga; artists included Oteiza, Chillida, Muñoz, Friar Xabier de Eulate and Basterrechea.

The present community is composed of forty friars. They plan to establish a museum about Arantzazu and its history in order to celebrate the 500-year presence of the sanctuary.

Nearby Tolosa, former capital of the province, is an industrial town. It shelters Roman remains and constructions of the Templars. Close to the sanctuary, the noble and elegant town of Bergara claims a rich historical and artistic heritage. It was the place where Generals Espartero and Maroto signed a peace treaty in the 1839 Civil War. A Christ attributed to Juan de Mesa dominates the Church of San Pedro de Ariznoa.

Accommodations
The hospedería belongs to the shrine but is managed by lay personnel. A one-star hotel, it contains 85 beds in 47 single, double and triple rooms, all with private bath. Both men and women are welcome.

Amenities
Towels and linens are supplied; some of the rooms have TV.

Meals
On request, all meals can be supplied.

Cost of lodging
Provisional cost per double room per night: $30.00-$36.00 (depending on type of room), no meals included. Closed in January.

Directions
By car: From Vitoria take route 240 north (about 5 kms) to a right on route 627. Continue approximately 25 kms to another right on route 2630 to Oñate. Once in Oñate ask for the santuary.

By train: Get off in Zumarraga and take a bus to Oñate. From Oñate take a taxi to the sanctuary (10 kms).

Contact
Anyone who answers the phone
Santuario de Nuestra Señora de Arantzazu
20560 Oñati (Guipúzcoa), Spain
Tel: 943/781313 / Fax: 943/781314
Email: ostatua@euskalnet.net

SANTÍSIMA TRINIDAD
Augustinian Nuns

Santísima Trinidad

Perched on a hill above the town of Rentería, along the coast between San Sebastian and France, the monastery's position offers views of the mountains, city and entrance to the port of Rentería.

"We are in a very good situation; we are in town but in a tranquil site. Behind us we have the mountain which protects us from being surrounded by new houses," said Madre María Carmen. Until the 1940s, Rentería was a small maritime town but it quickly became industrialized. "They used to call it a little Manchester," recalled the Mother Superior who grew up there and remembers when people from the nearby villages first started working in town. "There were only 10,000 inhabitants and today there are 45,000," she added. At one time, most of the ancient core was occupied by factories. Today, most have relocated to the outskirts of town.

The monastery was founded in 1543. "Despite the wars we have been through, we have lived here almost without interruption," commented the mother. The longest period the nuns had to live elsewhere was two years. That occurred during the 19th century when they took up residence in a nearby Benedictine monastery. Until a few years ago, the sisters ran a girls' boarding school. Due to the advancing age and small number of the order, they now rent the school for year-round courses. In 1972, the monastery was completely rebuilt. The well is the only ancient structure that remains. "I still remember that when I first came to the monastery in 1945, there weren't any faucets. We carried water from the well all the time," the mother added.

A Baroque church lies outside the monastery and is open to the public. Although most of its art was lost over the centuries, a 16th century sculpture of Christ and an 18th century image of San Augustin survived.

Not far from the monastery, the historic fishing port of Hondarribia is at the mouth of the Río Bidasoa. Protected by 15th century walls, the upper town is reached through the Puerta de Santa María. The walls encircle a cluster of alleys lined with brightly painted houses displaying coats of arms.

The center of the district is defined by Santa María de la Asunción. The church's façade is marked by huge buttresses and a Baroque tower; the interior is enhanced by a golden reredos. A 10th century castle once belonging to Charles V (now a parador), dominates the town from its highest point. Sited at the northeasternmost corner of Spain, the lighthouse on Cabo Higuer offers views of the sunset over the bay.

Rentería is close to the coastal town of San Sebastián. Once a fishing port, San Sebastián was transformed into an elegant city when Queen Regent María Cristina came to bathe in the waters of Spain's northern shores. The area quickly became a summer resort for royalty and aristocrats.

The cosmopolitan ambience of that period remains, enriched by the Belle Epoque mansions and manicured gardens, legacies of the town's golden period. The crescent-shaped Playa de la Concha is San Sebastián's largest beach and its most beautiful. The medieval town center, La Parte Vieja, is framed by steep mountains and graced with fine architecture. At its heart is the Plaza de la Constitución. A former bullring, the arcaded square is characterized by blue and orange shutters.

The Museum of San Telmo was once a Dominican monastery dating to the 16th century. Its church is arrayed with golden murals by Catalan artist Josep Sert depicting Basque legends and relating the history of the Basque people. Among its Basque art and artifacts, the museum also displays three El Grecos.

Some of the city's finest architecture can be found in the New Town along Avenida de la Libertad. Most of the buildings date to the 1800s and include neoclassical, French Revival and Art Nouveau designs offset by towers, turrets, steeples and domes.

In the mountain town of Hernani (quite close to San Sebastián), is a museum dedicated to the highly regarded sculptor Eduardo Chillida. Dozens of the artist's monoliths are strewn over a manicured hillside. A 16th century Basque farmhouse preserves some of the local legend's smaller pieces including sculptures of marble, iron and steel, stone blocks and alabaster statues.

Eduardo Chillida monolith

Accommodations

8 beds in 2 double and 4 single rooms, all provided with a sink inside the room. Baths are shared. Both men and women are welcome.

Amenities

Towels and linens are supplied. There is a kitchen, dining room and meeting room.

Meals

Meals are not supplied with the lodging but guests may use the kitchen at their disposal.

Cost of lodging

Voluntary contribution.

Special rules

Guests must have a reference from a parish or a religious representative. They are provided with a key to the guest house. Open year round, but in August the hospedería is reserved to the relatives of the nuns.

Directions

By car: From San Sebastián take highway A8 and exit at Rentería.

By train: Get off at Rentería and take a taxi to the monastery. Buses also run from San Sebastián to Rentería.

Contact

Madre Superiora
Santísima Trinidad
Avenida Agustinas, 2
20100 Rentería (Guipúzcoa), Spain
Tel: 943/516444

CANARY ISLANDS
(CANARIAS)

MONASTERIO DE LA SANTÍSIMA TRINIDAD
Cistercian Nuns

The complex anchors a hilltop about four miles from Santa Cruz de la Palma. Nestled in a landscape of trees, the monastery overlooks the sea. Originally founded in 1946 by a group of nuns from Gran Canaria, the nuns moved to the present location in the year 2000. The monastery is a new facility built in a classic style. It does not contain any works of art. "It is functional and has all the characteristics of a 'proper' monastery including a cloister and church," said one of the sisters. The nuns have become renowned for their culinary talents and supplement their income from the sale of homemade pastries, jams and spirits.

National Park of the Caldera del Taburiente

La Palma, the "Green or Lovely Island," as the Canarians have dubbed it, has the National Park of the Caldera del Taburiente at its center. An impressive geological formation, at more than five miles wide, it is one of the world's largest. Craggy, pine-covered ravines, pointed red needles and numerous streams create an unrivaled natural landscape.

Founded more than five hundred years ago during the reign of the Catholic monarchs, the heart-shaped island is acclaimed for its scenery and lush vegetation. In spite of its beauty, it remains largely unspoiled by tourism. The world's steepest island, it is encased by rugged cliffs which fall dramatically to the coast to meet a handful of coves and beaches of black sand. The interior is a verdant milieu of indigenous pine, giant fern and laurel.

Santa Cruz de la Palma

From the monastery, a serpentine road over Las Cumbres Mountains leads to Santa Cruz de la Palma, the island's capital and main port. An elegant town, it has preserved a number of colonial-style homes with intricately decorated wooden balconies typical of the island, numerous fine churches and 16th century buildings. The remarkable Iglesia El Salvador is installed on a cobbled street behind the seafront. Its interior shelters exquisitely detailed, Mudéjar-inspired coffered ceilings. A full-sized replica of the Santa María, Columbus' flagship, stands in Plaza Alameda.

Los Llanos de Ariadne is the island's second largest city. It is surrounded by thick banana plantations, almond and date orchards and verdant hillsides. The top of El Time offers vistas of the Gorge of the Angustias, the hidden town of San Andrés, the natural swimming pool of the Charco Azul and the Port of Espíndola.

The Canary Islands is an archipelago of seven large and six small islands in the Atlantic off Africa's northwest coast. They exist in a kind of perpetual spring. The Greeks and Romans called them the *Happy* or *Fortunate Islands, Garden of the Hesperides* and *Atlantida*. (Some historians suggest that the legendary continent Atlantis was located here.) Actually the tips of volcanoes that first erupted from the sea fourteen million years ago, the islands present a picture of rugged beauty and are graced with an outstanding range of scenery encompassing forests, sandy deserts, sheer rock faces and perfectly round craters. The coastline constitutes beaches and extensive palm-dotted dunes. The flora of the Canaries is quite unusual and includes plants from almost every vegetation zone in the world in addition to numerous endemic species. There are scheduled ferry services, hydrofoils and jet foils between the islands.

The island's original inhabitants were called *Guanches* and *Bimbaches of El Hierro*. A tall race with fair skin and blond hair, they once lived in the cliffs, natural caves and small settlements and made their living as shepherds and farmers. They practiced an elaborate cult of the dead and were masters of a sophisticated embalming technique, similar to that of the Egyptians. By the end of the 15th century, the Guanches were totally conquered by the Spanish and eventually most of their culture vanished.

Traces of their civilization are contained in mysterious inscriptions carved into the rocks of the Belmaco Cave in the south part of the island. Other cultural fragments are evidenced in the *silbo* (whistling), a strange language still used by the shepherds of La Gomera to communicate over long distances; and a primitive Canarian form of wrestling which originated in tribal custom. *Gofio*, a flour made of roasted cereals, once the staple diet of the natives, remains a typical feature of Canarian cuisine.

Santa Cruz de Tenerife

Mt. Teide

The largest island in the chain is Tenerife, locale of Mt. Teide, a monumental dormant volcano and the highest point in Spain (12,162'). Called White Mountain, it is laced with nearly two dozen hiking trails. Stunning views of the island can be had from the ridge road which begins at La Laguna and heads to La Esperanza, home of the *esperancera*, a traditional Canarian cape still worn by some locals. For a glimpse into the sulfurous crater, there is a funicular to the top of the volcano. In the town of Güimar, the archaeological park displays pre-Hispanic step pyramids. Santa Cruz de Tenerife, the island's capital, houses a number of worthwhile monuments including the 16th century Church of La Concepción. The archeological museum is highlighted by a collection of Guanche remains.

From Santa Cruz de Tenerife, an unusual route leads inland through a primitive landscape into the Anago land mass. It passes San Andrés, a small fishing village with ruins of a circular fortress and the enormous artificial Beach of Las Teresitas, made with tons of sand imported from the Sahara. The coast road through Punta de Los Organoz ends in Igueste de San Andrés, a quaint enclave with an unusual cemetery clinging to the rocks. Nearby are megalithic remains and stone circles dating to the Guanche civilization. Until recently the village of Taganana could only be reached on foot, by mule or by boat. Its inhabitants are believed to have descended from Nordic people who settled here in total isolation.

Candelaria's basilica and interior view of its dome.

A few miles inland from the capital is La Laguna de Tenerife, the cultural center of the islands and home to its university. Considered an architectural gem, La Laguna's streets are fringed with stately homes underscored by delicate galleries of Canarian pine called *tea*. Scores of monuments represent Gothic, Renaissance and Baroque periods. A beautiful basilica can be visited in Candelaria, located on the coast, south of Santa Cruz.

The island of La Gomera sustains a primitive charm combined with ancient customs. Fields carved into terraces carpet the valleys and expose a characteristic landscape. Before his final departure for the Americas, Columbus stopped in San Sebastián de la Gomera, the island's capital. His presence is unmistakable in several parts of the city including the house which provided him with his water supply for the long journey. Written on the well are these words: "With this water, America was baptized." La Gomera is also home to the National Park of Garajonay, a main habitat of silver laurel, a specimen which spreads thickly over the mountains and valleys. The forest claims more

National Park of Garajonay

than 400 species of flora. Hidden in one of the valleys is the tiny hamlet of Chipude, famous for its handmade pottery.

The smallest island of the chain is El Hierro. Pliny called it *Lagartaria* because giant lizards, remnants of extinct prehistoric creatures roamed the rugged terrain. Valverde, the capital, has a lovely square overlooking the sea. The Bimbaches continue to occupy scattered settlements over the wild landscape, a verdant milieu of sabine, a tree noted for twisted, gnarled trunks that brush the ground.

Accommodations

There are 30 beds in single and double rooms. Half the rooms have private baths. Both men and women are welcome. Maximum stay is 15 days. Open year round.

Amenities

Towels and linens are supplied on request. A meeting room is available to guests.

Meals

Breakfast, lunch and dinner are provided on request to guests seeking spiritual retreats or those staying for short periods (weekends). Other arrangements may be made upon arrival.

Cost of lodging

Costs vary depending on length of stay, number of meals, etc.

Products of the institution

Typical homemade pastries, jam and spirits are available for sale.

Directions

By car: From La Palma follow the directions to Breña Alta.
By ferry or plane to Palma: Take the bus from Santa Cruz de La Palma. The bus stop is a 5-minute walk from the monastery.

Contact

Anyone who answers the phone
Monasterio de la Santísima Trinidad
Encrujicada, 52
38710 Breña Alta (La Palma) Spain
Tel: 922/414500

ABADÍA CISTERCIENSE DE SANTA MARÍA DE VIACELI

Cistercian Monks

Abadía Cisterciense de Santa María de Viaceli

Installed in a breathtaking location between the sea and mountains, the monastery is a relatively new institution (completed in 1910). The first group of monks arrived in 1904. They came from an abbey in France to found a new monastery. This was made possible through the donations of Antonio and Manuel Bernaldo de Quirós who left their family possessions to the Benedictine Order.

Construction of the monastery took six years and was the first cement structure in Spain. This Cistercian monastery led to the forma-

tion of other monasteries including: Santa María de Huerta, Santa María de Sobrado and Santa María Evangelio in the Dominican Republic. "The complex is not artistic, but it is simple and pretty. It is a copy of a Gothic monastery, what you might call neoclassic style," said one of the monks.

During the Civil War, the monastery was the site of a martyrdom; Padre Pio Heredia and eighteen monks were killed. Canonization of the monks is currently underway.

Cóbreces is a tiny town west of Santander. It is quite close to the seaside resort of Comillas, known for its Modernista architecture. Framed by two beaches, Playa de Oyambre and Playa Comillas, the town center is a place of cobbled streets and arcaded sandstone mansions. The central feature of the ancient core is the paved Plaza Mayor.

Examples of Catalan Modernista architecture include Comillas' best-known monument, Gaudí's El Capricho. Now a restaurant, the Mudéjar-inspired fantasy features an unusual tower, half lighthouse, half minaret, covered in flowery yellow and green tiles. Overlooking the sea is the Universidad Pontificia, another building representative of the modernism era. The summer palace of the Marqués de Comillas is surrounded by an imitation castle wall with oubliettes and concealed dungeons.

To the west of Comillas is San Vicente de la Barquera, a small fishing port and resort noted for its 15th century bridge. On a hill near the Río Escudo, the old-world town is offset by arcaded streets and ramparts. The upper town is dominated by the Nuestra Señora de los Ángeles, a Gothic, rose-colored church. It shelters the sculpted Renaissance tomb of the inquisitor Antonio Corro.

Accommodations

1 triple, 7 double and 9 single rooms. All have private baths with showers. Both men and women are welcome. Closed Christmas week.

Amenities

Towels and linens are provided.

Meals

All meals are provided with the lodging.

Cost of lodging

To be arranged. Preovisional cost $16.

Products of the institution

The monks produce a semi-matured cheese, *Queso Trapa*, in their own factory near the monastery. It is sold locally and internationally. The factory phone number is 942/725055.

Special rules

Only adults are allowed inside the hospedería. Punctuality is required at meal times.

Directions

By car: From Santander take A67 west towards Torrelavega exiting on route C6316. Follow signs to Santillana del Mar and then to Cóbreces. By train: Get off at Santander and take the bus to Cóbreces.

Contact

Padre Hospedero
Abadía Cisterciense de Santa María de Viaceli
39320 Cóbreces (Cantabria), Spain
Tel: 942/725017
Fax: 942/725086
Email: ocsoacv@planalfa.es
Website: www.planalfa.com

SAN FRANCISCO
Trinitarian Nuns

San Francisco

The monastery is quartered in the old section of Laredo, a picturesque town of Cantabria and a part of Green Spain. Bathed in a golden light, the region is characterized by crashing seas and the snow-capped peaks of the Picos de Europa. The landscape in between includes Neolithic cave paintings, medieval towns, cobbled streets and stone farmhouses. Laredo is approximately thirty minutes from Bilbao and Santander.

"The old part of Laredo is still beautiful but they are building so much on the modern part," exclaimed the Madre María Teresa. The monastery was founded at the end of the 16th century by the Franciscan Order. As with many other institutions, it suffered from the religious suppression of 1835 which forced the community to leave. In addition, many works of art were lost during the French invasions. In 1884, it was reopened by the present order which has continued in residence since that time.

San Francisco

The hospedería of the monastery has always hosted pilgrims traveling to Santiago de Compostela via the northern branch of the route. Management of the guest house and the art of embroidery are the main activities of the sisters.

Laredo is beautifully situated in Santoña Bay. The inviting sandy beach has made the small town one of Cantabria's most popular coastal resorts. The fast growing modern district adjoins the old town, a section of narrow lanes edged with balconied houses. The 13th century Nuestra Señora de la Asunción preserves sculptures, a Flemish altar and an enormous bronze lectern.

Close to Laredo is the small port of Santoña. Relics of fortifications are reminders of Napoleon's plan to turn the port into a northern Gibraltar. Santoña is the hometown of Juan de la Cosa, the cartographer who sailed with Columbus on his second voyage to America.

Leaving Laredo, the road climbs and offers views of the town and Santoña Bay. It continues along a stretch of rocky coast to Castro Urdiales, a fishing village and popular resort built around a natural harbor. Distinguished by enormous buttresses and pinnacles, the fortress-like Iglesia de Santa María stands high above the port. The partially ruined castle was built by the Knights Templar and safeguards a lighthouse. The town is one of the oldest settlements on the Cantabrian coast and is delineated by handsome glass-fronted houses lining an elegant promenade.

Accommodations

There are two sections of the guest house (up to 50 beds):
1) 18 beds in a dormitory with 6 shared baths.
2) 32 beds in quadruple and double rooms. A few double rooms have private baths, the rest are shared. Both men and women are welcome. The guest house is often fully booked. Call well in advance.

Amenities

Towels and linens are supplied on request. Each section of the hospedería has a fully equipped kitchen which guests may use. There is a chapel, meeting room and garden.

Meals

Meals are not provided, guests may use the kitchen facilities.

Cost of lodging

Double with private bath: $12.00 per person (including towels and linens).
Quadruple: $11.00 per person (including towels and linens).
Dormitory: $9.00 per person (including towels and linens).
Prices without towels and linens average $2.00/$3.00 less.

Products of the institution

During the summer, the nuns sell embroidered items in the cloister of the monastery.

Special rules

Guests are provided with keys to the guest house.

Directions

By car: From Bilbao or Santander take highway A8 or route 634 and exit at Laredo. The monastery is in the old quarter of town.

By train/bus: Get off at Bilbao or Santander and take a bus to Laredo.

Contact

Madre Hospedera
San Francisco
San Francisco, 22
39770 Laredo (Cantabria), Spain
Tel: 942/606600 -942/606141
Mobile phone: 639/053072
Fax: 942/606600

MONASTERIO NUESTRA SEÑORA DE LAS CALDAS
Dominican Monks

Built on a small mountain and surrounded by a few structures, the monastery possesses a favorable position. The original hermitage (which contained the image of Mary) dates to medieval times. It was near the thermal waters of the Besaya River and was the property of the town of Barros. Las Caldas means "the hot" in Latin and referred to the waters.

In 1605, the Dominican friars of Santillana Del Mar were asked to settle in the hermitage. They accepted and became an independent monastery in 1611. After a pilgrimage, Prior Malfaz became devoted to the Virgin. In 1663, he laid the groundwork for the present structure. Funds were provided by Ana María Velarde de la Sierra, a local woman of means. The project was completed in 1683 and the 12th century statue of Mary was then transferred to the new church.

Like other religious institutions throughout the country, the monastery suffered the devastation of the French invasions and the suppression of the monastic orders during the 19th century. At that time, the friars were forced to leave. The order returned in 1877. During the Civil War, nine friars died trying to protect the convent and the image of Mary. Restoration of the complex began in 1943. The monastery was turned into a seminary/college for Dominican friars and a new hospedería was built. In 1970, the seminary was transferred to Valladolid.

The complex is composed of a Baroque 17th century church, cloister and convent (cells of the friars, refectory, chapter house and library). The simple cloister is adorned with a fine collection of Baroque paintings representing scenes from the life of Santo Domingo de Guzman. The church's impressive retablo was built to preserve the statue of the Virgen de Las Caldas. Each of the six lateral chapels has a retablo dedicated to a saint.

Santillana del Mar is about 7 miles from the monastery. Its inhabitants jokingly refer to it as the city of three lies: one, it isn't saintly;

two, it isn't flat (llana means flat); and three, it isn't by the sea. Despite its popularity and the fact that the city has become a tourist mecca, it is among the most perfectly preserved medieval villages in Spain. Santillana del Mar maintains an old-world atmosphere embodied by exquisite medieval buildings and cobbled streets. Its ensemble of 15th to 17th century golden stone mansions and palaces imbues the town with a distinctive character while offering a glimpse of the old country nobility of Spain. The houses are underscored by wooden galleries or iron balconies filled with flowers, their plain stone façades enlivened by coats of arms.

The Romanesque La Colegiata de Santa Juliana conserves the relics of Santa Illana, the martyr after whom the village was named. It straddles the entire north side of the Plaza de la Colegiata. Built in the 12th century, the interior was remodeled in Gothic style. The Romanesque cloisters are defined by twin columns and vivid biblical scenes sculpted on the capitals. The Plaza Mayor is the heart of town and the setting for the Museo Diocesano.

La Colegiata de Santa Juliana

The 400-year old Convento de Regina Coeli has been occupied since the 19th century by Clarist nuns. Gothic in style, the convent has a rich art collection featuring religious paintings and statues damaged or abandoned during the Spanish Civil War. Much of the restoration has been done by the nuns.

A short distance from town are the Altamira Caves which are embellished with prehistoric rock paintings renowned for their beauty, vivid coloring and excellent state of preservation. Written application must be made months in advance to arrange a visit. Even then, only a small number of visitors are admitted each day. A museum near the caves displays a variety of Stone Age materials and explains the significance of the paintings.

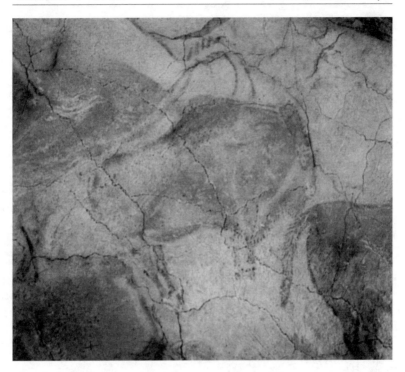

The cave paintings were accidentally discovered by a hunter in 1869. Four years later, archaeologist Marcellino Sanz de Sautuola happened upon the underground chambers containing the paintings, most of which date to the late Magdalenian period, c. 15,000-10,000 BC. Often referred to as the Sistine Chapel of Cave Art, the ceiling of the chamber is emblazoned with animals. The caves' most famous drawings are of bison. The artists used the rock contours to create shape and movement resulting in extraordinarily realistic figures. Predominantly painted in red, ocher, black and brown, the minerals used to create the paints were taken from the caves.

Accommodations

7 doubles (that can become triples) with private bath. Both men and women are welcome. The hospedería is the property of the monks, but is managed like a small hotel. Since it is often fully booked on weekends, the management suggests mid-week stays. Open year round.

Monasterio de Nuestra Señora del Río y San José

Cistercian Nuns (Congregation of San Bernardo)

Monasterio de Nuestra Señora del Río y San José

Occupying a mountain site, the monastery is about a mile from the small town of Liégarnes. The present community has inhabited the monastery for the past few years. The sisters were drawn to the verdant and tranquil scenery. "If someone comes here to meditate, we know that a walk in the country-side will bring a feeling of peace and serenity," said the madre. Once a farm, the building has been almost completely renovated.

Liégarnes is one of the most traditional towns of Cantabria. A spa town, its historic center and environs are rich in Roman ruins. It is part of what is considered Green Spain; approximately one-third of the region is comprised of protected areas. The varied landscapes and climates are characterized by crashing seas and the snowcapped Picos de Europa. Between the grandeur of the coastline with its beautiful

Monasterio de Nuestra Señora del Río y San José

bays, romantic fishing villages and impressive mountain range lies the Neolithic cave paintings of Altamira, Roman settlements, stone farmhouses and medieval towns. Cantabria's architectural patrimony covers a broad range of styles. Entire towns reflect the simple folk architecture of stone mansions with coats of arms and lathed wooden balconies placed to catch the sunlight. Many of the region's towns have been declared areas of artistic interest.

Attesting to Cantabria's interesting history, an abundance of Moorish, pre-Romanesque and Romanesque buildings remain. The simplicity of their designs presents an interesting counterpoint to the lavish splendor of Gothic, Baroque and Art Nouveau styles.

Accommodations

There are 2 types:

1) Inside the monastery: 6 doubles with shared baths, both men and women are welcome.

2) Outside the monastery: 20 beds in dormitories suitable for large groups. Guests must provide their own sleeping bags. Baths are shared. Men and women welcome.

Amenities

Towels and linens are only supplied inside the monastery. There is a meeting room, garden, orchard and chapel.

Meals

1) All meals are offered to guests staying inside the monastery.

2) No meals are offered to guests staying in the dormitory, however, there is a kitchen at their disposal.

Cost of lodging

1) Inside the monastery: $24.00 per person/per night, all meals included.

2) Dormitory: $6.00 per person/per night.

Special rules

Inside the monastery, punctuality is required at meal times and there is an 8:15 pm curfew. For all guests there is a minimum stay of two days, a maximum of eight. Open year round.

Directions

By car: From Santander take A8 east towards Bilbao and exit at Solares following signs to Liégarnes. From there follow the signs to the monastery.

By train/bus: Get off at Liégarnes and take a taxi or walk to the monastery.

Contact

Madre Hospedera
Monasterio de Nuestra Señora
del Río y San José
Barrio Los Prados 8
39722 Liégarnes (Cantabria), Spain
Tel: 942/528150
Fax: 942/528665
Email: ocsonsrsj@planalfa.es

CONVENTO-SANTUARIO DE
NUESTRA SEÑORA DE MONTESCLAROS
Dominican Friars

Convento-Santuario de Nuestra Señora de Montesclaros

The convent's location is high above the River Ebro. According to one of the fathers, "You can hear its low rumbling from the convent." Backdropped by mountains, the structure sits in the midst of a woodland a couple of miles from the dam of the river. "It's a good place for hiking and resting," said the Father Superior.

According to tradition, hundreds of years ago the area was settled by a group of Andalusians fleeing the invading Moors. During those tumultuous years, the religious images they carried were often hidden in caves to protect them from the marauders. Due to an apparition of Mary, one of the hiding places chosen by the fleeing Andalusians later became a pilgrimage site. Around the year 1000, a small chapel was built on the site. In the 16th century, the first community of Dominican friars founded the convent. They remained in residence until the mid-1800s when they temporarily abandoned the convent during the suppression of the religious orders.

The convent and most of the complex reflect the architecture of the Renaissance period, although the first chapel is pre-Romanesque. The original statue of the Virgin Mary is fashioned of golden wood set with precious stones. The present religious community consists of four friars who care for the church, conduct services and host guests of the convent. Twice a year, the convent has two special celebrations which attract many pilgrims: Fiesta de la Rosa, the last Sunday of May and Fiesta of the Procuradores, the second Sunday of September.

Located in southern Cantabria, wonderful views of high peaks, deep river valleys and lush green fields comprise the landscape. Reinosa, a handsome market town, is nearby. It is filled with old stone structures and is close to Retortillo and the remains of Roman Juliobriga, a town which

Reinosa

once provided protection from the tribes of Cantabria. Cervatos is also in the vicinity. Its former collegiate church has erotic scenes that warn against material pleasures. Towards Orbaneja del Castillo are the canyons of the Ebro. Sculpted by centuries of wind and rain, the rugged cliffs have been shaped into beautiful, intriguing forms. Arroyuelo and Cadalso are home to two churches built into the rock, structures that date to the 9th and 10th centuries.

Not far from the convent is the town of Alto Campoo. Occupying a lofty aerie in the Cantabrian Mountains, this winter ski resort is dominated by the towering *Pico de Tres Mares* (Peak of the Three Seas), so named because of the rivers rising near it.

Accommodations

There are 40 rooms with 1 to 4 beds each. Baths are shared. Men, women and families are welcome.

Amenities

Towels and linens are provided. There is a meeting room available to guests.

Meals

All meals can be included with the lodging. According to the father, "Our food is very good, some people come just to eat here."

Cost of lodging

$21.00 per person, full board. Other combinations can be arranged upon arrival.

Special rules
The guest house is open from 7 am to 12 midnight. Guests are expected to return no later than midnight. Open year round for large groups. Open from Easter until October for individuals and small groups.

Directions
By car: From Santander take route A67 west to route N611 south past Reinosa to Puerto Pozazal and then head southeast on route S614 to Polientes and the convent.

By train: From Madrid or Santander, get off at Reinosa and take a taxi to Montesclaros (20 kms).

By bus: From León/Salamanca/Bilbao there are buses to Reinosa. From Reinosa take a taxi to Montesclaros.

Contact
Padre Superiore
Convento-Santuario de Nuestra Señora de Montesclaros
39417 Montesclaros (Cantabria), Spain
Tel: 942/770559 - 770553
Fax: 942/770559 (call before faxing)

CONVENTO SANTA MARÍA DE LA MERCED
Mercedarian Nuns (Contemplative congregation)

Enveloped by the verdant countryside of the region, the convent is just outside of Noja, one of the beach towns skirting the coast of Cantabria. The convent is less than half a mile from the beaches but is far removed from the noise and crowds of the coast. "Just to give you an idea, our town has 1,600 inhabitants during the winter but more than 80,000 during the summer," explained the Mother Superior.

Santa María de la Merced was founded in 1988 as a branch of the Mercedarian Monastery of San José in Derio. The nuns transformed an old house into a monastery and are presently building a new chapel.

Convento Santa María de la Merced

Noja is a small port town with a stretch of sandy beaches and lagoons. According to local legend, the town's name is derived from Noah and the story that the Ark was found on one of the nearby mountains. During the 12th century, Noja was encircled by stone walls; traces of the once massive construction remain. Possessing a somewhat medieval flavor, the town reveals several old churches as well as a number of mansions including the Casa de los Churruachos and the Palacio Peña de Oro. Gothic San Martín displays an intricately sculpted façade and rose window. Santa María La Nova dates to the 14th century; its cemetery is remarkable for ancient carved headstones. East of Noja, the village of Ramales de la Victoria has prehistoric caves containing engravings and etchings.

Inland from the convent is Pazo de Oca, a grand country villa. Although the interior is not open to the public, the exterior of the house and grounds can be seen. The lavish 18th century manor is a montage of granite, greenery and lichens complete with a crenelated tower, serene garden and picture pretty lake.

Accommodations
4 beds in 2 double rooms, both with private bath. Both men and women are welcome but together only if married.

Amenities
Towels and linens are provided.

Meals
Meals are not provided with the lodging. There are many restaurants in town.

Cost of lodging
Voluntary contribution. The nuns said that they are spending a lot of money for the chapel and hoped the voluntary contribution would "be generous." Open year round.

Products of the institution
During the summer and by request, a large variety of homemade pastries typical of the region are prepared and sold by the nuns.

Special rules
The gate of the complex is open from 7:00 am until about 10:30 pm.

Directions
By car: From Santander head east following the signs to Noja (on coastal route S430). Before entering Noja there are signs indicating "Monjas Mercedarias" that lead to the convent.
By train: Get off at Santander and take the bus to Noja.
From Bilbao: During the summer, there are direct buses. During the winter, take a bus to Laredo and change to Noja.

Contact
Convento Santa María de la Merced
Madre Superiora
Cabanzo, 27
39180 Noja (Cantabria), Spain
Tel: 942/630086

Monasterio Casa de la Trinidad
Trinitarian Nuns

Amidst the verdant landscape of the northern coast, the monastery is a short walk from the village of Suesa. "There aren't any works of art but there is a splendid panorama which conveys a unique sense of spirituality," said the sister.

Monasterio Casa de la Trinidad

The structure was built in 1887 by a group of nuns of the Trinitarian Order. The nuns were originally from El Toboso. After a terrible epidemic of tuberculosis caused the death of many of their order, the remaining sisters journeyed to Suesa to build another monastery. Generous donations were made to the order's cause and within a year, the present building was completed.

Until 1974 the nuns taught school to the local population. At that time, they decided to devote themselves entirely to spiritual activities. "We would like to make the monastery a center of spirituality, as if we were living in the 12th century," said the sister. The monastery organizes concerts of classic music which are held in the church.

Cantabria is a region of rugged terrain, marked by high mountains such as the Picos de Europa, by broad valleys hugging a sinuous cliff-lined coast and by a series of quiet river estuaries through which the Bay of Biscay enters. Now a haven for historians and beachcombers, it was once a refuge for Christians during centuries of Moorish domination. Much of that period's religious architecture remains in the area's small towns and villages, evocative evidence of its diverse heritage.

Accommodations
The guest house was completely renovated and enlarged in 1998. It has 14 double rooms, each with private bath.

Amenities
Towels and linens are provided. There is a meeting room that guests may use.

Meals
All meals can be provided with the lodging.

Cost of lodging
To be arranged when reservations are made.

Special rules
There is no curfew, guests are provided with a key. During the winter months, only groups are hosted. The monastery is open year round.

Directions
By car: From Santander head east on the road along the coast (route S430) about 25 kms to Suesa. The monastery is on the edge of town.
By train: Get off at Santander and take the bus to the monastery (get off the "Nautilius" bar. It's a 5 minute walk to the monastery). From Santander there is also a ferry to Suesa that leaves every half hour during the summer, every hour during the winter.

Contact
Anyone who answers the phone (they speak some English)
Monasterio Casa de la Trinidad
39150 Suesa (Cantabria), Spain
Tel: 942/510021
Fax: 942/510129
Email: MONTRINI@santandersupernet.com

SANTA CRUZ O SAN ANTONIO
Clarisse Nuns

Not far from the coast of Cantabria, the monastery is on the outskirts of the small town of Villaverde de Pontones. The community inhabiting the monastery was originally founded in Santander in 1656. The nuns lived there until 1835. During the suppression of the monastic orders in 1835, the sisters were forced to leave. At that time, they joined another community in Santillana del Mar.

Santa Cruz o San Antonio

In 1917, the Bishopric asked the nuns to settle in their present location in an old house donated by a wealthy local family. Due to the deteriorating condition of the building, it had to be completely rebuilt. Of the original structure, only the 18th century chapel and Gothic vault remain. According to one of the sisters, "The building looks more like a house of the mountains than a classic monastery." The sixteen nuns who inhabit the monastery have established a Repostería where they make a large variety of sweets.

The nearby port of Santander occupies a beautiful protected bay enveloped by hills. In 1941, a devastating fire destroyed a portion of the city center. The area was rebuilt with wide boulevards, numerous parks and public spaces. The broad Avenida de Alfonso XIII runs inland from the harbor and ends in Plaza Porticada. The town's cathedral was restored after the fire. Although of modern vintage, the design reflects its former Gothic style and retains an early 12th century crypt with three naves.

La Magdalena is an English-style palace on the peninsula of the same name. It was once a royal residence for Alfonso XIII and his queen. The Museo de Bellas Artes has works by Goya including a portrait of King Ferdinand VII. The Museo de Prehistoria showcases relics from prehistoric caves in Cantabria as well as Roman coins and pottery. The collection of the Museo Marítimo includes rare whale skeletons, hundreds of species of local fish and an assortment of model ships.

The seaside suburb of El Sardinero is on the north side of the peninsula. A popular resort, it offers an inviting beach, an enormous Belle Epoque casino and seafront terraces. In the summer months, a dance and music festival featuring everything from jazz to chamber music takes center stage.

El Sardinero Casino, Santander

The Spa at Puente Viesgo

Not far from the monastery is the spa town of Puente Viesgo and its prehistoric grottoes. Dotted around the limestone hills above the town, the caves are a labyrinth of stalactites and stalagmites. The most spectacular, Cueva de Castillo, is open to the public. Its walls are covered with graceful drawings of stags, horses and bison. The colors used to draw the images were derived from minerals found in the cave. It is believed that these drawings predate the art at Altamira, the most famous caves in Cantabria.

Accommodations

6 beds in 1 double and 4 single rooms. Only the double room has a private bath; the rest are shared. Both men and women are welcome. Open year round. The guest house books early for July and August. Make reservations well in advance.

Amenities

Towels and linens are supplied and there is a kitchen.

Meals

No meals are supplied. Guests may use the kitchen or dine outside of the monastery.

Cost of lodging

$9.00 per person. Price for guests staying for long periods will be determined depending on length of stay.

Products of the institution

A large variety of pastries can be bought at the monastery. Special pastries are made during weekends, Christmas and on request.

Special rules

Guests staying for more than a week are required to send a 50% advance deposit. Maximum stay is one month. Guests are provided with a key to the guest house.

Directions

By car: From Santander take A8 and exit at Villaverde de Pontones. Once there ask for Monasterio San Antonio (or Santa Cruz).
By train: There is no public transportation to the monastery.

Contact

Madre Superiora
Santa Cruz o San Antonio
Prado, s/n
39793 Villaverde de Pontones (Cantabria), Spain
Tel/Fax: 942/508041

CASTILLA-
LA MANCHA

Convento de la Purísima Concepción y San José

Trinitarian Nuns

Convento de la Purísima Concepción y San José

The convent is in the center of El Toboso, a small village of La Mancha, a town strongly connected to the story of Don Quixote and the windmills made famous by Miguel de Cervantes. Dulcinea, alias Doña Ana Martinez Zarco, the woman who inspired Cervantes, was born in El Toboso. Her house has been restored to its original 16th century style and attracts many visitors each year. The town is also the locale for the Biblioteca Cervantina which shelters the masterpiece by Cervantes in eighty different languages.

Known as the "Little Escorial of La Mancha," the convent is an impressive structure built in Herreriano style. "Our walls are 1.5 meters thick," said the Mother Superior. The complex which includes the convent and church was built in 1680 by Ángela María de a Concepción who had a vision of the convent as it looks today. Nine years after having the vision, she came and built the convent and then reformed the order of the Trinitarian nuns. "The founder was a lady of great respect, a great writer and a woman of deep spirituality. She is still loved and worshipped by many people who think she is highly miraculous," commented the mother. The procedure of beatification for her, interrupted during the Civil War, has begun again. "We are working on it," the mother continued.

Convento de la Purísima Concepción y San José

The convent was deprived of many of its territorial possessions during the suppression of the monastic orders. The Civil War was yet another disaster for the nuns. "The convent was turned into a *cuartel* (barracks), the nuns were forced to leave and most works of art were stolen," the Mother Superior recounted. Some of the nuns were returned to the convent but most of the patrimony was lost. Nevertheless the sisters have established a museum for religious items and important paintings of the 16th and 17th centuries. There is a project underway to enlarge the museum.

The church also sustains some valuable artwork: the main retablo, a painting by a disciple of Coello and a painting representing Ángela María and the founding sisters. Since the nuns live in seclusion, the convent is not open to visitors but the cloister can be viewed through a grating in the museum. The guest quarters are in a separate area.

The drive along the plains between El Toboso and Ciudad Real evokes Cervantes' world of Don Quixote and Sancho. Campo de Criptana is a representative village of whitewashed dwellings sprawled on a hillside topped by windmills. The small town of Alcázar de San Juan has an archeological museum with an important collection of Roman mosaics.

Puerto Lápice is notable for its Manchegan fortifications and windmills. Near Villarrubia de los Ojos, in the heart of what is known as wet La Mancha, is the National Park of Las Tablas de Daimiel. A vast region peppered with inland lagoons, it is of considerable ecological value. The wetlands are covered with masiegas and reeds and provide wintering and resting places for thou-

Windmills

sands of migrating water birds. The Lagoons of Ruidera are also near-by. Comprised of fifteen linked waterways, the wetlands are separated from each other by natural barriers broken in places by spectacular waterfalls.

Ciudad Real, capital of the province, was founded in 1255. A frontier zone between Christianity and the Arab civilization, the town's past is reflected in the fortress-like Villa Real. Built by Alfonso X, it was walled and protected by one hundred and twenty towers.

Puerta de Toledo

At the entrance to the Alcázar Real, the Mudéjar-style Puerta de Toledo was built in what was the last part of the Jewish Quarter. It is among the largest alcázars in Spain. The town's noteworthy religious buildings include: the Romanesque Church of San Pedro, the oldest church in Ciudad Real; Iglesia de Santiago, an elegant Gothic-inspired building; and the Cathedral of Nuestra Señora del Prado, characterized by an enormous nave and Renaissance-style reredos.

North of the convent is the little town of Quintanar de la Orden. The corn and vine growing district of La Mancha, it was the region where Cervantes set the adventures of Don Quixote. Just east of the convent is Mota del Cuervo, a quintessential La Mancha village.

South of the convent are lagoons of great ecological interest as well as Tomelloso, one of the wine centers of La Mancha. The surrounding countryside is strewn with emblematic buildings called *bombos*.

Accommodations

15 beds in 5 single and 5 double rooms with private bath (only 1 single has its own bath outside the room). Both men and women are welcome.

Amenities

Towels and linens are supplied.

Meals

Only breakfast is provided with the lodging.

Cost of lodging

$18.00 per person.

Products of the institution

The nuns restore the antique objects of the monastery.

Special rules

Punctuality at breakfast is required (10:00 am). Guests have the key to the guest quarters. Open year round.

Directions

By car: From Madrid take NIV-E5 south to Ocaña and take N301 east past Quintanar de la Orden until the sign to El Toboso (CM3103 south).

By train: Get off at Madrid and take a bus to El Toboso.

Contact

Anyone who answers the phone
(Call in advance of your arrival)
Convento de la Purísima Concepción y San José
Padre Juan Gil 2
45820 El Toboso (Toledo), Spain
Tel/Fax: 925/197173

MONASTERIO DE SANTO DOMINGO
Dominican Friars

Main square, Ocaña

The Monastery of Santo Domingo lies in the center of Ocaña, a small town on the highway connecting Madrid with Andalucía. Its Plaza Mayor of Madrid is considered one of the most beautiful in Spain. Passing through the land of Don Quixote, the countryside is defined by windmills, vineyards and olive groves.

The monastery was founded in 1527 by the Dominican Order. Over the centuries, the institution grew in importance, much of its growth due to its central position near Madrid, Toledo and Cuenca. A novitiate center for missionaries to Asia (Vietnam, Japan, China), it wasn't closed during the suppression of 1835. Many friars educated in the monastery were sent to the Far East and many died during their mission; six were canonized on October 1, 2000.

Although they escaped the suppression, the monastery and church suffered greatly during the Civil War (1936-1939). The monastery was occupied during that time and valuable works of art were confiscated. Within the Renaissance-style church, the only artwork that remains is the choir and the painting of the main altar representing the founding of the Dominican Order.

The library, once considered among the richest of the entire country, lost most of its books and documents. A two-story cloister and a number of halls can be used by groups seeking spiritual retreats, workshops, etc. The large complex is inhabited by nine friars who, in addition to their spiritual activities, manage the guest house.

Very close to Ocaña is the town of Aranjuez. Conceived by King Fernando VI and based on the ideas of the Enlightenment Movement, the town was built in the 18th century and is underscored by a grid of streets and avenues that emanate from a central square. Gardens and Baroque and Rococo palaces run alongside the River Tagus and constitute an inviting picture. Built in 1761, the graceful Puente Largo spans the river.

The Palacio Real de Aranjuez, a royal summer palace and garden intended to emulate the grandeur of Versailles, grew up around a medieval hunting lodge. The present brick and white stone compound was built in the 18th century after several fires destroyed other structures on the same site. The main façade is Renaissance with Baroque influences. Valuable tapestries, porcelain, furniture and artwork adorn the rooms. The extraordinary staircase was designed by Giacomo Bonavia. The Throne and Porcelain Rooms are particularly beautiful; the latter richly endowed with hand-crafted porcelain. The Arab Salon closely resembles the Hall of the Two Sisters in the Alhambra and features Arabic inscriptions in stucco and a carved wood ceiling.

Gardens surround the palace and border the Tagus with centuries-old trees. The Parterre was styled in the French manner and laid out by Philip V in 1726. Busts of Roman Emperors and statues of gods enhance the garden grounds.

An artificial island in the Tagus is home to the Jardin de la Isla. An avenue of plane trees fringes the banks of the river. The Jardin del Principe is the largest and perhaps most captivating of the gardens. Designed by Etienne Boutelou, the same French landscape gardener who designed the Parterre, it is filled with sculptures, fountains and an array of specimen plants brought back from the Americas. At the far end of the garden stands the Casa del Labrador, a neoclassical hunting pavilion constructed by Carlos IV.

Cuenca

East of the monastery is the city of Cuenca, also called the *Casas Colgadas*, the city of hanging houses. Symbolic of the town, the houses are set on a promontory at the northern edge of La Mancha where they cling to the cliffside on the rocks that flank the Hoz del Huécar. Cuenca's streets lead upwards, a 300' difference in altitude between the lower part of the city and its crowning castle.

Cuenca is a dramatic fortress-like city with an arcaded plaza at its core. Its cathedral is considered a national monument. Initially built in Gothic-Norman style, it was later continued in Anglo-Norman. Among the cathedral's treasures (housed in the museum) are paintings by El Greco, Gerard David, several panels by Juan de Borgoña and a Byzantine diptych from the 14th century. The museum also preserves an important collection of tapestries, carpets and monstrances dating from the 15th to 18th centuries.

The Torre de Mangana, a watchtower at the top of town, is all that remains of an Arab fortress. The Archeological Museum houses relics from various excavations within the province in addition to an exhibition of Roman Cuenca. The Museum of Abstract Art is situated in the Casas Colgadas and has a collection of important abstract artists including Tapies, Viola, Chillida and Saura. The structure is graced with lattice windows and Mudéjar panels.

Ciudad Encantada, *The Enchanted City*, is not far from Cuenca. Set in a pine woods, it is an impressive mass of limestone rocks and outcrops. Over thousands of years, the rocks have been sculpted by wind, rain and snow to form spectacular and unusual shapes. In keeping with their form, they are named: *The Ships, The Seal, The Roman Bridge, The Tank, The Stony Sea.*

Accommodations
130 beds in a 3-story guest house. Rooms are all double; 22 have private baths, the remainder shared baths. Both men and women are welcome.

Amenities
Towels and linens are supplied.

Meals
All meals are supplied. Those staying out all day can request picnic lunches. Meeting rooms are available for guest use.

Cost of lodging
Provisional cost per person/per night: $21.00/$23.00 full board.

Special rules
Groups only (10 and up). Guests are provided with keys. Open year round.

Directions
By car: From Madrid take highway N4 and exit at Ocaña.
By train/bus: Get off at Madrid or Toledo. Buses to Ocaña are frequent. The bus stops very close to the monastery.

Contact
Padre Hospedero
Monasterio de Santo Domingo
45300 Ocaña (Toledo), Spain
Tel: 925/130055
Fax: 925/120871

SANTA ÚRSULA
Augustinian Nuns

In the very heart of Toledo, on a side street of Calle de la Trinidad, the monastery and church were built in the 13th century and have been declared Patrimonio Nacional. The monastery itself cannot be visited, however, the recently restored church is open to the public. It harbors a cache of paintings, Mudéjar decorations and a beautiful altar and retablo by Alonso Berruguete (1486-1561). "We are very close to the cathedral, the Taller del Moro, Santa Cruz and many interesting sites," said Madre Teresa, the sister in charge of the guest house and the Residencia Universitaria.

Toledo, panoramic view

Once the capital of Spain, Toledo is one of the country's architectonical treasures. Poised on a granite hill surrounded on three sides by a gorge of the Tagus River, the site forms a natural fortress. Historically and culturally, Toledo is one of Spain's most important cities. Of pre-Roman origin, it was known as Toletum and was captured by the Romans in 193 BC. Although Toledo prospered as a capital of the Visigothic empire in the 6th century, its golden age began during Moorish rule, from 712-1085. Under the Moors and then the kings of Castile, Toledo was a center of Moorish, Spanish and Jewish cultures.

The art introduced by Moorish craftsmen is evident today including their traditional gold and silver inlay work and the crafting of Toledo sword blades, highly regarded for their strength and design. The city was also the center of the mysticism symbolized by its adopted citizen, El Greco, who painted the famous *View of Toledo*.

Toledo's narrow medieval streets harbor a montage of monuments representing Moorish, Mudéjar, Gothic and Renaissance periods. One of the city's landmarks is El Alcázar, a huge square fortress easily recognized by its four pointed peaks. During the 16th century, it served as a residence for Charles V and Philip II. The structure was nearly destroyed during the Spanish Civil War but has since been restored.

The Mosque of El Cristo de la Luz is a gem of Hispano-Moorish architecture. Its interior displays horseshoe arches and caliphal-style vaulting. Small and square in design, a great apse was built at a later date, an addition which vastly increased the size of the mosque.

Toledo is surrounded by partly Moorish, partly Gothic walls and gates. The irregular pattern of its streets, alleys, iron-grilled windows and open courtyards reflects its Moorish heritage. Nine gates breach the medieval walls. The most commonly used is the *Puerta de Bisagra* (Gate of the Hinge), an arch flanked by two massive round towers. Erected in 1550 to welcome Emperor Charles V, it bears his royal coat of arms.

El Cristo de la Luz

Puerta de Bisagra

Gothic cathedral, Toledo

The landmark Gothic cathedral is considered one of the finest in Spain. Construction was begun in 1226 on the site of the Moorish Great Mosque and continued for more than 250 years. The church's steeple rises harmoniously above spires and turrets and defines the Toledo skyline. Vast and awe inspiring, it features nearly eight hundred stained glass windows. Running the length of a nave and four aisles, side chapels give way to one another, each ornamented with altarpieces, paintings and sculptures. The museum displays El Greco's *Expolio* and a collection of paintings by Titian, Velazquez and Ribera.

The Mudéjar-inspired Church of Santo Tomé was built in the 14th century at the behest of Don Gonzalo Ruiz de Toledo. A medieval nobleman, he was the central figure in El Greco's most famous painting, *El Entierro de Conde de Orgaz*. Regarded as a masterpiece of Baroque art, the painting was executed as a posthumous tribute two hundred years after the count's death and can be viewed in a chapel adjoining the church.

At one time, Toledo's Jewish Quarter was home to ten temples. Today only two remain. The Tránsito Synagogue was funded in the middle of the 14th century by a wealthy Toledan Jew, Samuel Leví, who held the post of Chancellor of the Exchequer under Peter I of Castile. The synagogue is graced with a large collection of wonderful adornments and one of the most beautiful coffered ceilings in Toledo. Built in Mudéjar style, it is now a Sephardic museum. Exhibits recount the arrival of Jews in Spain, their life under the Romans, Visigoths, Moors and medieval Christians, the start of the Inquisition and their expulsion from Spain in 1492.

Tránsito Synagogue

The synagogue is a singular embodiment of the architecture and art of Iberian Jewry, a synthesis of Islamic, Gothic and Mudéjar influences. Certain decorative motifs, such as the six-pointed star, are symbols peculiar to Jewish culture. The structure is one of great beauty with arches set into the side walls, a place where lattices allow light to filter through and create an aura of tranquility.

Synagogue, Santa María la Blanca

The Synagogue of Santa María la Blanca predates the Tránsito by almost two centuries. The simple exterior contrasts starkly against the lavish decor of its interior which has a luminous nave and four aisles divided by horseshoe arches. Believed to date to the late 12th or early 13th century, the building is a splendid work of art. It exudes an exotic Byzantine/Persian mood personified by the profuse ornamentation of its capitals and walls and elaborate configuration of its windows.

In Toledo and the surrounding region, numerous castles attest to centuries of conflict that swept to and fro across the land. The fortresses date from different periods and survive in varying states of preservation. San Servando Castle is within Toledo's city limits and has been perfectly restored. Its origins can be traced to the Visigoths. At one time, it was a royal seat and bastion of the Order of the Knights Templar.

Nearby castles include the Castle of Orgaz, a massive 14th century citadel enclosed by battlements. Manzaneque Castle, ca. 15th century, stands in the center of a small town and is visible from some distance away. The fortress is notable for its handsome entrance and neat proportions.

Impressive and well preserved, Guadamar Castle was constructed at the end of the 14th century by a Castilian nobleman. Its quarters provided lodging for many Castilian kings and for Emperor Charles I. The square keep is accented by six round towers. Enormous coats of arms adorn the walls and the sides of the main entrance. The castle has countless windows with flattened arches; its interior is comprised of grand rooms where psalms and Latin prayers are preserved on friezes and moldings.

Guadamar Castle

Maqueda Castle dominates its small, old-world town. The complex served Alfonso I as a base from which to sally forth and capture Toledo from the Moors. It is underscored by blind walls and four great corner towers. The quaint town of Oropesa is famed for its embroidery and is home to the recently restored Castillo Oropesa. Dating to the 12th century, the massive keep and twin round towers rise from the very center of town to form the silhouette of the castle.

Accommodations
There are two kinds:
1) Hospedería: 6 beds in 3 double rooms (one of which has a private bath) in a small apartment independent from the monastery. Both men and women are welcome.
2) Residencia Universitaria: 35 beds in single and double rooms with shared bath; only women are allowed. Students attending the entire academic year have priority. Arrangements should be made well in advance, accommodations book early.

Amenities
1) Hospedería: Towels and linens are supplied. The apartment contains a living room.
2) Residencia Universitaria: Towels and linens are not supplied to students staying for the academic year. Living room, study room and laundry room.

Meals
1) Hospedería: Meals are not supplied to guests in the apartment.
2) Residencia Universitaria: Meals can be supplied on request.

Cost of lodging
1) Hospedería: $12.00 per person/per night.
2) Residencia Universitaria: per person/per month: $271.00 double room; $313.00 single room (no meals included). Per person/per night: $12.00 (no meals included); $18.00 (all meals included). Closed in August.

Special rules
Guests staying in the apartment are provided with a key. Residencia Universitaria has a 10:30 pm curfew.

Directions
By car: Located in the center of Toledo.
By train: Get off in Toledo and take a bus to the center.

Contact
Madre Teresa
Santa Úrsula
Santa Úrsula, 3
45002 Toledo (Toledo), Spain
Tel: 925/222235

Monasterio San Juan Bautista

Benedictine Nuns

Monasterio San Juan Bautista

In a verdant valley on the outskirts of the small town of Valfermoso, the monastery is encompassed by the mountains of northern La Mancha. "The surroundings are beautiful, ideal for excursions," said the Madre Hospedera. "There are many interesting historical sites nearby," she added.

The monastery was founded in 1186 by a Benedictine community which settled here during the *reconquista*, the time when Christians reconquered the land from the Arabs. "As the reconquista advanced, monasteries were founded," the madre explained. The nuns lived uninterruptedly until 1936 when a fire (during the Civil War) completely destroyed the complex and the valuable artwork accumulated over the course of seven centuries. The monastery has been entirely rebuilt. "It is a pretty building but it is the nature around us that is the most beautiful," the madre continued.

Close by is historic Guadalajara, principal town of the province. Formerly *Arriaca* (place of stones), the town was founded by the Iberians. Traces of its walls can still be seen in the turrets of Alvar and el Alamin. The Palacio de los Duques del Infantado is its most characteristic building and the place where the Mendoza family held court. Built in 1461 by Jean Guás, the architecture reflects Renaissance and Mudéjar details. The façade is an paragon of Gothic-Mudéjar style. The interior harbors the Museo de Bellas Artes and a collection of 15th to 17th century works.

The 13th century Santa María de la Fuente was built using the remains of a mosque and possesses a minaret-like tower executed in Mudéjar style. The parish church of San Nicolás dates from the 17th century; it is enhanced by an elegant Baroque reredos on the high altar. Iglesia de Santiago reveals a Plateresque chapel by Alonso de Covarrubias. Iglesia de San Francisco was built on the site of a mosque and contains the mausoleum of the Mendoza family.

There are several interesting villages in the countryside near the monastery including Cogulludo, a charming village with a 16th century main square and the Palace of the Duques de Medinaceli, one of the earliest Renaissance buildings in Spain.

Heading north from the monastery is medieval Sigüenza, a town of Celtic origins. The heart of the old town is defined by the cobbled Plaza Mayor and Plaza del Obispo Don Bernardo, locale of the massive cathedral. Begun in the 12th century, work continued on the church for four centuries. Delineated by two battlemented towers, the structure resembles a fortress; its architecture represents Romanesque, Gothic, Mudéjar and Plateresque. The cathedral shelters the famous Doncel tomb and a chapter house covered with rib vaults. The Capilla del Espíritu Santo's doorway combines Plateresque, Mudéjar and Gothic styles. The chapel houses the *Anunciación* by El Greco.

Accommodations

The guest house has been recently renovated. There are 36 single and double rooms with private bath. Both men and women are welcome. During the winter, it primarily hosts guests seeking spiritual retreats. In July, August and September, it is open to all.

Amenities

Towels and linens are supplied. There is a meeting room and chapel that guests may use.

Meals

All meals can be supplied with the lodging.

Cost of lodging

To be arranged upon arrival.

Special rules

Curfew at 11:00 pm. Punctuality is requested at meal times. Closed from December 20th until January 10th.

Directions

By car: From Madrid take highway N2 past Guadalajara and exit Valfermoso de Las Monjas.

By train: Get off in Madrid and take the bus to Valfermoso. The bus only runs on Mondays, Wednesdays and Saturdays. Other times, get off in Jadraque and take a taxi to the monastery (about 20 kms).

Contact

Madre Hospedera
Monasterio San Juan Bautista
Extramuros, s/n
19196 Valfermoso de Las Monjas (Guadalajara), Spain
Tel: 949/285002

CASTILLA - LEÓN

CASA DE ESPIRITUALIDAD NUESTRA SEÑORA DE LOURDES

Franciscan "Alcantarinas" Nuns

**Casa de Espiritualidad
Nuestra Señora de Lourdes**

Founded in the 1960s, the casa lies at the entrance to the village of Arenas de San Pedro. A modern building, it is encompassed by a pretty garden in a mountainous landscape. "We are making improvements all the time," said one of the sisters who emphasized the efforts of the nuns to make every stay a pleasant one for their guests. The main activity of the casa is hosting groups seeking spiritual retreats but guests wishing to enjoy a relaxing stay are also welcome.

The countryside is bounded by the huge mountain chain of the Sierra de Gredos, a milieu of craggy, snow-capped summits, green rolling hills and rocky outcrops. Lush vegetation grows on the slopes while forests of pine, oak and holm oak tower over the bare rugged peaks. Arenas de San Pedro has become the "capital of Gredos." Reached via the Puerto del Pico, a pass at over 4,000', the village is filled with leafy streets made all the more charming by a square castle sitting beside the Plaza Mayor. The town is well known for its leather-work and ceramics.

A number of medieval villages can be reached via twisting mountain roads. They include El Arenal, Guisando, El Hornillo and Mombeltrán where a well-preserved 14th century castle can be visited. South of town, near Ramacastañas, are the limestone caverns of the Cuevas del Águila. In the east near El Tiemblo stand the Toros de Guisando, four stone statues resembling bulls believed to be of Celtic/Iberian origin.

Along the western edge of the Sierra de Gredos, not far from the casa, are several appealing towns. The itinerary follows roads that twist through woodlands of chestnut, almond and olive groves passing rural villages of stone and wood. La Peña de Francia is the highest point in the range. Atop the peak is a Dominican monastery which shields a Byzantine-style statue of the Virgin and Child. Miranda del Castañar is a fortified village lined with houses offset by wide eaves.

Nearby Talavera de la Reina is a centuries-old pottery center. The ceramics are celebrated for their high artistic value and quality. The workshops continue to pro-duce the yellow and blue *azulejos* (tiles) that have distinguished the town's artisans for hundreds of years. Some of the loveliest azule-jos are sheltered within the Ermita del Virgen del Prado.

Azulejos

A busy market town, Talavera de la Reina stretches alongside the Tagus River where a 15th century bridge marks the entrance to the old part of town. The town preserves four Gothic-Mudéjar churches, the largest of which is the Colegiata de Santa María la Mayor. Built in 1194, the structure is remarkable for its fine rose window. The 14th century Iglesia de Santiago el Nuevo represents another example of Mudéjar architecture.

Accommodations
40/50 beds in single, double, triple and quadruple rooms, all with private bath. Both men and women are welcome.

Amenities
Towels and linens are supplied, but younger guests on a budget may use their own sleeping bags and towels.

Meals
All meals are supplied on request.

Cost of lodging
To be arranged according to the size of the group, length of stay and time of year.

Special rules
Guests are provided with keys to the guest quarters. Open year round. Since the nuns participate in an annual spiritual retreat (dates vary), advance reservations are required.

Directions
By car: From Ávila take route N502 south. After about 70 kms, turn right following the signs to Arenas de San Pedro.
By train: Get off in Ávila or Talavera de la Reina and take a bus to Arenas de San Pedro.

Contact
Madre Superiora (or anyone who answers the phone)
Casa de Espiritualidad Nuestra Señora de Lourdes
Camino de Sotillos s/n
05400 Arenas de San Pedro (Ávila), Spain
Tel: 920/370626

Monasterio Santa María La Real
Cistercian Nuns (Trappist Congregation)

The monastery is just outside the small town of Arévalo. The present institution is a modern construction (1973) but one that claims a long history. Thanks to a donation by the Naron family who rebuilt La Lugareja (an old Benedictine church), a community of Cistercian nuns settled in Arévalo in the 13th century. The first name of the monastery was Santa María de Gomez-Roman. The name was changed to Santa María La Real when the nuns moved to the palace of San Juan II

Square in Arévalo

(donated by King Carlos V), a safe haven from bandits who once roamed the countryside.

The sisters remained in residence until 1835 when the suppression of religious orders forced them to leave. By the time they returned in 1951, a great deal of progress had taken place in the countryside. The once small village had grown into a town and the palace was surrounded by houses. The townspeople decided to build a new home for the nuns in the quietude of a pine woodland.

The monastery conserves several paintings dating to the 14th century. A 16th century choir is housed in the chapel. The original church, still called La Lugareja, is situated on a hill a short distance from the town center. Declared a national monument, the building is a fine example of Mudéjar architecture and is open to visitors.

At the junction of the Río Arevalillo and the Río Adaja and surrounded by the typical landscape of the Castilla plains, the historic town of Arévalo is home to a 14th century castle. The edifice is marked by an imposing keep and is the place where Queen Isabel spent her childhood. Arévalo's old town has also been declared a national monument. Its spacious, porticoed Plaza de la Villa is enhanced by attractive, half-timbered buildings. The plaza itself is defined by emblematic arcades and is the site of the church of San Martín which features two large Mudéjar towers and traces of Romanesque frescoes.

Nearby Coca occupies a pine forest setting. Originally an Iberian settlement, the town was known to the Romans as Cauca and is marked by the extraordinary 15th century Castillo de Coca. A classic Mudéjar fortress built for the Fonseca family, it is constructed entirely of brick and includes countless Moorish details. The gate of the wall sur-

Castillo de Coca

rounding the keep has a horseshoe arch inside a pointed brick arch. The general style of the building is late-Gothic with a multitude of defensive battlements and polygonal towers. The structure was built on a square plan laid in decorative patterns; it serves as an example of Mudéjar military architecture. A bridge spans the deep moats and leads through the Arco de la Villa, the main gateway.

Madrigal de las Altas Torres

A short distance from the monastery is Madrigal de las Altas Torres, birthplace of Isabel la Católica, an historic village with numerous Mudéjar-inspired remains.

An interesting itinerary heads north from the monastery into the Province of Valladolid. The town of Olmedo was immortalized by Lope de Vegas in his play *El Caballero de Olmedo*. Typically Mudéjar, it is enclosed by a curtain of walls. Seven gates dating from the 12th and 13th centuries allow entrance into the town. Among its seven churches, the most outstanding are the Mudéjar churches San Miguel and San Andrés and the Gothic Santa Maria.

Medina del Campo is where the Catholic monarchs established their official residence. It is also where Queen Isabel died. The Mudéjar structure of the restored Castle of La Mota towers over the town. The Ayuntamiento, Royal Palace and Collegiate Church of San Antolín are sited on the Plaza Mayor. Known for its fine white wines, the village of Rueda has a series of brick houses dating from the 17th and 18th centuries. The Baroque Church of La Asunción has a sacristy designed by Churriguera.

The town of Tordesillas shelters the Royal Monastery of Santa Clara. Built by Alfonso XI in the 14th century, it was used as a residence by Pedro I and as a refuge by Juana la Loca. The trefoil arches and interlace decoration of the Gothic church of San Antolín are attributed to builders from Toledo. The sebka panel on the façade is a reference to Almohad art. The town witnessed the historical Treaty of Tordesillas between Spain and Portugal which established the meridian by which land (already discovered and to be discovered) would be divided.

Accommodations
2 double and 4 single rooms, each with private bath. Both men and women are welcome.

Amenities
Towels and linens are provided.

Meals
All meals are provided with the lodging.

Cost of lodging
$21.00 per person/per night, all meals included.

Products of the institution
The nuns do embroidery.

Special rules

Maximum stay is 8 days. Guests are accommodated in a building separate from the monastery and are provided with keys to the guest house. Open year round, however, due to heating costs, the nuns prefer to host guests in the warmer months.

Directions

By car: From Madrid go north on highway A6 (Carretera Madrid-La Coruña) to exit 129 and signs to "Trapa" (an indication for the monastery).

By train: Get off at Arévalo and take a taxi.

Contact:

Madre Hospedera
Monasterio Santa María La Real
Apartado 50
Ctr. Madrid-La Coruña, km 129
05200 Arévalo (Ávila), Spain
Tel: 920/300231
Fax: 920/328006
Email: ocsoavi@planalfa.es
Website: www.planalfa.es

CONVENTO SANTA MARÍA DE JESUS
Clarisse Nuns

Ávila

The monastery is in the southern section of Ávila, a walled city of Old Castile on the upper Adaja River. Ávila's high altitude equates to cold winters and very pleasant summers. "Many people come here to spend the summer," said one of the sisters.

The community inhabiting the monastery was founded in the 15th century and until thirty years ago occupied another residence in the heart of Ávila. The order moved because the maintenance of the old building had become too costly. "It was so costly that it was less expensive to build a new one," said the Mother Superior. "We originally chose the new site because it was far from the city but the city eventually reached us. Fortunately our new home is on a hill where we have beautiful views of the countryside and the Sierra," she continued. The nuns live in seclusion; their main activity is making and selling homemade pastries typical of the area.

Ávila is one of the great religious centers of Spain. It is the home town of the highly venerated and mystic Saint Teresa (1515-1582), prioress of the Convent of Encarnación. A chapel was erected over her cell in 1630. There is also a museum containing relics of the saint. Nearby is the Convento de Santa Teresa; its plain Baroque façade is highlighted by a statue of the namesake saint.

Like stepping back in time, the walled city of Ávila exudes the atmosphere of medieval Castile. Sprawled on a hill at 3700' in the midst of a stark landscape, Ávila is surrounded by high hills on three sides and is known for its climatic extremes. Within the 36-foot walls that encircle the old city is an array of sober Gothic palaces, Romanesque churches, convents and monasteries. Built of stone, these structures are representative of the tough and austere Castilian spirit.

Originating as the Roman town of Avela, for more than three centuries after the Moorish invasion in 714, it alternated between Arab and Christian rule. The massive Romanesque fortifications contain eighty-eight semicircular towers and nine gates that allow entrance into the city. There is also access to a walk along the ramparts which offers panoramic views. The walls of the city, backdropped by towering, snow-covered mountains, can be appreciated in their full dimension from the Cuatro Postes viewpoint outside the city.

Alcázar gate

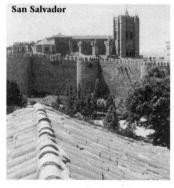

San Salvador

Standing against the walls is the imposing Cathedral of San Salvador. Featuring Romanesque and Gothic design elements, the fortress-like structure is built of granite, its interior underscored by red and white granite stonework. It consists of three covered naves with Gothic vaults, a transept and double ambulatory around the chancel. Many renowned artists are credited with the decoration of the church including Pedro Berruguete and Santa Cruz who painted a large reredos showing scenes from the life of Jesus.

The main façade has two 15th century Gothic towers, one unfinished. The work of architect Juan Guas, the tower was later renovated in Baroque style. The choir stalls are Renaissance. The cathedral museum showcases sculptures and a monstrance by Juan de Arfe.

Artistic architecture can be seen throughout the city. The Palacio de Polentinos has a rich Plateresque façade; the Renaissance Mansión de los Deanes and the Dávila are enriched by patios; the house of the Guzmanes claims the most beautiful turret in the city. The old town harbors the Jewish Quarter and the arcaded Plaza Mayor.

Just outside the walls is the Iglesia de San Vicente, considered one of the finest Romanesque buildings in Spain. Begun in the 12th century, it was not completed until the 14th. The church contains three naves, an outstanding transept and a tall, sober sanctuary covered with barrel vaulting. The western façade is highlighted by Romanesque sculpture.

San Vicente

The name Castile is derived from the many castles built by the Christian nobles during the reconquest from the Moors. The area is also known for unique stone gravemarks called *verracos* carved in the shape of boars or bulls and attributed to the Celts who once inhabited the region.

Accommodations

12 beds in single and double rooms, each with private bath (two of the rooms have a private bath located outside the room). Both men and women are welcome.

Amenities

Towels and linens are supplied. The facility includes a chapel, garden, meeting room, TV/reading room and a dining room with a microwave oven and refrigerator.

Meals
Meals can be prepared on request, however, they are not served by the nuns who live in seclusion. Guests can be provided with pre-cooked meals which they can heat in the microwave.

Cost of lodging
Provisional cost per person/per night (meals included): $24.00. Open year round.

Products of the institution
A large variety of pastries including *turron*, typical Spanish Christmas treats, are prepared by the sisters. A desert specialty of the monastery is *Corazones de Santa Teresa* (Santa Teresa's hearts). Similar to the renowned Yemas de Santa Teresa sweets made with egg yolk, the sisters' version has almonds in their "heart."

Special rules
Curfew at 10:00 pm.

Directions
By car: The monastery is in Ávila.
By train: Get off at Ávila. The N1 bus stops close to the monastery. Or take a taxi from the train station; average cost is about $2.

Contact
Madre Superiora
Convento Santa María de Jesus
La Luna, 3
05003 Ávila (Ávila), Spain
Tel: 920/220583
Email: mtp.fcclarisas@planalfa.es

REAL MONASTERIO SANTO TOMÁS
Dominican Friars

Real Monasterio Santo Tomás

The monastery is outside the walled city of Ávila, one of the main historical cities of Spain. A stately complex, the monastery's foundation (1479) has been attributed to different people. Recent studies credit it to Don Hernán Núñez Arnalte, secretary and treasurer to the Catholic monarchs, Don Fernando and Doña Isabel. Although Don Arnalte was certainly the original founder, it is obvious that such a vast undertaking would not have been possible without the intervention and support of the royal family.

Real Monasterio Santo Tomás

The majority of the structure was built between 1480 and 1483 although several additions were made at a later date. It is divided into three parts; the first and most somber is composed of the Claustro del Noviciado and the rooms that surround it. Its style is defined as Tuscan and most likely, it was built with money donated by Don Arnalte. The second section reflects the splendor and extravagance associated with the royal family. Gothic in style, it includes the church, choir, Claustro del Silencio, refectory, sacristy, chapter hall and cells.

The third part is the Royal Palace. Renaissance in design, it consists of the Claustro de los Reyes, halls and rooms. The façade of the church forms the letter "H" for "Hispanidad".

The first cloister, Claustro del Noviciado, is the smallest of the three. Claustro del Silencio is the most elaborate and is earmarked by a double series of arches. Its name is derived from use as a cemetery for the monks. The third and largest, Claustro de los Reyes, was once used as a university. Today it hosts the Museum of Oriental Arts.

During the French invasion at the beginning of the 19th century, the church was turned into a hospital. The interior displays a retablo by Pedro Berruguete and several engraved tombs: the alabaster tomb of Prince Don Juan, only male child of the Catholic kings; the tomb of Don Juan and Doña Juana, grandparents of Prince Juan; and the tomb of Don Hernan Arnalte, founder of the institution. The reredos on the high altar is attributed to Pedro de Berruguete.

The complex encompasses a large modern residencia with 180 single rooms, most of which are normally occupied by students and locals working in Ávila. The balance of the rooms are open to visitors, to groups seeking retreats and to individuals participating in conferences. Guests are invited to enjoy the gardens of the monastery.

Ávila is the capital of the province. Enveloped by walls and built on a hill along the banks of the Adaja, the city holds the distinction of being the highest in Spain. Of Celtic origin, numerous sculptures depicting bulls and pigs evoke this ancient heritage. Near El Tiemblo, *Los Toros de Guisando* (The Guisando Bulls), provide the most representative examples of this Celtic art form. On the Salamanca Road (a short distance from Ávila), stands the observation platform known as *Los Cuatro Poster*, a site offering the best view of the city.

Ávila is considered among the best-preserved walled cities in the world. At the end of the 11th century, under orders of Raimundo de Borgoña, work began on the ramparts. Rectangular in shape, with a perimeter of about 1.5 miles, the walls themselves form an impressive monument. Reinforced by ninety stout turrets, the most important is *Cimorro* (cathedral apse). Nine gates allow entrance into the city, including the monumental San Vicente and Alcázar. Ávila has been the residence of various kings of Castile and the seat of several courts.

Accommodations
60 single rooms, some with private bath. Both men and women are welcome but housed separately.

Amenities
Towels and linens are supplied. There are many meeting and reading rooms.

Meals
All meals can be supplied with the lodging.

Cost of lodging
$28.00 per person, full board (rooms with private bath).
$24.00 per person, full board (rooms with shared bath).

Special rules
Guests are provided with a key. Open year round.

Directions
By car: Near the center of the city.
By train: Get off at Ávila. Take a public bus, taxi or walk (1 mile) to the monastery.

Contact
For reservations contact the Residencia directly
Real Monasterio Santo Tomás
Apartabo 10
Plaza de Granada, 1
05003 Ávila (Ávila), Spain
Residencia - Tel: 920/221006 Fax: 920/257269
Convent - Tel: 920/220400 Fax: 920/254162

Monasterio Inmaculada Concepción
Concepciónistas Franciscanas

Monasterio Inmaculada Concepción

Monasterio Inmaculada Concepción

The monastery is in Ayllón, a small historical town at the foot of the Sierra de Ayllón in the province of Segovia. In addition to being a place of natural beauty, the town is surrounded by important historical sites. "Along the banks of the Río Duratón, there are many beautiful places but this beauty must be seen to be appreciated. It cannot be described," the sister said. "There are so many tourists, it is incredible to see how many there are... but our place is still serene. We are isolated from the noise and the crowd by the high walls which surround the monastery," said one of the nuns. "Moreover, within the walls there is a very large garden and sports grounds for visitors who come here year round," she added.

The large Renaissance complex was built in the 15th century by a noble family to host the nuns of the Dominican Order. Although many of the monastery's works of art and possessions were lost during the war against France, the nuns remained in residence during that turbulent period. The monastery has two double-storied cloisters; the lower floors are reserved for the nuns, the upper ones house guests. The interior shelters a statue of the Virgin Mary attributed to the school of Alonso Cano (1601-1667), an architect and sculptor who lived and worked in Seville, Granada, Toledo and Madrid.

Ayllón is a picturesque village with venerable reminders of the past. The arcaded main plaza is the heart of town and close to the 15th century Palacio de Juan de Contreras, a grand Plateresque structure, once completely encircled by a wall. The town of Ayllón and its Renaissance church have been recognized as national monuments. Nearby are the ruins of the San Francisco Convent, founded by St. Francis of Assisi. In the vicinity is the characteristic village of Maderuelo. Its houses form a unique oval-shaped cluster within clearly established boundaries.

Sitting in a landscape of rolling countryside, nearby Pedraza preserves its medieval air, as if time had come to a standstill at the entrance to the city. The quintessential Castilian town, it is enclosed by medieval walls and dominated by a huge castle perched on a rocky outcrop. The charming old town is filled with mansions graced with colorful coats of arms. The porticoed Plaza Mayor is an idiosyncratic Castilian square and the locale of the Romanesque Torre San Juan. Every September, the square is used as a bullring.

Castle of Pedraza

The castle of Pedraza is famous for having been one of the most impregnable castles in the country. It is completely inaccessible from three sides. A wide esplanade separates the fortress from the village. The coat of arms of the Valesco family (Pedraza residents in the 16th century) are featured on a solemn Gothic arch between two projecting guard houses.

Segovia

Segovia

When the province of Segovia was resettled in the 12th and 13th centuries, Romanesque architecture flourished throughout the countryside. Hardly a single village exists without some trace of that period. Outstanding among them is Sepúlveda. A weekend retreat for Madrileños, it remains an inviting town. Its houses line a ridge carved by the gorge of the Río Duratón and are ornamented with colorful coats of arms. A circuit of Roman walls and vistas of the Sierra de Guadarrama enhance the already scenic setting. Warm, ocher-tone public buildings instill a welcoming atmosphere to the old part of town. The 11th century Iglesia del Salvador is of Castilian Romanesque design. It has one of the first atria of this period and is underscored by a single-arched portico and free-standing bell tower.

Segovia, chief town of the province is about fifty miles from the monastery. Among the most beautiful cities in Spain, it is a UNESCO World Heritage Site. Surrounded by two rivers, the town is built along a ridge on the northern slopes of the Sierra de Guadarrama. The alluring locale encompasses medieval buildings, lofty city walls and an unusual Roman aqueduct. Slicing through the very heart of the city, the 2000-year old Roman waterway is a granite block bridge composed of more than a hundred arches. Constructed with Roman know-how and attributed to Trajan, the granite blocks were cut so perfectly that not a drop of mortar was used to join them. Nearly one hundred feet high and twenty-seven hundred feet long, the aqueduct is an exemplary engineering feat.

Occupying the highest point in town, the landmark Gothic cathedral is a dazzling structure offset by pinnacles, flying buttresses, a squarish bell-tower and elegant dome. The opulence of its interior is portrayed by vivid stained glass, fine sculpture and ironwork grills which enclose the side chapels.

One of Spain's most famous castles, the Alcázar represents the distinguished military architecture of Old Castile. The fortress ascends on a steep-sided crag between the valleys of the Eresma and Clamores. Rising above the towering crags, a multitude of gabled roofs, turrets and crenelations imbue the structure with a distinctive silhouette.

For centuries, the Alcázar was the favorite place of the monarchs. Gothic in design, much of the interior reflects a Mudéjar influence. Two opposing towers, Don Juan II and the keep guard the ship-like castle. Don Juan, the highest of the two, was designed

Alcázar

on a rectangular plan with twelve round towers and ornamented balconies. Views from the tower take in the town, Sierra de Guadarrama and the Meseta. The small towers of the keep are covered with conical slate spires topped with weather vanes. The Torre del Homenaje features pointed turrets, atypical of Spanish castles.

Accommodations
There are two types:
1) 75 beds in single and double rooms with private bath, both men and women are welcome.
2) 60/80 beds in a large dorm for groups with sleeping bags; both men and women are welcome. Baths are shared.

Amenities
Towels and linens are supplied in the single and double rooms, not in the dorm. Facilities include a large meeting room (up to 100 seats), smaller meeting rooms, garden, sports grounds, patio and a well-equipped kitchen.

Meals
All meals can be supplied on request (the nuns prefer that large groups use the kitchen, but arrangements can be made for meals).

Cost of lodging
To be arranged depending on type of accommodation, size of the group, length of stay, number of meals and time of year. Open year round. Provisional cost $15 per person.

Special rules
Each group or individual can set their own rules. If the nuns are doing the cooking, punctuality is required at meal times.

Directions
By car: From Madrid take highway N1 north towards Burgos. At exit 104 take N110 northeast following the signs to Soria and Ayllón.
By train: Get off in Segovia or Madrid. Buses run daily from both cities.

Contact
Madre Hospedera
Monasterio Inmaculada Concepción
San Juan, 4
40520 Ayllón (Segovia), Spain
Tel/Fax: 921/553039

MONASTERIO DE SAN JOSÉ
Benedictine Nuns

Monasterio de San José

"The institution was founded in 1601 and is very near the cathedral but far from the noisy area of the center," one of the sisters stated. Until 1813 when it was destroyed during the war, the monastery flourished and contained many works of art. By the 1820s, restoration of the complex was completed and the nuns returned. The community is one of the few that did not suffer from the suppression of 1835. "The suppression was not as bad for the nuns as it was for the monks," said the mother. "We were allowed to live here and continue our mission." Due to the destruction of the original building, the present institution does not contain any works of art. "Although our building is not beautiful, it is a large stone house that is quite functional," she continued.

The Burgos area claims to be home to Europe's oldest known human remains. They were found at the Atapuerca archaeological site a few miles from the provincial capital. A number of digs bear testimony to the presence of humans in pre- and protohistoric times.

Burgos was founded in the ninth century, a time when it huddled beneath the protective might of the castle erected by Diego Rodríguez Porcelos. In the following century, Fernán González declared the city the capital and the Kingdom of Castile under the rule of King Ferdinand I. Situated on a mountainous plateau, Burgos is known for its architecture and great historic tradition. Undoubtedly though, it is most famous for its cathedral. Prominently situated on a terrace at the foot of Castle Hill, the handsome church soars above a landscape of wheat fields. The edifice represents one of the finest examples of Gothic architecture in Europe. Founded by Ferdinand III on the site of an earlier Romanesque building, the cathedral's lofty, filigree spires dominate the city while the interior showcases many works of art, relics and religious artifacts.

Among its architectural splendors is the large Golden Staircase by Diego de Siloé. Featuring lavish gilded banisters by Hilaire, the French master ironsmith, the stairs were built to compensate for the difference in height between Calle Fernán González and the cathedral. In the transept over the crossing, the lantern was erected following the collapse of the original dome and is the work of Juan de Vallejo. It forms an eight-pointed star worked in filigree and rises on four massive columns above the tombstones of El Cid and his beloved Doña Jimeña. A rose window encircles a six-pointed Star of David superimposed by the sculpted figures of the eight Kings of Castile. The ensemble is flanked by twin towers that support openwork spires designed by Johan of Cologne.

From the mirador, views of Burgos embrace the old quarter, the Carthusian Monastery and Las Huelgas Reales Convent. The latter was founded in 1187 by Alfonso VIII and Eleanor of Aquitaine (daughter of Henry II of England). A small cloister is delineated from the original construction by semicircular Romanesque arcades. Other highlights include the San Fernando Cloister, chapter house and richly decorated Mudéjar chapels.

Burgos

The ancient core of the city is the Plaza Mayor. With the spires of the cathedral peeking out from behind the grand buildings lining the arcaded square, the setting is reminiscent of the days of monarchs and *hidalgos*, claimants to noble lineage. Reached through narrow lanes from the plaza, the Church of San Gil is considered one of Castile's prized parish churches. Built in the 14th/15th centuries, its nave, two aisles and transept served as a canvas for cathedral sculptors and artists who created a montage of images and paintings ranging in style from Gothic to Baroque.

Church of San Gil

With Burgos at its center, the Pilgrims' Way travels east and west through a myriad of historic towns. Heading west, Tardajos' roots can be traced to the Romans. Its parish church was built between the 13th and 16th centuries. The town plan of Hornillos del Camino is evocative of the Jacobean Age, with an old pilgrims' hospital and two medieval bridges. Castrojeriz was originally Roman and one of the great cities of the area. Its past glory is witnessed by a castle, town walls and an abundance of churches including the 13th century Collegiate Church of Santa María del Manzano built by Berenguela the Great. On the banks of the Pisuerga River, Itero del Castillo is the last town along the Pilgrims' Way. Once an important frontier outpost, it retains a 13th century hermitage chapel and a bridge built by order of Alfonso VI.

Itero del Castillo

Traveling east from Burgos, Ibeas de Juarros is close to the well-known Atapuerca cave and archaeological dig. Agés' parish church contains the remains of King García of Navarra who was defeated and killed by Ferdinand I. The hamlet of San Juan de Ortega is home to a 12th century church completed in the 15th century. At 5:00 pm on the day of the spring and autumn equinoxes, pilgrims come to see the *Milagro de la Luz*, the time when the sun's rays stream through the church windows and illuminate the *Angel of the Annunciation*.

Accommodations
16 single rooms (some of which can become doubles), with private bath. Both men and women are welcome.

Amenities
Towels and linens are supplied. There is a meeting room, chapel and parking.

Meals
All meals can be supplied on request.

Cost of lodging
To be arranged upon arrival.

Special rules
Open year round for spiritual retreats and to students of the University of Burgos; other guests are welcome in July.

Directions
By car: The monastery is in the center of Burgos, near the hospital San Juan de Dios.
By train: Get off at Burgos and take a taxi or bus to the monastery.

Contact
Madre Superiora
Monasterio de San José
Emperador, 9
09003 Burgos (Burgos), Spain
Tel/Fax: 947/205373

CONVENTO DE SANTO DOMINGO
Dominican Friars

Lying in the heart of Castilla - León, the small village of Caleruega is the setting for the monastery as well as the birthplace of Santo Domingo de Guzmán (1170-1221), founder of the Dominican Order. The church of the Dominican Mothers was built on the site where the saint was allegedly born. The nuns' convent was established in 1266 after the death of the saint. Until the 20th century, the monastery of nuns was the only one in Caleruega and visitors to the birthplace of the saint were attended by a small group of religious representatives living in the Vicariate beside the house.

In the 1920s, the order built a large institution and expanded the old Vicariate. The convent was completed in 1957. During the early years, it served as a novitiate for the Dominican Order. As the number of vocations decreased, the convent became a house for spiritual retreats, peaceful meditation and meetings.

In addition to the monastery, the complex is composed of the Cellar of Beata Juana, where tradition holds that St. Dominique's mother performed the miracle of the "Multiplication of Barrels of Wine" which she distributed to the poor; the 16th century Baroque church which unified the new structure with the 13th century building; the sacristy and the crypt which preserve the remains of Santo Domingo and his brother Antonio; the Well of Santo Domingo, considered the exact birthplace of the saint; and the cloister, recently restored to appear as it did in the 13th century.

Not far from Caleruega is Baños de Valdearados where, in 1972, a villa dating from the late Roman period was unearthed. The villa is embellished with an enormous mosaic depicting Dionysian scenes. Near the baths is the town of Gumiel de Hizán which is distinguished by a medieval town plan. The parish church has an imposing façade; its museum exhibits a Romanesque Madonna attributed to the Silos school.

Further south is Aranda de Duero, a town that traces its period of splendor to the reign of Henry IV. It rose to its pinnacle under Isabel the Catholic. Situated in the old part of town, the Isabelline Gothic-style Church of Santa María is graced with an heraldic portal and a cornice of major proportions. The interior has a lovely Renaissance retablo credited to Simon of Cologne.

Accommodations
60 single and double rooms with private bath. Both men and women are welcome.

Amenities
Towels and linens are supplied and there is a meeting room.

Meals
All meals are supplied with the lodging.

Cost of lodging
To be arranged according to the size of the group, length of stay and number of meals included.

Special rules
Curfew at 11:00 pm. Open year round. Due to the cost of heating during the winter, only groups are accepted.

Directions
By car: From Burgos or Madrid take N1 to Aranda de Duero and take BU920 northeast following the signs to Santo Domingo de Silos and Caleruega.
By train: Get off at Burgos or Aranda de Duero and take a bus to Caleruega (there is only one each day).

Contact
Padre Hospedero
Convento de Santo Domingo
Plaza de Santo Domingo, s/n
09451 Caleruega (Burgos), Spain
Tel/Fax: 947/534061
Email: caleruega.es@dominicos.org
Website: There is no official website for the convent, but there is one about Caleruega that contains information about the convent and the history of Caleruega - www.lanzader.com/caleruega

CASA DE SPIRITUALIDAD NUESTRA SEÑORA DE BELÉN

Hermanas Filipenses

Casa de Spiritualidad Nuestra Señora de Belén

Nuestra Señora de Belén is located on the outskirts of Carrión de Los Condes, a small town on the Santiago de Compostela. Built in 1967, it was once a private boarding school for the children of Carrión. According to the sister, "we were the last to open a boarding school and the first to close, because there weren't enough children in Carrión and in this part of Spain." The school was closed in 1990 and since then has served as a house of spirituality to host retreats and guests seeking a restful stay. In front of the casa is an antique Jewish synagogue. Founded by Dom Sem Tob, a rabbi who lived in Carrión in the Middle Ages, the synagogue is no longer a religious site, but can be visited at various times during the year and at Easter.

The casa does not contain any works of art but is very close to the Sanctuary of Nuestra Señora de Belén, patroness of the town. During the summer months, volunteers open its medieval church to visitors coming to worship the Virgin Mary or to admire the building, a one-time fortress. The interior conserves a Romanesque altar and several paintings.

Carrión de los Condes was the birthplace of the Marquis of Santilliana. One of the old towns of the kingdom of León, it has retained a distinct atmosphere as witnessed in its monuments. The town's oldest church, the 12th century Santa María del Camino contains an assortment of sculptures, a Plateresque main reredos and 17th century tombs. The Church of Santiago is an important example of Romanesque architecture. Its portal is an exceptional work, due in part to the naturalistic facial expressions of the sculptures and to the artistic effect created by the folds of the robes and tunics. The Monastery of San Zoilo was founded in the 10th century. Over the years, it has been renovated several times including the conversion of the cloisters into Plateresque style in the 16th century.

Heading north from the casa is a string of monument-rich towns and villages. In Moarves de Ojeda, the Church of San Pedro showcases a Romanesque façade with a beautiful frieze. The town of Aguilar de Campóo is a place of historic and artistic importance. Although accounts trace its beginnings to the 9th century, many Roman and Visigothic remains have been unearthed which predate that period. Just outside of town is the Romanesque Monastery of Santa María La Real. After laying in ruins for years, it was recently restored, a restoration which led to the Europa Nostra Award. Founded in the 9th century, its Gothic church dates from the 13th. The latter has painted capitals and a lovely cloister.

Nearby Palencia stretches along the banks of the River Carrión and appears as an oasis amidst the extensive wheat fields of Tierra de Campos. In medieval times, the city was a royal residence and the site of Spain's first university. The aura of that period can be sensed in the city's center. Once encircled by fortified walls, Palencia was founded under the name of Pallantia. In Celtic times, it was the capital of the Vaccei people; during the Roman occupation, it was an important town of the Tarraconense people.

Catedral de San Antolin

Palencia's grandest monument is the Catedral de San Antolin, known as *La Bella Desconocida* (The Unknown Beauty). Built over the Crypt of San Antolin, it incorporates the remains of a 7th century Visigothic construction with the relics of an 11th century church. Gothic in style, it was begun in the 14th century and completed in the 16th. The cathedral has fine works of art ranging from Flamboyant-Gothic and Isabelline to Plateresque and Renaissance. The structure consists of a nave, two aisles, a transept and an ambulatory with five side chapels. Its museum has four 15th century Flemish tapestries, a painting of San Sebastian attributed to El Greco and Romanesque and Gothic paintings, images and sculptures.

The Church of San Martín de Fromista was built during the Romanesque period. The interior has a basilica with three naves and three apses in the sanctuary, the first round-shaped apses in western Spanish Romanesque style. Half-point arches rest upon pillars adjoining lavishly carved columns. Wider columns rise above the others in characteristic Romanesque form. The dome in the transept reflects Oriental inspiration. The windows, placed high on the walls, are long and slender and provide the only illumination.

Accommodations
75 single and double rooms, only a few with private bath but all with sinks inside the room. There are numerous shared baths. Both men and women are welcome.

Amenities
Towels and linens are supplied. Meeting rooms and chapel.

Meals
All meals can be supplied on request.

Cost of lodging
To be arranged upon arrival, depending on length of stay and number of meals included.

Special rules
Curfew at 11:00 pm. Open year round.

Directions
By car: From Palencia take route C615 north to Carrión de Los Condes. From Burgos take N120 west to Carrión de Los Condes.
By train: Get off in Burgos or Palencia and take a bus to Carrión de Los Condes.

Contact
Madre Hospedera
Casa de Spiritualidad Nuestra Señora de Belén
Avenida Mons. Leopoldo María de Castro, 6
34120 Carrión de Los Condes (Palencia), Spain
Tel: 979/880031

MONASTERIO SANTA MARÍA DE CARRIZO
Cistercian Nuns (Trappist Congregation)

Situated in the hamlet of Carrizo de la Ribera, the monastery is about 13 miles from León. "The surroundings are quite lovely and the Orbigo River offers the possibility of relaxing walks along its banks," said the Mother Superior. "Although we provide a very simple hospitality at our casa, people are usually very happy... perhaps because they find this a peaceful atmosphere," she continued. Since the nuns live in strict seclusion, visits to the monastery itself must be made by special arrangement.

Founded in 1176 by Doña Estefania Ramirez, the building was donated to the Cistercian Order. It flourished during the 15th, 16th and 17th centuries and became a large spiritual center inhabited by as many as eighty nuns. During the suppression of the 19th century, the nuns were forced to leave. They returned after an absence of three years and have inhabited the complex since that time.

A stone structure, its church has a Baroque organ and Romanesque apse. The archive is the most important room of the complex. Eight centuries of history are documented in parchments, books, contracts and illuminated papers. For more information on these artifacts, a book by Doña Concha Lobato titled *Colección Diplomatica del Monasterio de Carrizo* details the monastery's collection.

Carrizo is not far from Astorga. Once the Roman town of Asturica Augusta, it was a stopping place on the *Vía de la Plata* (Silver Road) and linked Andalusia to northwest Spain. It later became one of the towns on the route to Santiago, the most famous Christian place of pilgrimage in the Middle Ages.

Palacio Episcopal

The Palacio Episcopal was designed by renowned architect Antoni Gaudí. Its interior is embellished with stained glass and ceramic tiles and portrays the architect's originality and stylish beauty. The palace shelters relics attesting to Astorga's Roman heritage as well as an array of medieval religious.

Towering above the medieval walls in the upper part of town, Catedral de Santa María displays architectural styles ranging from Gothic and Plateresque to florid Baroque. A golden retablo by Gaspar Becerra underscores the Spanish Renaissance design. The church's museum conserves the 10th century carved casket of Alfonso III and many religious artifacts.

Astorga is the capital of La Margatería, a Spanish district composed of forty towns scattered over an area of 240 square miles. The inhabitants are believed to be descended from 8th century Berber, Celtic or Mozarabic invaders. For centuries they have married among themselves and preserved their customs; these entail singular family rites, solemn weddings, colorful costumes and distinctive dances. Their traditional dress includes elaborately embroidered garments: broad bottomed breeches and red garters for the men, crescent-shaped caps covered with a mantilla and heavy earrings for the women. Many of their homes are constructed of local stone with arched doorways and windows highlighted by white stucco or stone.

Castrillo de los Polvazares is thought to be the most beautiful Maragato town; Santa Colomba de la Vegas is a close second. The latter boasts a parish church with a polychromed coffered ceiling dating from the 14th century.

Very close to the monastery is León, a city whose origins can be traced to the year 68 AD, a time when the Roman *Septima Gemina* (the legion formed by the Emperor Galba), was quartered here. León lies on a fertile plain surrounded by woods, orchards and meadows. An intriguing composite of two cities, Roman and medieval walls accentuate the contrast between the old with its charming squares and historic monuments and the new, with broad avenues, modern buildings and spacious parks.

The symbolic monuments in León are its cathedral, the Collegiate Church of San Isidoro and the Convent of San Marcos. The cathedral is classic Gothic, representative of the architecture that spread throughout Europe during the 13th and 14th centuries. Its design is based on a Roman cross, with a nave, two aisles and a transept.

The cathedral is considered the "Beauty of León." Its design was greatly influenced by the cathedrals of Reims, Amiens and Sainte-Chapelle. The similarities are most evident in the purity of its lines and the surprising dimensions of its stained glass windows which illuminate the church's interior. The main façade is flanked by the Towers of El Reloj and Las Campanas.

León cathedral

The main reredos is attributed to Nicolás Francés, ca 15th century. The altar holds a silver urn by Enrique de Arfe which preserves the remains of San Froilán, patron saint of León. The cloisters were built in Renaissance style; frescoes from that period adorn some of the walls. A Plateresque stairway leads to the cathedral museum and more than fifty Romanesque carvings of the Virgin.

The Collegiate Church constitutes an example of early Romanesque art in Spain. The Pantheon of the Kings is its oldest section and forms a portico of the church founded by Fernando I and Doña Sancha. The original church, erected over an earlier pre-Romanesque construction dedicated to St. John the Baptist, was later destroyed by Almanzor. The interlaced vaults of thick marble columns form a series of Romanesque arches. Although the paintings on the vaults were completed in the 12th century, the bright colors have survived the centuries and are considered superb examples of Romanesque painting.

The Convent of San Marcos was originally founded in the 12th century for the Knights of the Order of St. James. The present day construction was designed by Pedro Larrea in 1513. Its Plateresque façade is covered with medallions, columns and pilasters; the chapter house is marked by a Mudéjar coffered ceiling. The façade of the church is covered with scallop shells, symbolic of the pilgrimage route to Santiago de Compostela.

San Marcos Convent

East of León in the direction of Gradefes, the Monastery of San Miguel de Escalada is a singular specimen of 10th century Mozarabic architecture. Rebuilt by monks from Cordova, its nave and two aisles are separated by rows of horseshoe arches.

Nearby are the Valporquero Caves. They can be reached via Felmín. The action of water and time on the limestone landscape has created a world of capricious forms complete with stalagmites, stalactites and what are known as *coladas* paintings, art created with pigments from local iron and sulphur oxides.

Accommodations
4 single and 5 double rooms, each with a sink and shower. Only 2 have private toilets. Both men and women are welcome, together only as a family. Arrangements must be made at least 5 days in advance of visit.

Amenities
Towels and linens are supplied.

Meals
Only breakfast is supplied, guests must take other meals out. There are several restaurants in the village.

Cost of lodging
To be arranged upon arrival.

Special rules
Curfew is flexible and will be arranged upon arrival. Closed mid-October to May.

Directions
By car: From León take route LE 441 west to Carrizo.
By bus: From León take the bus towards Benavides de Orbigo. It stops in Carrizo de la Ribera.

Contact
Anyone who answers the phone
Monasterio Santa María de Carrizo
24270 Carrizo de la Ribera (León), Spain
Tel: 987/357055
Fax: 987/357872
Email: matrapen@planalfa.es
Website: www.planalfa.es

Monasterio - Santuario de Nuestra Señora de la Peña de Francia

Dominican Monks

Crowning the windswept peak of La Peña de Francia, the monastery has been inhabited by the Dominican Order since 1437. Located at the highest point in the range, it overlooks the hills and valleys on the western edge of the Sierra de Gredos.

The monastery was built on the site where images of Mary, Santiago, San Andres and Jesus were discovered in 1437. They were probably buried by Christians during the Arab invasions but once found were considered miraculous and therefore worshipped by the local populace. Since Mary's image was considered the most important, the monastery was named after it. Like Catalonia's Virgin of Montserrat, the Madonna is black. Stolen in 1872, it was recovered a few years later in a severely damaged state. In 1900, a replica was made to replace the original. The Capilla de la Blanca was erected in 1767 to commemorate the site where the images were found. The imposing structure, decorated with Tuscan-style pilasters, contains a bas-relief relating the story of the images.

Until a few years ago, the monastery ran a small guest house to accommodate pilgrims to the shrine. Since that time, the facility has been completely renovated into a three-star hotel managed by a lay company.

The monastery is outside the town of La Alberca. Considered one of the most beautiful villages in Spain, its streets are lined with overhanging, half-timbered houses which lend the town an air of antiquity. The Church of the Assumption was built in the 18th century. It shelters a granite pulpit, Gothic processional cross and a figure of Cristo del Sudor attributed to Juan de Juni.

La Alberca lies in the Meseta, a cool, mountainous region in Spain's central plateau. Wheat fields and dry, often dusty plains dominate the landscape broken here and there by woodlands, lakes and scenic gorges. The area is characterized by narrow roads which wind through a countryside laced with tiny, atmospheric villages.

A popular driving route travels from La Peña de Francia to Candelario with stops along the way. Miranda del Castañar is a completely walled village with a parish church, castle and the Plaza de Toros. The cobbled streets of Candelario present a picture of well-preserved village architecture. The 16th century church of Our Lady of the Assumption reveals a central absidal chapel with a Mudéjar coffered ceiling.

To the west of La Alberca is Cuidad Rodrigo, a city with one of Spain's longest recorded histories. At one time, it was inhabited by Neolithic settlers. In 1100, Count Rodrigo González Girón gave the city his name. In the 12th century, King Ferdinand II rebuilt the Roman bridge and had the city walled. Its cathedral has stellar vaulting over the main chapel and choir stalls bearing the stamp of maestro Rodrigo Áleman.

Salamanca, Spain's great medieval university town, is about 60 miles north of the monastery. The town's history is reflected in its Renaissance architecture, often referred to as Plateresque because the details resemble ornate silver work. Renaissance elements give structure to Elizabethan forms, which in turn mix Flamboyant Gothic and Mudéjar features. The most extraordinary example of Plateresque style is the 16th century Iglesia-Convento de San Esteban. A single nave church, the façade's delicate relief was carved by Ceroni in 1610. A frieze embellished with medallions and coats of arms graces the area directly above the door.

Salamanca

Roman ruins

Founded as an Iberian settlement in pre-Roman times,
Salamanca's Roman heritage
is evidenced by the Puente
Romano. Built in the first
century AD, fifteen of its original twenty-six arches remain.
The illustrious work of the
Churriguera brothers (a family of architects), can be admired in the
golden stone buildings, particularly those in Plaza Mayor. The stone is
actually *piedra de Villamayor*, an initially soft and pliable sandstone
that eventually hardens and darkens to a deep, golden brown patina.

Salamanca is also home to the Catedral Vieja and Catedral Nueva.
Although joined together, the architectural style of each is quite different. Begun in the 12th century, the Catedral Vieja has a richly colored
altarpiece by Nicolás Florentino; its Torre del Gallo is one of the rare
Romanesque/Byzantine domes in Spain. The Catedral Nueva was
begun in 1513; its western façade is offset by laced stone with three
semicircular arches and Churrigueresque archivolts.

Accommodations
40 double rooms with private baths. The guest house is open year round.

Amenities
The hospedería is a three-star hotel. Towels and linens are provided. All rooms have TV, minibar and telephone. There is private parking, restaurants and a cafe as well as conference rooms, a sauna, garden, gym and facilities for the handicapped.

Meals
All meals can be provided at an additional cost.

Cost of lodging
A double room is $60.00 plus 7% VAT per room. Breakfast is an additional $5.00 per person. The cost of other meals varies.

Directions
By car: From Salamanca take route 630 south to Béjar and head east on SA515 following the signs to La Alberca and then to the monastery.
By train: Public transportation to the monastery is not available. Most guests arrive by chartered bus or by car.

Contact
Anyone who answers the phone
Monasterio - Santuario de Nuestra Señora de la Peña de Francia
37624 La Alberca (Salamanca), Spain
Hotel:
Tel: 923/164000
Fax: 923/164001
Monastery:
Tel: 923/164179
Website: www.estancias.eom/nu98.htm
Email: pdefrancia@verial.es

MONASTERIO DE SANTA MARÍA DE LA VID

Augustinian Monks

Monasterio de Santa María de la Vid

Nestled in a woodland setting above the small village of La Vid, the Monasterio de Santa María de la Vid is on a high hill alongside the banks of the Duero River. Founded in 1162, it was inhabited by the Premonstratenses monks until 1835 when the religious suppression forced the order to abandon the monastery.

Monasterio de Santa María de la Vid

After thirty years of military occupation (1835-1865), the Philippine Province of the Augustine Order acquired the monastery and dedicated it to the education of missionaries destined to work in the Philippines. In 1926, the Spanish Augustine Province replaced the Philippine missionaries and turned the monastery into the headquarters of the Inter-Provincial Noviciate.

The monastery's history reflects the changing times in Spain. It prospered under the protection of Alfonso VII and VIII and their successors. In 1288, Sancho IV provided funds to renovate and enlarge the complex and extend its power. The abbots became something akin to feudal lords. Over the course of seven hundred years, the monastery grew in importance and in the 16th century was declared an Imperial Convent.

In 1600, under the patronage of the Counts of Zúñiga y Avellaneda, the complex was enlarged and enriched with many works of art in the Baroque style. The enlargement embodied a new cloister and the present church, which was begun in 1522 and completed in 1737. During that time, it was enhanced by Spanish and international artists including a new façade designed by Domingo de Izaguirre and Diego de Horna.

The present cloister (ca. 1517), replaced the original Romanesque one. A two-story structure, the lower level is Renaissance, the upper dates from the 18th century. The chapter hall was built in Romanesque style while the sacristy and library reflect 17th century design. The once medieval refectory was restructured in the 18th century and continues to be used by both monks and guests.

Monasterio de Santa María de la Vid

Nearby Peñaranda de Duero is one of the most endearing villages in old Castile. Once a Celtic fortress village, the main square is flanked by porticoed, timber-framed buildings and is home to the 16th century Palacio de los Zúñiga y Avellaneda, a regal Renaissance palace featuring a Plateresque portal. The plaza is also the site of the Church of Santa Ana, another example of Spain's Golden Age classics. The church is graced by a Baroque portal,

Peñaranda de Duero

Roman columns and white marble busts. Very close to the plaza is Botica de Jimeno, the second oldest pharmacy in Spain. It sustains a cache of antique apothecary jars.

Roman ruins of Clunia

The village of Coruña del Conde harbors the Hermitage Chapel of Santo Cristo, a 12th century Romanesque structure with a square apse and blind arches. A short distance away are the ruins of Clunia. Founded at the time of Augustus on the site of an earlier Arevaci settlement, it once had a population of 30,000. It was in Clunia that Galba was proclaimed emperor after spearheading an uprising against Nero. Excavations have unearthed houses, mosaic inlays, hot baths and a theater.

Accommodations

1) Inside the hospedería: 60 beds in single and double rooms, each with private bath and heating.

2) Independent of the monastery: A youth hostel with 114 beds (shared baths) in large dormitories.

Amenities
1) Inside the hospedería: Towels and linens are provided.
2) Youth hostel: Guests must supply their own towels and linens or sleeping bags.
3) Camping area: There is a kitchen and bathing facilities.

Meals
1) Inside the hospedería: All meals are provided with the lodging.
2) Youth hostel: Guests must supply their own meals.
3) Camping area: There is a kitchen which campers may use.

Cost of lodging
1) Hospedería: $24.00 per person.
2) Youth hostel: To be arranged when reservations are made.
3) Camping area: To be arranged when reservations are made.

Special rules
Inside the hospedería: There is a curfew at 11:00 pm. Minimum stay during the winter is two days; summer one week. Children under 8 are not permitted. Punctuality at meals is required. Closed from December 20th until January 10th.

Directions
By car: From Burgos take highway 1 to Madrid, exit at Aranda de Duero and take route N122 east towards Soria about 18 kms to La Vid de Aranda.
By train: Get off at Aranda de Duero. There are local buses to La Vid leaving daily at 1:30 and 8:00 pm.

Contact
Padre Hospedero
Monasterio de Santa María de la Vid
Ctra. De Soria, s/n
09491 La Vid (Burgos), Spain
Tel: 947/530510 - 947/5300514
Fax: 947/530429
Email: For reservations - licet@retemail.es
Email: For information only (no reservations) - licet@mx3redestb.es
Website: http://personal.redestb.es/licet/

MONASTERIO SANTA CLARA
Clarisse Nuns

Monasterio Santa Clara

Monasterio Santa Clara

The monastery was founded in 1491 at the entrance of Medina de Rioseco, an ancient town north of Valladolid. It has been inhabited by the Clarisse nuns since that time with the exception of a short period when the sisters were forced to leave because of the French invasion. During that turbulent period, the institution lost much of its precious art including the retablo of the main altar.

Since the nuns live in seclusion, the monastery cannot be visited but the church is open to visitors. "The church doesn't contain any valuable works of art but on the other hand, the entire town is a work of art," said the Superiora of Santa Clara. "Many interesting towns can be visited in the area as well," she added. Two houses in a patio area of the complex host guests.

Medina de Rioseco grew wealthy from its wool trade. During the Middle Ages, many leading artists (mainly of the Valladolid school), were commissioned to adorn its churches, six of which date from the 15th to 17th centuries. Situated near the center of town, the Isabelline Gothic Iglesia de Santa María de Mediavilla shelters some of the finest work of that period. The church's star vaulting and woodwork are particularly beautiful. The main retablo is by Esteban Jordán and Juan de Juni. The Plateresque Benavente Chapel displays a vivid stucco ceiling by Jerónimo del Corral and altarpiece by Juan de Juni. The stellar design points to a late revival of the Mudéjar style.

The Iglesia de Santiago has a Plateresque portal; the interior displays a triple altarpiece by the Churriguera brothers of Salamanca. Calle de la Rúa is the town's main street. Its buildings are supported on wooden pillars and form shady porticoes, emblematic of Castilian architecture.

The environs of Medina de Rioseco are sprinkled with a variety of interesting sites. Montealegre boasts an Early Gothic castle. Austere and solid looking, the namesake fortress occupies a hill towering over the hamlet. Villalón's Mudéjar monuments were mainly built with rammed earth or brick. The Rollo de Justicia is a stone column once used to indicate jurisdiction. The churches in Wamba and San Cebrián are rare examples of Mozarabic architecture. Just outside the walled village of Urueña, stands the Hermitage of La Anunciada, the only example of Catalan Romanesque in Castile.

Valladolid, capital of Castilla - León is close to the monastery. Once the Arabic city of Belad-Walid, it sits at the confluence of the rivers Esgueva and Pisuerga and preserves some of the country's best Renaissance art and architecture. The city itself is monumental and many castles can be seen in the immediate area. Fernando and Isabel were married and proclaimed king and queen in the Gothic-Mudéjar building of the Vivero family. The city is also the place where Christopher Columbus died.

Valladolid cathedral

Valladolid's university was established in 1346, its Baroque façade built by Antonio Tomé and sons, Narciso and Diego. The statues represent the branches of learning and the kings who protected the institution. A cultural center, the university maintains a valuable library with Baroque shelving by Alonso Manzano. Among its treasures are 520 manuscripts, 355 incunabula and over 10,000 volumes from the 16th to 18th centuries.

The Convent of Las Huelgas Reales was founded by Queen María de Molina in 1282. The interior of the church includes reliefs by Gregorio Fernández, paintings by Tomás de Prado and works of art by Juan de Juni. San Pablo and San Gregorio colleges are representative of Spanish Isabelline style, a combination of Flamboyant Gothic and Mudéjar elements characteristic of the reign of the Catholic monarchs. San Pablo is designed in the form of a Latin cross with a vault and 17th century marble retablo. The centerpiece of the church is its façade. Distinguished by the purest Isabelline style, it is festooned with angels and coats of arms. San Gregorio College is an Isabelline building with an elaborate façade and spacious inner courtyard.

Castle at Torrelobatón

Of the numerous castles in the vicinity of Valladolid, the Castle at Torrelobatón is the best conserved in all of Castile. Built by King Juan II in the 15th century on the ruins of an older castle, it is a sober and solid structure, its design simple and pure. Erected on a square plan, it was protected by a wide moat. Three massive round towers stand at three corners while a keep with eight smaller towers occupies the fourth.

The Castle at Simancas dominates its namesake village. It was converted by Charles V into Spain's national archive and has a vast collection of political documents of modern Spain. Built on flat land, the castle belongs to the mountain variety. To compensate for its lack of elevation, the polygonal structure was surrounded by high walls and a very deep moat.

Castle at Peñafiel

The Castle at Peñafiel is shaped like a ship. Extremely long and narrow, the Romanesque fortress occupies a ridgetop. Underscored by a double wall and thirty towers, the structure represents a solitary and elegant picture. It was captured from the Moors in the 11th century. Legend holds that its conqueror, King Sancho, drove his sword into the highest point and said: "From today, this will be the faithful rock (*peña fiel*) of Castile."

The Castle of La Mota was designed by master builder Fernando Carreño. Composed of brick, the golden colored citadel was built on a polygonal plan. The walls feature round towers, loopholes and a drawbridge leading up to the gates. Traces of the elaborate interior design include arches, small cupolas and plinths in Mudéjar style. The "Dressing Room of the Queen" has a barrel vaulted ceiling with Gothic ribs. Another room belonged to the famous Caesar Borgia. The epitome of a Renaissance Italian, he lived by the motto engraved upon his sword, "Caesar or nothing," Borgia was imprisoned in the castle but escaped by climbing out of the window and down the walls.

In Baños de Cerrato, between the towns of Valladolid and Palencia, the tiny Iglesia de San Juan Bautista was founded by King Recesvinto in 661. It is the oldest church in Spain and one of the remaining models of Visigothic architecture. Carved capitals and horseshoe arches adorn the interior of the stone structure.

Accommodations

There are two small houses. Each one contains 7 double rooms, a living room, 3 baths and a kitchen. One of the houses does not have central heating, it is heated by stoves. Both men and women are welcome.

Amenities

Towels and linens are supplied.

Meals

Meals are not supplied, guests must cook their own.

Cost of lodging

$15.00 per room/per night.

Special rules

The guests are independent from the monastery and have their own key. Maximum stay 1 month. Open year round.

Directions

By car: From Valladolid take N601 North and exit at Medina de Rioseco.

By train: Get off at Valladolid and take a bus to Medina de Rioseco. Buses of the Madrid-Valladolid line run every hour and stop at Medina de Rioseco.

Contact

Madre Superiora
Monasterio Santa Clara
Extramuros, s/n
47800 Medina de Rioseco (Valladolid), Spain
Tel: 983/700982

MONASTERIO NUESTRA SEÑORA DEL ESPINO
Redentorist Fathers

According to tradition, a miraculous apparition of Mary appeared in 1399 and over the years attracted an increasing number of pilgrims. In the early 15th century, the Monasterio Nuestra Señora del Espino was built on the site of the apparition. A document that "certified" the truthfulness of the sighting is preserved in the Vatican. "In most cases, tradition tells us about apparitions, but in this case, we have an official document signed in 1399 by a Royal Officer, we can prove it," stated Padre Antonio.

Monasterio Nuestra Señora del Espino

The monastery originally belonged to the Benedictine Order and between the 16th and 18th centuries was an important spiritual center. Closed during the suppression of the religious orders, it later passed to the present order. The monastery and its church are Gothic in design, simple but quite beautiful. The complex preserves the miraculous statue of Mary. The 17th century refectory now serves as a dining room for guests.

Miranda de Ebro is a major town in Castilla. Since ancient times, its strategic riverside location has made it a gateway between Spain and its European neighbors. Many of the houses in town have glass balconies which hang over the waterway. Mirando de Ebro's most stunning monument is the 16th century church of Santa María.

A smattering of small towns and villages are nearby. Frías traces its origins to the 9th century when Alfonso VIII repopulated the valley to bolster the frontier between Castile and Navarra. From the heights of its rocky emplacement, a castle overlooks the cobbled streets of the village. The medieval town center is the site of the Church of San Vincente and the Convent of Santa María de Vadillo. Crossing the River Ebro just below the town is a striking medieval bridge featuring an unusual and elegantly arched defensive tower.

The town of Medina de Pomar offers a rich architectural assemblage of churches, stone walls and the Alcázar de los Velasco, a 14th century Moorish palace. Inside are ruins with Mudéjar stucco decorations, Arabic inscriptions and a crenelated tower.

Oña grew in the protective shadow of San Salvador Monastery, founded in the 11th century by the Benedictine Order. The Church of San Salvador is marked by Romanesque windows and a Gothic-Mudéjar arch. The interior is particularly noteworthy for the royal pantheon where King Sancho the Great of Navarra and Sancho García are interred. In the summer, *Cronicón de Oña*, (a theatrical repre-

San Salvador Monastery

sentation of the town's history), is performed. The 16th century cloister is the work of Johan of Cologne.

Roman in origin, the walled town of Briviesca is the capital of the La Bureba district. Built on a perfect grid in imitation of Santa Fe de Granada, the town has an arcaded main square and elegant mansions. Among its notable monuments is the Shrine of St. Casilda, a 16th century structure housing a collection of votive objects and a statue of the saint sculpted by Flemish artist, Gil de Siloé.

Accommodations
There are 30 double and 14 single rooms, each with private bath. Only groups are allowed, minimum 15. Closed between December 24th and January 7th.

Amenities
Towels and linens are provided.

Meals
All meals are included with the lodging.

Cost of lodging
$21.00 per person including all meals and heating.

Directions
By car: From Burgos go north on highway 1 to Miranda de Ebro. Follow the signs to Puentellara and then to the monastery.
By train: Get off at Miranda de Ebro and call the monastery. They will provide transportation.

Contact
Anyone who answers the phone
Monasterio Nuestra Señora del Espino
El Espino, Apartado 12
09200 Santa Gadea - Miranda de Ebro (Burgos), Spain
Tel: 947/359015
Fax: 947/359041

MONASTERIO DE SAN SALVADOR
Benedictine Nuns

Monasterio de San Salvador

Situated on the Santiago de Compostela, the monastery is on the outskirts of Palacios de Benaver, a small village approximately twelve miles from Burgos. It resides at the foot of a hill which offers protection from the long cold winters and short hot summers typical of the area.

Monasterio de San Salvador

The origins of the monastery have been lost in the mists of legend. According to tradition, a group of Benedictine nuns settled in the monastery in 537 and remained until 834. At that time, all three hundred inhabitants were brutally martyrized by the Moors who destroyed the dwelling. After a miraculous apparition of a cross grew over the ruins of the original monastery, the institution was rebuilt in 968. This structure was also devastated by the Moors. During the 13th century, after the monastery was once again rebuilt, the Manrique family restored it and with the help of many donors, enlarged the facility.

The institution prospered between the 16th and 18th centuries. During the suppression of the religious orders (1835), the nuns continued to live in the complex although the majority of their possessions were confiscated. At the end of the 19th century, they founded a boarding school which operated until a few years ago.

The complex is well preserved. The church is the result of the various interventions and renovations which took place between the Romanesque and Renaissance periods. A simple structure, it harbors a large golden retablo and an array of valuable wooden sculptures and paintings. The most interesting artifact is the miraculous wooden cross. The tomb of the Manrique family is contained in a Gothic chapel.

The area southeast of the monastery is home to many historic towns and hamlets. Once a pre-Roman settlement, Lerma began its long ascent under Fernán González, a process that culminated with the Duke of Lerma. Classical in style, the Ducal Palace, the Church of San Pedro, the Piedad Hermitage Chapel and two 17th century monasteries reflect the town's heritage.

Medieval walls surround the old center of Covarrubias, an archetypical Castilian town with arcaded streets and Tudor-like timbered houses. The Collegiate Church of San Damián is remarkable for its pantheon and 16th century cloister. The museum exhibits a Flemish Gothic triptych, *The Adoration of the Magi*.

Nearby, at the base of the crag known as Peña Lara, stands the hermitage chapel of Santa María of Quintanilla de las Viñas, a prime example of Visigothic art. The east end, square ground plan and bas-reliefs all date from the 7th century.

Santo Domingo de Silos is also close. Its Abadía Benidictina de Santo Domingo is a world famous monastery whose monks are renowned for their mastery of Gregorian Chant. The monastery's two-

Abadía Benidictina de Santo Domingo

story cloister marks a watershed in the history of European Romanesque art; it is defined by carved capitals and arabesques. The Mudéjar ceiling portrays scenes from medieval life.

Not far from the monastery is the Yecla Gorge, a deep ravine gouged from the local limestone by the Arlanza River. A protected area of outstanding natural beauty, walkways lead to the juniper-fringed Arlanza.

Accommodations
The hospedería has been recently enlarged and renovated with 22 rooms (3 singles and 19 doubles), each with private bath. Both men and women are welcome. There is also a dormitory reserved for large groups.

Amenities
Towels and linens are provided.

Meals
All meals can be included with the lodging.

Cost of lodging
$24.00 per person, full board.

Products of the institution
The monastery owns a small farm where they raise chickens. The nuns prepare sweets, jam and honey. They also produce terra cotta vases. All services are held in Gregorian Chant.

Special rules
Punctuality is required at meals. Curfew at 10 pm.

Directions
By car: From Burgos go west on 120 towards León. After approximately 15 kms there is a turnoff to Palacios de Benaver.

By train: Get off at Burgos and take the bus from Palacios de Benaver (5:30 pm). Taxis are also available. A bus returns to Burgos from Palacios de Benaver every day at 9:00 am (holidays excluded).

Contact
Madre Superiora
Monasterio de San Salvador
Plaza del Monasterio, 1
09132 Palacios de Benaver (Burgos), Spain
Tel: 947/450209
Fax: 947/450262

CASA DE ORACIÓN VILLA BETANIA
Cooperatrices Parroquiales de Cristo Rey Nuns

Piedrahíta

The casa is near the center of Piedrahíta, a town of the Ávila Province. "Piedrahíta is very pretty. It lies in the Valdecorneja Valley at the foot of the mountains. The air is very pure and the casa is ideal for a relaxing stay," said the sister in charge.

Founded less than twenty years ago, the mission of the casa is to guide adults during spiritual retreats. However, the house has always been open to all guests. The building is relatively modern (ca. 1950s) and is surrounded by a garden imbued with a peaceful aura. Not far from the casa is the area of Las Navas del Marqués where extensive pine groves blanket the region. A popular summer resort, it is highlighted by a castle and Gothic-styled parish church.

The surrounding small towns and villages blend historic and artistic elements with varying landscapes, all dominated by the majestic mountain massif of the Sierra de Gredos. The towering peaks are almost permanently snow covered and reach their highest point in the Pico de Almanzor. The legendary town of Mombeltrán preserves the 14th century castle of the Duques de Albuquerque, one of the most characteristic castles of Castile. The village of Candeleda is notable for its picturesque nature while tradition claims that El Barco de Ávila owes its name to the boat used to cross the River Tormes.

A number of side trips in the adjoining province of Salamanca include the *Ruta de la Plata* (Silver Route). Along the centuries-old itinerary is the town of Alba de Tormes, home to four churches built in Romanesque-Mudéjar style and the Convent of the Discalced Carmelites. Founded in 1571 by St. Teresa, it is where she lived and died and where her remains are preserved. The Armoury Tower stands as a reminder of the palace that once belonged to the powerful Duke of Alba.

Ensconced along a ridge at the foot of the Sierra de Béjar, namesake Béjar is the main town of the district. A textile center with 19th century factories and mills, it is famous for its capes, woolens and blankets. Within the town's old walled section is the Palace of the Dukes of Béjar. Rebuilt in the 16th century over the still visible remains of a castle, its entrance bears the look of a fortress.

Béjar's old quarter reveals a delightful main square. Nearby La Antigua Park adjoins the 13th century walls which provide panoramic views of the mountain scenery. El Bosque is an exquisite Italian Renaissance-style garden with promenades, an ornamental palace and pond.

The town of Candelario is just outside of Béjar. Its streets harbor some well-preserved village architecture. The 16th century parish church is underscored by a central absidal chapel and Mudéjar coffered ceiling.

Accommodations
18 single rooms with private sink. Baths are shared. Both men and women are welcome, but housed separately.

Amenities
Towels and linens are supplied.

Meals
All meals are supplied on request.

Cost of lodging
Provisional cost $18.00 per person, full pension.

Special rules
Curfew at 10 pm. Closed in August.

Directions
By car: From Ávila go southwest on N110 and exit at Piedrahíta. Once there ask for Villa Betania.
By train: Get off at Ávila and take a bus to Piedrahíta. There are three buses a day.

Contact
Encargada de la casa
Casa de Oración Villa Betania
Virgen de la Vega, 10
05500 Piedrahíta (Ávila), Spain
Tel: 920/360239

MONASTERIO SAN PEDRO DE CARDEÑA
Cistercian / Trappist Monks

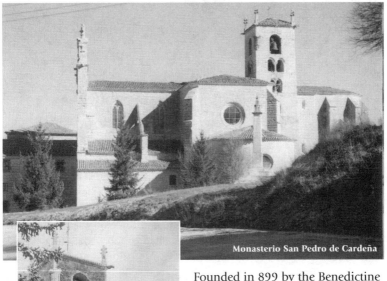

Monasterio San Pedro de Cardeña

Founded in 899 by the Benedictine Order, the monastery is now inhabited by the Trappists. After King Alfonso VI banished El Cid from the territory of Castile, the Spanish hero led his family to safety within the confines of San Pedro de Cardeña. The monastery once contained the remains of El Cid and his wife Jimena, but for safety's sake, they were moved to the cathedral in Burgos. The original tombs housing their effigies reside in the chapel of the Cloister of Martyrs, regarded as one of the finest Romanesque structures in Spain.

Monasterio San Pedro de Cardeña

An important stop along the Santiago de Compostela pilgrimage route, the monastery is also the site of a famous massacre; two hundred Benedictines were beheaded during a 10th century Moorish raid. Tradition holds that the statue of Mary shed blood tears. The devoted continue to visit the monastery to see the miraculous statue.

At the time of the religious suppressions (1835), the Benedictine monks were forced to leave. During the civil war, the monastery was used as a concentration camp by the Francoists. In 1942, the Cistercian/Trappist monks restarted the institution and have continued in residence since that time. The monastery's troubled history is evident in the dissimilar architecture. Years of suppression also caused serious damage to the buildings. Nevertheless, the simple Gothic church and the 16th century exterior of the complex are still lovely. The sacristy has a Renaissance lavabo by Diego De Siloé.

Burgos is about six miles from the monastery. Once the old capital of Castilla, it exudes a medieval Castilian ambience. Founded in 884, Burgos is remarkable for its collection of Gothic art and monuments. The Arco de Santa María was originally part of the walls. The white gateway is bedecked with statues and turrets. Behind the arch stands one of Spain's great Gothic cathedrals, its distinctive gray spires visible throughout the

Monasterio San Pedro de Cardeña

city. The church showcases an assortment of artwork including statues of Spanish kings and stone tracery incorporating two Stars of David, a reflection of the fact that two of the city's bishops were of Jewish descent. The interior overflows with masterpieces and contains the remains of El Cid and his wife. The diamond-shaped Plateresque Golden Staircase (ca. 1523) is the most dramatic interior element.

Although the main square has been refurbished, the true heart of the city is the shaded, riverside Paseo del Espolon. A pretty promenade, the walkway is defined by topiary and an equestrian statue of El Cid. Across the bridge, Casa Miranda is home to the Museo de Burgos and its archaeological collection of relics from the Roman city of Clunia.

Two lavish monasteries are just outside the town of Burgos. The first and closest is the Cistercian Monasterio de Las Hueglas. Guided tours (in Spanish) offer an education on the monastery's artwork and architecture. The other, La Cartuja de Miraflores, was founded during the 15th century and is inhabited by the Carthusian Order. Its church preserves the tomb of Juan II and Isabel of Portugal. Commissioned by the queen, it was built in honor of her parents. The alabaster work on

Monasterio de Las Hueglas

the tomb is particularly outstanding. *The Annunciation* by Pedro Berruguete and a wooden statue of St. Bruno carved by Portuguese artist Manuel Pereira are on exhibit. Perhaps its most unique work is Gil de Siloe's polychrome altarpiece. Legend holds that it was gilded with the first gold brought from the New World.

South of Burgos, the town of Lerma was founded in the 8th century. Once a pre-Roman settlement, it is filled with impressive monuments. A massive gate flanked by two round towers leads into the atmospheric, cobbled streets of the old quarter, locale of the grand palace of the Dukes of Lerma. Contained within a circuit of walls, the palace is on a large square with attractive courtyards. A walk on the ramparts affords views of the countryside and the Río Arlanza.

Accommodations
15 rooms, each with private bath. Most are single, but there are some doubles. All guests are welcome.
Note: Contact Padre Hospedero well in advance, particularly in the summer months. Spiritual retreats have priority.

Amenities
Towels and linens are supplied.

Cost of lodging
$18.00 per person, full board.

Meals
All meals are included with the lodging.

Products of the institution
The monks are famous for their wines and spirits. The *Licor Tizona Del Cid* is made with 28 different herbs. The wines are called *Valdevegòn* and are aged in Romanesque wine cellars. The monastery shop also sells products of other religious institutions.

Special rules
Minimum stay 3 days, maximum 10 days. Curfew at 8:30 pm. Guests are also required to be respectful of silence and be punctual at meal times.

Directions
By car: From Burgos go east on Route BU800 approximately 10 kms to the monastery.
By train: Get off at Burgos and take a taxi to the monastery.

Contact
Padre Hospedero
Monasterio San Pedro de Cardeña
09193 San Pedro de Cardeña (Burgos), Spain
Tel: 947/290033 / Fax: 947/290075

MONASTERIO DE SAN PEDRO APÓSTOL
Benedictine Nuns

Monasterio de San Pedro Apóstol

The monastery is in the center of San Pedro de las Dueñas, one of the main stops on the Camino de Santiago. A small town, San Pedro sits on a plain enveloped by fields, a familiar setting in this part of Spain. Founded in 973 by the Benedictine community, the order has inhabited the institution since that time. Its Romanesque church was begun in the 12th century and completed many years later in Gothic style. Visited by thousands each year, the church is the most important part of the complex.

One of the oldest female monasteries in the area, its proximity to the Camino de Santiago contributed to its importance during the Middle Ages. The daughters of the most important noble families (including Sancha, daughter of Alfonso VII) were educated at the institution.

The most pleasing decorations of the church can be seen in the columns. Twenty-two in all, the capitals were sculpted by the schools of San Isidro de León. A three-storied tower bell rises from the center of the church. Although the statue of Mary behind the altar is a copy of the original by San Miguel de Escalada, it is a remarkable work of art.

Close to the monastery, a section known as *La Ruta de la Plata* (The Route of Silver), connected Zamora to the Roman roads of Zaragossa in the north. Benavente, a town characteristic of medieval Castile, is along the route. Illustrious monuments include the 12th century church of San Juan del Mercada and the relics of the 16th century Castle of the Counts of Pimentel. A mixture of Gothic and Renaissance styles, the fortress was set afire during the War of Independence. Only the Torre del Caracol remains. It has since been restored and is now a parador.

Many sites and villages are nearby including Las Lagunas de Villasfáfila. The lagoons form the National Game Reserve and contain an assemblage of birds ranging from wild geese, mallards and herons to white storks and cranes.

The town of Sahagún was once the main settlement of the district known as Tierra de Campos. Its strong Mudéjar roots are reflected in two churches: 12th century San Tirso and 13th century San Lorenzo. Constructed of brick (a new building medium at the time), both structures have square bell towers with arches, triple apses and shaded porticoes. Sahagún was home to a powerful Benedictine abbey, one of the largest and oldest within the Kingdom of León. Its Romanesque design dates to the 12th century. Beside the monastery is the Convent of Benedictine Sisters which houses the Museum of Sacred Art as well as a Gothic monstrance, the work of Enrique de Arfe.

The area east and west of Sahagún is part of El Camino de Santiago, a string of quaint towns and monuments. The village of Castrojeriz is dominated by a castle. Its collegiate church is a sober 12th century Cistercian building displaying a medieval carving of the Virgin and a painting by Carduccio.

Monasterio de San Pedro Apóstol

Accommodations
20 single and double rooms. A few have private baths, most have a sink inside the room and shared baths.

Amenities
Towels and linens are provided.

Meals
All meals can be included with the lodging. Provisional cost of meals: breakfast $3.00 per person; lunch and dinner $12.00 per person.

Cost of lodging
$18.00 per person, meals excluded.

Products of the institution
The nuns produce hosts.

Special rules
Curfew 11:00 pm (summer), 10:00 pm (winter). Punctuality at meals. Maximum stay 1 month.

Directions
By car: From León take route 601 South. After about 30 kms, turn left heading east on route A231 and follow the signs to Sahagún. From there go south to San Pedro de las Dueñas.
By train: Get off at Sahagún and take a taxi to San Pedro.

Contact
Madre Hospedera or Madre Superiora
Monasterio de San Pedro Apóstol
24329 San Pedro de las Dueñas (León), Spain
Tel: 987/780150

MONASTERIO DE SANTA MARÍA DE HUERTA
Cistercian Monks

Monasterio de
Santa María de Huerta

The monastery sits beside the banks of the River Jalón in the center of the small village of Santa María de la Huerta. "Typically Castellano and very dry, we are surrounded by a landscape of mountains and pine forests. A remarkable complex, it is distinguished from others because of its architecture and the austere and simple spirituality of our order," said Padre Hospedero.

Monasterio de
Santa María de Huerta

Founded in 1162 by Alfonso VII of Castilla, the mainly Gothic design of the monastery has been preserved. It was inhabited by the Cistercian Order until 1830 when the monks were forced to leave during the religious suppression. They returned in 1930 and since that time have restored and revived the spiritual life of the monastery.

Although the monastery is not as renowned as other religious sites, it is nevertheless a gem of Spanish Gothic architecture and sculpture. There are three cloisters: the 13th century Gothic one is decorated with simple stone vaults; the two-story Plateresque cloister has an unusual Lacunar ceiling (a ceiling composed of square tiles, usually made of wood); the third was designed by Juan de Herra and built between 1582 and 1630. There is also a 13th century kitchen containing an enormous stone fireplace.

The monastery is akin to a small museum of Gothic sculpture, finely depicted in the vaulted refectory (ca. 1215) and in the 16th century Plateresque cloister. The church has a Romanesque-Gothic façade with a Baroque interior that houses the tombs of the Dukes of Medinaceli.

The old-world town of Soria is not far from the monastery. Situated alongside the Duero River, the reddish color of the roof tiles (made from local clay), accentuates the look of the town. Originally formed around a castle which no longer exists, traces of the square, a great cistern and ruins of the wall remain. Medieval Soria was once an important Jewish enclave; many headstones remain as testament to this ancient lineage.

The town is home to several Romanesque churches. San Juan de Rabanera dates from the 12th century and represents Romanesque Castilian. Santo Domingo was built in the second half of the 12th century and is ornamented by a handsome Romanesque façade. Near the Duero River is the Concatedral of San Pedro, highlighted by a Plateresque façade and Romanesque cloister. The chapel of St. Saturio safeguards a Flemish triptych representing the Crucifixion (ca. 1559).

Plaza Ramón y Cajal connects the old town with the new. It faces the Alameda de Cervantes and the Museo Numantino which showcases finds from the ancient city of Numantia. The history of Numantia is underscored by a year-long Roman siege in 132 BC. When defeat was close at hand, the citizens of Numantia chose an heroic climax to the battle. Instead of surrendering, they set fire to their town and themselves.

Soria's riverfront is a tranquil section peppered with groves of poplars, an island and a low dam. An old stone bridge leads to the relics of a ruined monastery and one of the most original monuments of Romanesque art, San Juan de Duero. Founded by the Knights of St. John, its cloister is mainly Gothic in design and highlighted by lavishly carved interlacing arches. The church's capitals represent scenes of the *Massacre of the Innocents*. The Romanesque-Oriental design is an extremely complex specimen of Spanish art.

Beginning in Soria, a travel itinerary known as the Duero Route encompasses a number of attractive towns and villages. The town of Almazán occupies a natural elevation that dominates the landscape. As a citadel, it was one of the best fortified places in antiquity. It sustains ruins of the Roman wall, Romanesque churches and Renaissance palaces. Quartered on the characteristic main square, the 16th century Palace of the Hurtado de Mendoza is a paragon of secular architecture. Also on the square is the Romanesque St. Michael, now a national monument. Its exterior is carved in stone and depicts the martyrdom of Saint Thomas of Canterbury.

The village of Berlanga is overlooked by a 15th century castle with two walls and a tower. The town's collegiate church was built in Gothic/Renaissance style in 1526. The chapel's altarpiece was carved at the beginning of the 15th century. A few miles south of Berlanga is the famous Hermitage of St. Baudilio. Defined by its original Mozarabic plan, it once housed 10th century mural paintings now at the Prado in Madrid.

Burgo de Osma is one of the oldest Episcopal Sees in Spain. Already founded in the Visigothic era, the small village retains a medieval atmosphere with arcaded streets and a Gothic cathedral. Considered among the most important religious monuments of the province of Soria, the structure is composed of three aisles in a Latin cross layout. It is delineated by an ornate Baroque tower which dominates the village. The interior is remarkable for its filigree iron work and altarpiece, a monumental work of imagery attributed to Juan de Juni. The cathedral shelters a Gothic cloister; the library/museum maintains a collection of illuminated manuscripts.

Accommodations
There are 13 double and triple rooms with bath. Both men and women are welcome.

Amenities
Towels and linens are provided.

Meals
All meals are included with the lodging.

Cost of lodging
Prices vary according to guest requirements. To be determined upon arrival.

Products of the institution
The monks produce wooden icons and the famous *Dulce de membrillo,* a sweet made with quince. The monks also produce jams and marmalades.

Special rules
Guests are required to return by dinner. Minimum stay 2 days, maximum 8. The facilities are closed during the week of the monastery's spiritual practice. This week normally coincides with the last week of November, but is subject to change.

Directions
By car: Exit at Santa María de Huerta (km 177 on the Autovia 2 between Madrid and Zaragoza).
By train: Get off at Arcos de Jalón and take a bus to Santa María de Huerta. Getting to the monastery by public transportation can be difficult; contact the monastery for additional information.

Contact
Padre Hospedero; mobile phone: 616/738864 (during office hours)
Monasterio de Santa María de Huerta
42260 Santa María de Huerta (Soria), Spain
Tel: 975/327002
Fax: 975/327397
Email: huerta@planalfa.es
Website: www.planalfa.es

ABADÍA BENIDICTINA DE SANTO DOMINGO
Benedictine Monks of the Congregation of Solesmes

Abadía Benidictina de Santo Domingo

Erected over the ruins of a Visigothic abbey destroyed by the Moors, the tranquil setting and spiritual aura of the monastery has roused a myriad of poets to sing its praises. The Romanesque cloisters are among the most beautiful in Spain. Built around an ancient cypress tree, the capitals are sculpted in an array of designs, many in the shape of animals. The corners depict Biblical scenes while the ceilings are a reflection of Moorish style and are painted with scenes representing life in the Middle Ages.

Abadía Benidictina de Santo Domingo

Abadía Benidictina de Santo Domingo

"The most beautiful thing in our monastery is the Romanesque cloister, which is unique in the whole world," said the Padre Hospedero. "The double cloister (upper and lower) was edified between the 11th and 12th century during the time Santo Domingo was in residence. Each of the columns is a work of art, an unusual mixture of Arab and French Romanesque," he continued.

The Silos Cloister has a trapezoidal layout consisting of two floors with bays covered by wooden structures in keeping with Castilian tradition. The most attractive reliefs are portrayed on the capitals of the eastern bay. Fifteen in all, they depict monsters, witches, gazelles and four-legged creatures. All are carved with great style and artistry.

In this museum of Romanesque beauty, the superb bas-relief panels are particularly outstanding. They decorate, in pairs, the corners of the bays and reflect a medley of themes. The scenes are framed within a simple arch; a gentle rhythm animates the figures. The lines of moustaches and beards are perfectly differentiated in each person. Emotional motifs abound throughout the other panels, a singular feature in Romanesque art.

Abadía Benidictina de Santo Domingo

The monastery is in the small town of Santo Domingo de Silos amid a landscape of rolling hills. It was founded in 954 after a donation to San Sebastian. From 1041 to 1073, the Abbot Domingo lived in the monastery. He was a monk from the La Rioja region of Spain and had ruled several monasteries in Navarra. His body rests in a sarcophagus supported by Romanesque lions. A charismatic leader, the institution's name was changed to honor him. Over the ensuing centuries, the complex was enlarged and enhanced with works of art and continued as an important cultural and spiritual center until its closure in 1835 during the religious suppressions.

In 1880, it was reopened by a community of French monks from Solesmes, a village in northwest France. They restored the spiritual life of the monastery and introduced a style of singing known as plainsong or plainchant, an ancient and austere unharmonized melody in free rhythm. Throughout the day, services are sung in plainchant. Less strictly systemized than Gregorian Chant, the origins can be traced to early Christian times and are derived from Jewish and Greek music. In

1903, Pope Pius X decreed the use of the chant in the Solesmes version as the official music of the Catholic Church. In the early 1990s, the monks recorded their very distinct music. It became a Platinum CD and to this day, remains popular on international music charts. The CDs are sold at the monastery.

The monastery has contributed to the foundation of new monasteries such as Valle de Los Caídos and the rebirth of others like San Salvador de Leyre. Visits to the complex include the cloister and museum which display medieval manuscripts and historical documents related to the monastery.

Accommodations
22 single rooms with private baths. Only men are allowed. Make reservations well in advance; the guest house books early.

Amenities
Towels and linens are supplied.

Meals
All meals can be provided with the lodging.

Cost of lodging
$21.00 per person. Provisional cost only, subject to change. All meals are included.

Special rules
Minimum stay one weekend, maximum 8-10 days. Punctuality is required at meals although guests may choose not to dine at the monastery.

Directions
By car: From Burgos or Madrid take route State 1 and exit at Lerma. From there head east following the signs to Silos and the abbey.
By train: Get off in Burgos and take the local bus to Silos. It departs once a day at 5:30 pm.

Contact
Padre Hospedero
Abadía Benidictina de Santo Domingo
09610 Santo Domingo de Silos (Burgos), Spain
Tel: 947/390049 - 390068
Fax: 947/390033

MONASTERIO SANCTI SPIRITUS EL REAL
Dominicas Nuns

Monasterio Sancti Spiritus el Real

Ensconced in Toro, an historical site of the Zamora province of Castilla-León, the monastery was built by the kings of Castilla (hence the name "el Real"). Protected by the royal family, it flourished during the ensuing centuries and often hosted members of the noble families of Castilla. During the 19th century, the nuns were forced to leave due to the suppression of the religious orders. They returned after a few years and have inhabited the monastery since that time.

Monasterio Sancti Spiritus el Real

The complex is composed of different sections from different periods: "13th, 14th, 16th, 17th and of course, 20th century," said Madre María Dolores. "In fact, part of the 16th century section has been recently restored and turned into a hospedería," she added. The monastery's museum has many precious works of art as well as the striking alabaster tomb of Queen Beatriz of Portugal who died during the reign of the Portuguese kings. "In reality, it is all a work of art, the Gothic tomb, the monastery, the Mudéjar church," said the madre. Of particular note are the Moorish-inspired coffered ceilings and Renaissance cloister.

Monasterio Sancti Spiritus el Real

A natural fortress near the border of the Portuguese kingdom, Toro was an important city during the 14th century when the Spaniards were often engaged in battles over the territory. In 1471, the Army of Isabel I defeated the Portuguese and established the Spanish succession to the throne of Castilla. "In ancient times, there were three different communities cohabiting here: Christian, Arab and Jewish. I think that they fought over the possession of the land for more than just religious reasons," the madre continued.

Occupying a picturesque setting on red cliffs above the Duero, Toro is a delightful city in the heart of the wine region. The red grapes of Toro produce the renowned wines cited by Cervantes. Thick and dark, they can be sampled at centuries-old wineries. Toro has been declared a town of historic-artistic interest. Its Collegiate Church of Santa María la Mayor is a Romanesque treasure from 1160 with a dome resting on pendentives of Byzantine origin. The nearby 10th century Alcázar preserves its walls and seven towers.

Iglesia de San Lorenzo dates from the 13th century. A Mudéjar-Romanesque structure, it contains a Gothic altarpiece. Also located in Toro, the Monastery of Santa Sofía is the only Spanish monastery of the Premonstratensian Order. Exceptional civil buildings include the clock tower, stone bridge and 1828 bullring (one of the oldest in the country).

The province of Zamora was settled by the ancient civilizations of the Duero Valley. Of all the archeological remains to be found, perhaps the most important is the so-called Tesoro de Arrabalde which dates from the Iron Age. The region was also inhabited by the Romans, Visigoths and Moors. As a result of its location close to the border with Portugal, Zamora was of great strategic importance and the scene of many historic events: the internal struggles within the kingdoms of Castile and León during the 11th century, the war between the followers of Queen Isabella in the 15th century and the uprising of the Comuneros (supporters of the comunidates in Castile) against Carlos I during the 16th century.

Zamora was settled by the Vaccei people followed by the Carthaginians and Romans. Legend holds that Viriato, a famous Roman warrior, was born here. A medieval town, it is surrounded by ancient walls and gates including the Doors of Zambranos, the house of Cid, Romanesque churches and Renaissance palaces. The cathedral was founded by King Alfonso VII in 1135 and reflects a unity of style of the transition from Romanesque to Gothic. Additions include the 13th century El Salvador Tower, the Gothic west end (ca. 15th century), the 17th century Herrerian cloisters (built in the style of Juan de Herrera) and the neoclassical north façade. The only original Romanesque portal is on the south side at the gate known as Puerto del Obispo.

The most intriguing aspect of the cathedral is the dome of the lantern which is embellished with fish-scale tiles. As in Toro, the use of pendentives to support the dome denotes a Byzantine influence. The interior is composed of a nave and two aisles in the shape of a Roman cross. In addition to a 16th century silver monstrance, the museum has a collection of Flemish tapestries. One depicts the *Parable of the Vineyard*, another, the *Story of Hannibal*.

Several Romanesque churches reflect Mozarabic influences as witnessed by the poly-lobed arches. The Church of San Cipriano has a stained glass window, semicircular arches, columns with capitals and an outstanding screen. The Church of Santa María La Nueva has an original construction that probably dates to the 7th century. The Church of La Magdalena exhibits a portal with a rose window and archivolts bearing an unusual vegetable design.

The old quarter of Zamora is a place of steep, stone-paved streets and small, serene squares lined with eminent buildings. Overlooked by the Byzantine dome of the cathedral, the aura evokes the splendor of the 12th century. The Renaissance Palace of the Counts of Alba de Aliste is in the Plaza de Viriato. Its austere façade conceals a double-galleried courtyard. The lower gallery has columns with bas-reliefs depicting mythological, biblical and historical characters. The upper gallery safeguards the family coat of arms. The palace is now a parador.

Situated on the secluded Plaza de Santa Lucia, El Cordón Palace dates from the 16th century and is now the Zamora Museum of Fine Arts. The museum's collection includes bell-shaped vessels, Roman mosaics and Visigothic liturgical objects.

About 12 miles from Zamora is the 7th century Church of San Pedro de la Nave. One of the oldest and rarest Visigothic churches in Spain, its simple exterior is built from a reddish sandstone with ashlars that have no mortar. Designed in the form of a Roman cross with a nave and two aisles, there is a symbiosis between its Roman and Oriental elements. The horseshoe arches in the portal and interior reflect the church's Spanish origins.

Accommodations
The guest house has been recently restored and enlarged. At present there are 30 beds in double rooms with private baths. Both men and women are welcome.

Amenities
Towels and linens are supplied. There is a meeting room, reading room, dining room and chapel.

Meals
Breakfast is included with the lodging.

Cost of lodging
$15.00 per person per night.

Products of the institution
The nuns produce a large variety of homemade pastries that are sold at the monastery and in the gourmet section of El Cortes Ingles, a well-known Spanish department store.

Special rules
Maximum stay 5 days. Open year round, except on Christmas Day and during the week of spiritual retreat of the nuns (dates vary).

Directions
By car: From Zamora take N122 east to Toro.
By train: Get off at Toro. There are buses to Toro from Madrid, Zamora and Salamanca.

Contact
Madre Hospedera
Monasterio Sancti Spiritus el Real
Canto, 27
49800 Toro (Zamora), Spain
Tel: 980/690304
Fax: 980/691752
Email: dominicas@rolole.com

CATALONIA

MONASTERIO SANTUARIO EL MIRACLE
Benedictine Order

Built in 1901, the history of the monastery and shrine can be traced to August 3, 1458. According to legend, the Virgin Mary appeared to a six-year old girl and warned the local populace about their morality and asked them to build a chapel in honor of the apparition or face castigation.

A chapel was promptly erected on the site of the venerated shrine. In 1553, a guest house was also built, the same structure that exists today. A larger church was built in 1590 but destroyed at the end of the 18th century. A few stones of the original wall are all that remain of the second church. These stones are contained within the present complex. The church's Renaissance retablo is preserved in the chapel of the Santissim Sagrament. Composed of various wooden paintings dedicated to Mary and the Rosary, it is quite different in appearance from the later Baroque structure.

The third and final church was begun in 1652 and completed in 1774. Baroque in style, the retablo was executed by sculptor Carles Marató and took fourteen years to complete.

Several nearby villages offer interesting side trips. The town of Cardona is known as the "Capital of Salt," because of Montanya de Sal, an enormous deposit mined since Roman times. Cardona Castle dominates the landscape from its hilltop perch and provides views of the town, the green hills and the chimneys of old factories. The stone structure is one of the best exponents of a medieval castle. Rebuilt in the 18th century, it is now a parador. The Església de Sant Vincenç sits beside the castle; it contains the remains of the once powerful Dukes of Cardona.

Solsana is a welcoming town accented by moated fortifications; nine towers and three gateways enclose noble mansions within the battlements. Its old town is marked by a medieval church and arcaded square where market day still takes place every Friday. The church, with its single nave, is a fine example of Catalan Gothic. The east end of the building, however, is still plainly contained inside a Romanesque shell. The church's interior conceals a black stone Virgin. The adjoining Episcopal Palace overlooks a small square; its museum is filled with priceless Romanesque paintings and archaeological finds.

Crossing the Portal del Pont on the way out of town, a road leads to Sant Llorenç de Morunys, the beginning of a wild countryside near the Pyrenean heights. The journey from Solsona to Berga by way of this road ranks among the most beautiful excursions in the Catalan Pyrenees. There is a Romanesque church in San Llorenç and two medieval sanctuaries, La Pietat and Santa Creu.

Pyrenean countryside

In May and June, the village of Berga celebrates La Patum, a Fire Feast which takes place in the streets and small square of town. Local men form long dragons, giants and monsters and parade through town, chasing and spitting fire over the public. In nearly every town and village throughout Catalonia, Midsummer's Eve (June 23rd) is celebrated with bonfires and fireworks.

Accommodations
There are 2 types:
1) Apartments Les-Cels: 20 apartments with 4 to 8 beds, for singles and families. The apartments have very simple furnishings and are equipped with toilets and sinks. Some do not have a shower (renovation of the baths is planned). There is a kitchen in each apartment.
2) Casa d'Espiritualitat (religious use only): 37 single and double rooms with bath. Both men and women are welcome.

Amenities
Apartments: Towels and linens on request and only if guests are staying more than one week.
Casa d'Espiritualitat: Towels and linens are provided.

Meals
Apartments: No meals are provided.
Casa d'Espiritualitat: All meals are provided.

Cost of lodging
Apartments: Provisional cost per apartment per day, minimum $10.00 (4 beds, no shower); maximum $19.00 (8 beds with shower).
Casa d'Espiritualitat: To be arranged when reservations are made.

Products of the institution
There is a small laboratory used for the production of ceramics.

Special rules
Apartments: Guests are independent but required to be respectful of the religious site.
Casa d'Espiritualitat: To be determined.

Directions
By car: From Barcelona take highway A18 to Manresa. From Manresa follow the signs towards Cardona/Solsona. From Cardona follow the signs to the Santuari del Miracle.
By train: Get off in Barcelona or Manresa. From there take a bus to either Solsona or Cardona and then a taxi to the monastery.

Contact
For the apartments:
Anyone who answers the phone
Monasterio Santuario El Miracle
25287 El Miracle (Lleida/Lérida), Spain
Tel: 973/480002
Fax: 973/481756
Email: elmiracle@mx2.redestb.es
Website: http://personal.redestb.es/elmiracle/
For the Casa d'Espiritualitat:
Anyone who answers the phone
Tel: 973/480045
Note: This number is different from the monastery.

MONASTERIO DE SANT DANIEL
Benedictine Nuns

Monasterio de Sant Daniel

The monastery is near the ancient barrio in the center of Girona. Known as Vall Sant Daniel, the monastery has been declared a Spanish national monument because of the beauty of its Romanesque church and cloister which date from the 13th and 12th centuries respectively.

It was founded in 1018 by the Benedictine Order which is still in residence. Apart from their spiritual activities, the nuns decorate and restore linens and make religious vestments. They also manage the "residencia universitaria" a place for Spanish and international students (preferably female) who come to study in Girona during the academic year.

"It is a very attractive complex because we have succeeded in blending ancient and modern architecture... especially in the residencia. All the students and professors who come here love it. It is pretty, inexpensive and very clean. Even the food is very good," the sister added.

Girona across the Onyar River

Sant Feliu Cathedral

Crossing the Onyar River from the newer part of town, a climb of nearly one hundred steps ascends to Sant Feliu Cathedral. Begun in the early 14th century, the church was completed towards the end of the 16th century. It took the place of a Romanesque structure of which only the cloister and Carlomagno Tower remain. Two hundred steps lead to the top and views of the red tile roofs of old town and the more modern architecture across the river.

The cathedral's solid west face is pure Catalan Baroque, the remainder of the structure is Gothic. Comprised of a single nave built in 1416 by Guillem Bofill, it has a rectangular ground plan. Its colossal vault is supported by interior buttresses and is one of the largest vaulted spaces in Gothic architecture. The high altar has a gilded retablo, a precious work of 14th century art. It is surmounted by a beautiful silverplated baldachin.

Beyond the cathedral is an atmospheric labyrinth of medieval streets reminiscent of Girona's past. Lying in the shadow of the cathedral is the Jewish Quarter, known as the *Call*. A warren of arched streets, steep stairs, little piazzas and solid stone buildings, until recently, this gem of ancestry lay concealed under a patina of more modern construction. Today it is among Spain's best-preserved testimonies of the Middle Ages and of its once flourishing Jewish community. On Carrer de la Forca, the historic main thoroughfare of the *Call*, is the Centre Bonastruc de Porta. Once a synagogue, it is now an information center and bookstore on the district's Jewish heritage.

From the cathedral, *Passeig Arqueológic*, a signed archaeological trail, offers a garden-like stroll along the walls leading to the important sights in the old town. The walk begins near the 12th century Monestir de Sant Pere de Galligants. A former monastery of the Benedictine Order, the cloister is home to an archaeological museum with exhibits from prehistoric to medieval times including Roman mosaics and medieval Jewish tombstones.

Throughout the pre-Romanesque period, Catalonian buildings combined artistic elements of Hispano-Arabic and Carolingian civilizations. The Church of the Monastery of San Pedro de Roda was the most illustrious example of this style of architecture. The edifice has three naves; the central one soars to a grand height and is crowned with barrel vaulting supported by ribbed arches and thick pillars.

Girona is close to the Costa Brava, a collection of popular beach towns and attractive inland scenes. Northeast of Girona is the resort town of L'Escala, a small fishing port sited above the sea on a small promontory in the Gulf of Roses.

Heading south is L'Estartit and Illes Medes. The former has a long, wide beach; the latter is a group of rocky islets. The shores and waters around the seven islands are home to the most abundant marine life along this part of the Mediterranean coast. The islands are a continuation of the limestone Montgri hills and protected as an underwater nature reserve. Nearby Pals Beach is fringed by dunes and pine forests.

Just inland, the tiny hilltop town of Begur is built around a castle. Dating from the 10th century, the fortress sits on a cone-shaped crag with views of the coast. Dotting the village are half a dozen towers built for defense against 16th and 17th century pirates. Other inland towns such as Peratallada and Ullastret have also preserved their ancient heritage. On the outskirts of Ullastret, an Iberian settlement was discovered in the 1930s. Excavations have revealed stone walls, six large round towers and six gates. Now an archaeological park, it is one of the largest of its kind in northeastern Spain. Its museum occupies the highest point of the acropolis and displays relics of the Iberian period.

Further inland is ancient Pals, a medieval hamlet composed almost entirely of Gothic-style structures. Resting on the slope of a hill, its urban layout and streets present an altogether charming picture. At the highest point in the village, Las Horas Tower was once used to keep watch over the coast and plain. The church beside the tower is an example of Catalan Gothic.

Castell De Púbol is also in the vicinity. A Gothic and Renaissance structure, it was bought in 1968 by Salvador Dalí for his wife Gala. The castle adornments are representative of the artist's style: lions' heads on cupboards and statues of elephants with giraffes' legs. The motif throughout the house also reflects Dalí's passion for his wife who lived in the castle until her death.

The journey south along the coast to Tossa de Mar is an endless succession of twists and turns and exceptional views. The origins of Tossa de Mar can be traced to the Romans. Situated in a bay, it is sheltered by Mont Guardi, a pine-dotted headland crowned with medieval stone walls and towers. A picturesque village of archetypical whitewashed houses, the castle and the layout of the streets have been maintained in a perfect state of preservation. Its center, Vila Vella, is a maze of crooked alleys lined with stone houses. The setting is enriched by a 12th century crenelated wall, three towers and ancient cottages. The old quarter lays claim to the Museu Municipal, a treasure trove of local archaeological finds, Roman mosaics and modern art including *The Flying Violinist* by Marc Chagall.

Accommodations

There are two types:

1) Residencia Universitaria: 27 beds in single and double rooms with private baths. Only students or scholars of the University of Girona are admitted. Closed in August.

2) Hospedería: Reserved for men and women seeking spiritual retreats. Open year round.

Amenities

Towels and linens are provided. There is a washing machine which may be used by the students. A TV room and library are also available.

Monasterio de Sant Daniel

Meals
All meals are provided with the lodging.

Cost of lodging
$18.00 per person/per day, meals included.

Special rules
1) Residencia Universitaria: Younger students (18/19 years), arrangements to be determined. Older students and scholars are given a magnetic card which allows them to enter and exit at all times.
2) Hospedería: To be arranged.

Directions
By car: From the south: Exit 7, Girona Sud on A7 and follow signs to Palamós. After crossing the bridge over the Onyar River, turn right and follow signs to Vall Sant Daniel and Museum Sant Pere Galligants (less than 1 km).

From the north: Exit 6, Girona Nord on A7 and follow signs to Palamós. Exit at Girona Campdurá and pass Pont Major and Pedret. Before crossing the bridge over the Onyar River, turn left and follow signs to Vall Sant Daniel and Museum Sant Pere Galligants (less than 1 km).

By train: Get off in Girona, walk to the monastery (30 min) or take a taxi. There is also a bus station near the train station. Ask for the bus to Sant Daniel.

Contact
Madre Hospedera
Monasterio de Sant Daniel
De les Monges, 2
17007 Girona (Girona), Spain
Tel: 972/201241 (Monastery)
Tel: 972/485380 (Residencia Universitaria)
Email: rsantdaniel@virtualdomus.com
Website: www.virtualdomus.com/rsantdaniel/

MONASTERIO DE SANTA MARÍA DE PUIGGRACIÓS

Benedictine Nuns

Monasterio de Santa María de Puiggraciós

The monastery is in a quiet, secluded setting three miles from the tiny village of L'Ametlla. Its name is derived from its location (Puiggraciós in Catalan means gracious mountain or mountain of grace). The monastery dates to 1700 and is annexed to a sanctuary dedicated to an image of Mary. Legend holds that the image was miraculously discovered in the 18th century. The monastery shelters a 14th century statue of the Virgin in Gothic-Catalan style.

The monastery is quite near Montseny Natural Park, the only park in Catalonia declared a Biosphere Reserve by UNESCO. Holm oak, cork oak, beech and pine groves blanket the region. The woods provide a habitat for boars, genets, dormice and a large variety of birds.

Situated in the foothills of the Pyrenees, a mountain range along the border of France and Spain, the small town of Vic is a short trip north of the monastery. The landscape is marked by a scattering of oaks surrounding solitary and grand, classically proportioned country houses called *masías*.

The town of Vic is highly regarded for its historic center which has been preserved somewhat like an island. Its 18th century cathedral, a complex of Romanesque and Gothic structures, was built around El Cloqueran, an 11th century tower. The interior of the church is embellished with bold red and gold murals depicting biblical stories by Josep María Sert. As they have since the 10th century, market days are held each Tuesday and Saturday in the Gothic-style Plaza Major.

Monasterio de Santa María de Puiggraciós

Accommodations
1 single and 3 double rooms with shared baths. Both men and women are welcome. There is heating but the monastery may be closed during the winter.

Amenities
Towels and linens are provided.

Meals
All meals are included.

Cost of lodging
Voluntary contribution. (A basic donation should be $18.00/$21.00 per person, per night.)

Products of the institution
The nuns produce laminated icons sold in Barcelona and at the Monastery of Montserrat.

Special rules
Guests are required to be punctual for meals.

Directions
By car: From Barcelona take route 152 towards Vic (L'Ametlla del Vallés is approximately 38 kms north of Barcelona). From there follow the directions to the monastery. Part of the road is unpaved.
(Note: The roads around Barcelona are like a maze. Road signs at intersections are located ON the intersection.)

By train: Get off in Barcelona or la Garriga and take the local bus to L'Ametlla del Vallés. From there take a taxi to the monastery. FYI: there are very few taxis.

Contact
Anyone who answers the phone
Monasterio de Santa María de Puiggraciós
Santuario de Puiggraciós
08480 L'Ametlla del Vallés (Barcelona), Spain
Tel: 93/7445030
Email: puiggracios@teleline.es

Monasterio Santa María de Bellpuig de Les Avellanes

Maristas Fathers

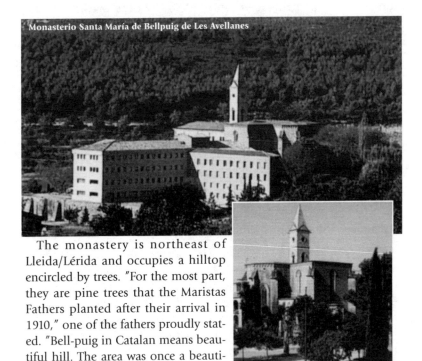

Monasterio Santa María de Bellpuig de Les Avellanes

The monastery is northeast of Lleida/Lérida and occupies a hilltop encircled by trees. "For the most part, they are pine trees that the Maristas Fathers planted after their arrival in 1910," one of the fathers proudly stated. "Bell-puig in Catalan means beautiful hill. The area was once a beautiful place and we have tried to recapture that beauty," he continued.

Founded in 1166 by the Premonstratenses Fathers who obeyed the rules of Saint Augustin, the order came from Premontré, France during the Spanish reconquista. They came to help the church resettle the territories once occupied by the Moors. As a sign of gratitude, the kings donated the land to build the monastery. At one time, it was the burial place for the Counts of Urgell.

"Just to give you an idea of the long history of the monastery, there have been seventy-two abbots since the monastery was founded," said the father. The 19th century brought wars and suppressions of the religious orders. Three times the Premonstratenses Fathers had to abandon the monastery but each time they returned. Bad conditions finally forced them to leave a few years after 1835; they never returned. The monastery remained vacant until 1910 when the Maristas Order bought it. They too had their share of troubles and suffered the vicissitudes of the Civil War which brought the monastery to the point of destruction. The fathers eventually restored the structure and turned it into the Catalan Noviciate and Seminary of the Maristas Order.

"As the vocations decreased, the monastery emptied and we had to decide what to do with it," said Padre Jaume. "We turned it into a hospedería which opened in July 2000. Most of the rooms have been completely renewed and are like those of a three or four star hotel," he continued. "There are also very comfortable rooms that are simpler and some dormitories for large groups."

Most of the monastery has been restored. The complex embraces a pretty Romanesque church and cloister, library and chapter hall. The remainder of the rooms are utilized as conference and dining rooms.

The region around the monastery is scattered with worthwhile towns and sites. To the south, Balaguer is the main town of the Noguera district. It is home to the Monasterio de Santo Domingo, a fine example of Catalan Gothic architecture. The town sustains the atmosphere of an old commercial center with frequent references to nobility. Of particular interest is the arcaded Plaza del Mercadal. The ancient walls and remains of the Formós Castle, once home to the counts of Urgell, attest to the town's noble heritage. Characterized by a single nave, the Gothic Church of Santa María is a paragon of Catalan Gothic architecture.

Overlooked by a castle, the village of Salás de Pallars reveals totally conserved medieval streets and numerous façades displaying coats of arms. Further north, the landscape is surprisingly reminiscent of southern Spain, with trained vines, fig trees and geranium-filled balconies. The village of Gerri de la Sal grew around the salt works operated by the monks who once lived in the nearby monastery. The salt works, the church of the convent and a medieval bridge add to the allure of the small village.

Accommodations
35 double rooms with private bath, TV, telephone. 14 single and double rooms with shared baths. 80 beds in large dormitories for groups. Both men and women are welcome.

Amenities
Towels and linens are supplied in the rooms but not in the dorms. The complex also includes conference rooms, dining rooms, a swimming pool and sports area.

Meals
All meals are supplied.

Cost of lodging
35 double rooms: $19.00 per person - no meals included; $42.00 per person - full pension ($6.00 additional if a single guest occupies a double room). Other prices to be determined when reservations are made.

Special rules
Punctuality at meals. Curfew at 11:00 pm. Open year round.

Directions
By car: From Lleida/Lérida take C1313 northeast to Balaguer. From there take L904 north following the signs to the monastery.
By train: Get off at Balaguer. There is only one weekday bus which leaves Balaguer at 5:00 pm (no weekends). Transportation by taxi is recommended. The monastery is approximately 13 kms from Balaguer.

Contact
Anyone who answers the phone
Monasterio Santa María de Bellpuig de Les Avellanes
25612 Les Avellanes - Os de Balaguer (Lleida/Lérida), Spain
Tel: 973/438006
Fax: 973/438038
Email: avellanes@maristes-cat.es
Website: www.maristes-cat.es/avellanes
Reservations can be made between 9:00 am - 1:00 pm via telephone, internet or fax. It is best to write or email.

ABADÍA DE NUESTRA SEÑORA DE MONTSERRAT
Benedictine Monks

Abadía de Nuestra Señora de Montserrat

Montserrat is the incredible setting for Catalonia's holiest place, the Monastery of Montserrat. An essential part of the Catalonian identity, the monastery is one of the most famous in Spain and the spiritual heart and symbol of Catalan nationalism. Many Catalan girls are named Montserrat after the site, a name often shortened to Montse. Situated at more than 4,000', the complex enjoys a spectacular view over the landscape which is dotted with chapels and ancient caves. Montserrat appears as if carved out of the rock. Its name, "serrated mountain" is derived from the Catalan mont and serrat, which describe the sharp profile of the rock site. A massif of jagged pinnacles, it rises precipitously over deep gorges, domes and shallow terraces. Every year, thousands of pilgrims travel to Montserrat for religious reasons and to behold the grandeur of the surroundings.

According to tradition, the monastery was founded by the Benedictines around the 9th century. Historical data, however, traces its founding to the Abbey Oliba da Ripoll in 1025. Over the years, the importance of the monastery grew and in 1410, it was declared an independent abbey.

In 1811 when the French attacked Catalonia during the War of Independence, the monks were killed and the monastery nearly destroyed. In 1844, it was rebuilt and repopulated. The Renaissance cloister, a notable section of the complex, is the only remaining part of the original edifice. Built by the Italian, Giuliano della Rovere, he later became Pope Giulio III. The monastery also hosted many opponents of the Regime of Franco. It was the place where the first Bible in Catalan was printed (1918) and continues to be an important center for the preservation and diffusion of the Catalan language and culture. Under Franco's rule, the church was the only religious institution permitted to celebrate mass in Catalan. To this day, thousands of couples of Catalan descent are married in Montserrat in a service conducted in their very distinct language.

The soul of Montserrat is the Virgin, a small wooden statue called *La Moreneta* (the dark one). It is believed to have been made by St. Luke and brought to the monastery by St. Peter in 50 AD. Centuries later, the statue was supposedly hidden from the Moors in the nearby Santa Cova. In 1881, Montserrat's Black Virgin became patroness of Catalonia.

The basilica was built in 1592 with a Plateresque façade. In 1900, the façade was changed to a Neo-Renaissance design and enhanced with a sculpted *Christ and the Apostles* by Agapit and Vananci Vallmitjana. The interior is Baroque and graced with an enameled altar and paintings by Catalan artists.

Twice each day, the Escolania, a choir of fifty boy choristers, sings in the basilica. Escolania was founded in the 13th century and is the oldest church music school in Europe. Beginning near the Plaza de l'Abat Oliba, the *Vía Crucis* (Way of the Cross) passes the fourteen stations of the cross before ascending the mountain in a narrow corridor carved out of the rock.

Abadía de Nuestra Señora de Montserrat

The grounds of the monastery include shops, cafes, a hotel and museum containing a collection of 19th and 20th century Catalan paintings and works by Italian artists. There is a funicular which travels from the Plaza de la Creu to the Cova Santa and Cappella San Joan. The monastery holds Gregorian Chant, classic and sacred music concerts.

Accommodations
There are three types:
1) Outside the monastery: Hotel Abat de Cisneros has 54 single and double rooms (100 beds), each with private bath. Both men and women are welcome.
2) Celdas Abat Marcet; 94 apartments with 1 to 4 beds each. They can accommodate up to 275 people. All apartments are equipped with bath, kitchen, heat, TV and telephone.
3) Inside the monastery: 48 beds, some with private bath. Only men are permitted and only for religious use.
Note: Hospitality at the monastery is only for religious use. The monastery's 3-star Hotel Abat Cisneros and Celdas offer lodging to all.

Amenities
Towels and linens are provided.

Meals
All meals can be included with the lodging.

Cost of lodging
1) Hotel Abat de Cisneros (prices are for double room, price range depends on season):
Breakfast included: from $34.00 to $70.00.
Two meals: from $66.00 to $101.00.
Three meals: from $88.00 to $124.00.
2) Celdas Abat Marcet (price range depends on season):
1 bed - min. $10.00 to max. $29.00 (high season).
4 beds - min. $42.00 to max. $67.00 (high season).
3) Monastery: cost of lodging to be arranged.

Products of the institution
A bakery and shop sell liqueurs made by the monks and nuns. A specialty of the monks is Aromas de Montserrat, a liqueur distilled from mountain herbs.

Directions

By car: From Barcelona take highway A18 towards Manresa and follow the signs to Montserrat. There is a toll station for the last kilometer of the route to the monastery. It is also possible to reach the monastery by funicular near the village of Monistrol de Montserrat.

By train: Get off in Barcelona and take the bus to Montserrat.

Contact

Central de Reservas
Abadía de Nuestra Señora de Montserrat
08199 Montserrat (Barcelona), Spain
Tel: 93/8777777 (For reservations only)
Tel: 93/8777701/ Fax: 93/8777724
Email: informacio@larsa-montserrat.com
     reserves@larsa-montserrat.com
Website: http://www.abadiamontserrat.net

MONASTERIO DE SAN BENET
Benedictine Nuns

Monasterio de San Benet

The monastery is situated on the same mountain as the famous Monasterio de Montserrat, the main Catalan shrine (see previous listing). Although it is about two miles lower on the mountain, San Benet's ideal setting offers vistas of the beautiful environs.

It was founded in 1954 by two Catalan Benendictine communities who were forced to abandon their monasteries during the Spanish Civil War. Designed by Jordi Bonet, the church is considered a monument of modern architecture. Composed of wood and stone, it is completely integrated into the natural elements and is offset by a large glass window with views of Montserrat.

Accommodations
The monastery is mainly a spiritual center. Nevertheless, the nuns host men and women coming for a pilgrimage, a period of study or to meditate. There are 9 rooms, 7 of which are doubles. All baths are shared.

Special rules
Curfew at 9:00 pm; maximum stay 10 days.

Amenities
Towels and linens are provided.

Meals
All meals can be provided for an additional cost.

Cost per person/per night
$16.00 per person.

Directions
By car: From Barcelona take highway A18 towards Manresa and follow the signs to Montserrat. The monastery is located at km 70 of the road to Montserrat.
By train: Get off in Barcelona and take the bus to Montserrat.

Contact
Madre Superiora
Monasterio de San Benet
Carretera de Montserrat (Km 10)
08199 Montserrat (Barcelona), Spain
Tel: 93/8350078 / Fax: 93/8284229

SANTUARIO DE LA MADRE DE DIOS DE NÚRIA
Property of the Church

Santuario de la Madre de Dios de Núria

Surrounded by towering mountains in an enchanting valley of the Pyrenees, the sanctuary constitutes one of the most important Catalan shrines. As with Montserrat (described earlier in this region), Núria is a popular name for Catalan girls. The town of Núria is inaccessible by car. In the past, the complex could only be reached via Els Pelegrins Trail through a verdant, albeit rocky valley of the thundering Río Núria. Now it can be accessed by a cable train (Little Cremallera Railway) from Ribes de Freser or Queralbs, an attractive stone village. The steep seven-mile journey rises over 3,250'.

Santuario de la Madre de Dios de Núria

Santuario de la Madre de Dios de Núria

According to tradition, the Greek hermit Saint Gil (later appointed abbot in Nimes, France), lived here in solitude between 700 and 703. During that period, he sculpted an image of Mary. Forced by the persecution of the times, he fled Núria and left the image hidden in a small cave.

In 1072, a man called Amadeo was inspired by a divine vision and began his search for the relics of the Virgin Mary and other possessions of the hermit. When Amadeo's mission proved unsuccessful, he built a chapel on the sacred site. The chapel was finished in 1079 and then, as legend has it, the relics he had been seeking miraculously appeared in the chapel. They included a cross, the pot used by the saint to cook his meals and the bell that later became the symbol of Núria.

Over the ensuing centuries, devotion to the image grew. Saint Gil and the image are believed to be patrons of fertility. In order to be blessed with children, an unusual rite is performed. It consists of putting one's head inside the pot once used by the saint while simultaneously ringing the bell.

The first reconstruction of the shrine took place in 1629 and was followed by a second enlargement in the 19th century. Part of the complex is occupied by a three-star hotel, property of the sanctuary but managed by lay personnel.

Núria is an important religious site as well as a holiday resort. Ensconced in a lofty, mountain-ringed bowl, the region is particularly popular with hikers and mountaineers during the summer, skiers in the winter. Other sports such as river fishing, horseback riding and paragliding contribute to the appeal of the area.

The sanctuary is very close to the principality of Andorra in the eastern Pyrenees between Spain and France. Andorra La Vella, its capital, provides the opportunity of experiencing a touch of France, Spanish style.

Many nearby towns offer interesting day trips including: Ribes de Freser, a spa in a wooded setting on the Río Freser and La Molina, an exceptional winter sports area. Puigcerdá is a fortified frontier town sited on a hill (Puig is Catalan for hill) at the junction of the ríos Segre and Carol. Encircled by majestic mountains, it is home to a 12th century monastery. The charm of the town is amplified by a pretty swan-filled lake. Not far from Puigcerdá is the medieval town of Llivia, now a national monument. Its heavily fortified church dates from the 1400s. Since 1659, Llivia has been a Spanish enclave lying inside French territory. Its museum contains what is reputed to be the oldest pharmacy in Europe, a structure marked by elaborate woodwork, painted ceilings and antique apothecary jars.

Once a tiny mountain base from which raids against the Moors were conducted, the town of Ripoll is notable for its Benedictine monastery,

Santa María de Ripoll, an example of Catalan Romanesque architecture. Founded by Count Wilfred the Hairy in 888, it achieved prominence in early medieval Catalonia. Its scriptorium has an enormous number of classical texts. The great Romanesque church of the monastery was begun in the 12th century and is characterized by a five-naved basilica and stone portal. In 1835, the church was severely damaged in a fire but the west portal and two-storied cloister remain. The portal is underscored by intricate biblical carvings, the cloister by extravagant capitals.

The Romanesque architecture found throughout Catalonia originated in Lombardy, Italy and was called "the first Romanesque art." Its significant diffusion can be attributed to a phenomenon which continued throughout the Romanesque period, a time when groups of quarriers and architects organized into brigades and worked wherever their services were required.

The Lombards crossed the Pyrenees and in less than twenty-five years covered Catalonia with their emblematic churches. Referred to as the *Romanesque Route*, more than seven hundred civil and religious constructions from that period can be seen in the region. These simple, inexpensive and practical structures soon triumphed over the complex and highly personal Mozarabic style. The architectural traits display a rustic appearance distinguished by irregular ashlars. The decoration was based on blocked arcades and serrated sides, barrel vaulting and the absence of sculptures. Many of the churches had a single, vaulted nave; others were built with a basilical design consisting of three naves separated by pillars and at times, a transept covered by a dome. Nearly all had slender towers with geminated (combined in pairs) windows which served as bell towers, a la Italian style.

Accommodations
The hotel has 65 double, triple and quadruple rooms each with a private bath. There are also 10 apartments, each with 4-5 beds, a private bath and dining room. Both men and women are welcome.

Amenities
All hotel rooms have satellite TV and telephone. There are meeting and TV rooms. Towels and linens are supplied.

Meals

All meals can be supplied on request. There are two restaurants, one is open only on the weekends.

Cost of lodging

Per double room: $36.00 to $72.00 depending on season and number of meals included. Per apartment per day: $57.00 to $87.00 depending on the season (for updated information on prices, consult the website).

Products of the institution

The liqueur of Núria is sold by the order. It is produced with locally grown and cultivated herbs.

Special rules

Minimum stay 2 nights. Closed in November.

Directions

By car: From Barcelona take N152 north to Ribes de Freser or Queralbs and take the cable train to Núria.

By train: Get off at Barcelona and take a bus to Ribes de Freser. From there take the cable train to Núria.

Note: The cable train runs every hour during the summer, every two hours during the winter.

Contact

Oficina de Reservas
Estación de Montaña Vall de Núria
17534 Núria -Queralbs (Girona), Spain
Tel: 972/732020 - 972/732000
Fax: 972/732024
Website: www.valldenuria.com

SANTUARI DE LA MARE DE DÉU DELS ANGELS
Property of the Bishopric of Girona

Dedicated to the Virgin of the Angels, the sanctuary was founded on a peak of the Gavarres Mountains. "The view is glorious, you can see the sea and many small towns along the Costa Brava up until Figueres and Roses," said the man at the desk. The shrine is a few miles from Girona and can be reached by driving up one of two winding roads. Although it dates from the 15th century, nothing of the original structure survived the wars of the 19th century, not even the original image of Mary (it disappeared during those turbulent times). The present structure was built after the war with France and doesn't contain any valuable works of art. "What is beautiful here is the view," commented the host. The hospedería is managed by lay personnel. Many visitors come to hike the old route from Girona.

The most striking feature of the region is the scenic Costa Brava. Winding down from the French border as far south as Blanes, the coastal range was strongly associated with the first Greek and Roman settlements in Spain. This classical heritage is evidenced by the archeological finds at Roses, Iloret de Mar, Tossa de Mar and Empúries where a sprawling composite of pine-fringed ruins sits beside the sea.

There are many picturesque towns and villages throughout the area. Castelló d'Empúries preserves numerous Gothic buildings. Palafrugell is an important cork-producing town and the birthplace of writer Joseph Pla. Torroella de Montgri has a walled area while the town of La Bisbal is known for its ceramics industry. Just north of Palafrugell are several villages and woodlands running right down to the sea. Charming Calella de Palafrugell is lined with traditional houses, its coastline dotted with hidden coves.

Northwest of the sanctuary is the region known as Gorrotxa, locale of the medieval town of Besalú. Situated across a fortified bridge which spans the Río Fluviá, the heart of the old town is the arcaded Plaza Mayor. A short distance from the plaza is the Romanesque Sant Vincenç, underscored by a 16th century tower. Also nearby is the 11th century Santa Pere, the single remnant of the town's Benedictine monastery. The columns on either side of the middle window of the church feature lavishly carved figural capitals flanked by lions.

Cadaqués

Backdropped by the rugged beauty of El Cabo de Creus, nearby Cadaqués is an art colony once favored by Dalí. Its skyline of white-washed buildings is offset by the brightly colored boats in the harbor. The small town of Roses shelters the ruins of the Greek town of Rhode and the Romanesque Monastery of Sant Pere de Rodes. Empúries reveals numerous Greek ruins and the Roman city of Emporion.

In the 1960s, a *mikvah* (ritual Jewish bath), was discovered in Besalú. Dating to the 13th century, it is only one of three from that period that have survived in Europe. Just outside of town is the beautiful lake of Banyoles, site of the 1992 Olympic rowing contests. On the opposite side of the lake, tiny Porqueres has a gem of a Romanesque church.

Accommodations

15 double rooms and 4 shared baths. Both men and women are welcome.

Amenities

Towels and linens are supplied.

Meals

All meals are supplied in a restaurant annexed to the shrine.

Cost of lodging

Provisional cost: $24.00 per person /per night, all meals included.

Special rules

Minimum stay 2 days. The hospedería is only open in July and August; the restaurant is open year round.

Directions

By car: From Girona take C255 north to Bordils. From Bordils follow the signs to San Martí Vella and from there to the shrine.

By train: Get off at Girona and take a taxi to the shrine (there is no public transportation). The cost of the taxi is approximately $15.

Contact

Anyone who answers the phone
Santuari de la Mare de Déu dels Angels
17462 San Martí Vell (Girona), Spain
Tel: 972/190205

SANTUARI DE SAN RAMON
Mercedarios Fathers

The shrine is at the entrance to the small town named after the saint, "a town which stretches along the road," explained one of the fathers. San Ramon was born in Portell in the 13th century, just a couple of miles from the sanctuary. When the saint was a little boy, he tended the sheep of his family and spent many hours at prayer in a nearby chapel. When he died (after having lived elsewhere), the church wanted him to be interred in Barcelona. His family and the people of Portell wanted him to be buried in his home town. According to legend, the dispute was resolved by loading his body onto a mule and following the direction the mule chose which was towards Portell.

The present shrine was begun in 1674; the relics of the saint were placed in a chapel of the church in 1695. The church and the convent were completed in the 18th century. During the Spanish Civil War, the church was almost destroyed by an explosives charge. Tradition holds that an unknown person, someone with an Andalusian accent, cut the burning fuse and saved the shrine. The church and convent are in the Herrerian style which owes its name to architect Juan de Herrera, 1530-1597. Inspired by classic Italian architecture, Herrera participated in building the Escorial in Madrid and the Cathedral of Vallodolid.

The relics of the saint are longer in the church. They disappeared during the Civil War. "What is more interesting," commented the father, "is the collection of images tied to the Religiosidad Popular, the manner in which people express their devotion and religiousness. Paintings, pictures, photographs and ex-voto, which relate the story of the saint and the miracles, are on display. Since Saint Ramon is the patron saint of pregnant women, many of the votive offerings are related to births.

The Province of Lérida stretches from the high peaks of the Pyrenees in the northeastern part of Catalonia to the plains of the Central Catalan Depression. The dramatic Pyrenees range constitutes lake-filled cirques and green valleys highlighted by a patchwork of meadows and forests and a smattering of characteristic villages.

The town of Lérida is less than twenty miles from the monastery. Capital of the Terres de Ponent, it is an important agricultural, industrial and commercial center. Poised on the banks of the Segre River, the town is crowned by the old castle of La Suda. From its lofty site, the Moorish-built fortress envelopes the once magnificent church, La Seu Vella. Dating to the 13th century, the church is a specimen of transitional style from Romanesque to Gothic and is defined by a massive octagonal tower and Romanesque-Gothic cloister. Twelve one-of-a-kind arches with delicate stone tracery further enrich the beauty of the structure. The carved capitals in the nave reflect the once prevalent Moorish influence.

An elevator travels from the church to Plaça de Sant Joan, the town's main square. The area claims the new cathedral and a collection of grand buildings such as Paeria, the 13th century town hall.

Lérida was once the capital of an important Iberian people called the Ilergetes. Two famous chiefs, Indibil and Mandonio, fought in the service of Hannibal against Scipio and rose up against Roman domination in 206 BC. Llera, as the city was known in Roman times, became established as a *municipium*, (a free town). It was a key city during the civil conflicts involving Julius Caesar and Pompey. After the conquest of the Moors, it became the center of a powerful Islamic taifa and was a stronghold against the Christian-controlled areas. The consequences of four centuries of Moorish domination are evident throughout the city.

Accommodations
25 beds in 18 single and double rooms, 9 with private bath. Both men and women are welcome.

Amenities
Towels and linens are supplied.

Meals
Meals are not supplied with the lodging.

Cost of lodging
Spring and summer - $6.00 per person; winter - $7.00 per person.

Directions

By car: From Lleida/Lérida take NII East. After about 50 kms take C25 and follow the signs to San Ramon. The shrine is located along the main road.

By train: Get off in Cervera and take a taxi to San Ramon.

Contact

Anyone who answers the phone
Santuari de San Ramon
Avinguda Santuari, 26
25215 San Ramon (Lleida/Lérida), Spain
Phone/Fax: 973/524005
Email: mersanram@moebius.es

MONASTERIO DE SANTA MARÍA DE VALLBONA
Cistercian Nuns

The monastery is among the most important Cistercian communities of Catalonia. Founded in 1153, the complex is nestled in a hilly landscape. "The setting reminds many visitors of an area near Jerusalem," said one of the nuns. It was originally inhabited by a male and female community of hermits who lived according to the Cenobitic rules of San Benito under the auspices of founder Ramon de Vallbona.

In 1175, the male community was transferred to Montsant and the remaining female community converted to the Cistercian Order. The nuns dedicated themselves to working the land and the monastery prospered under their guidance. Its fame was so widespread that it hosted kings like Alfonso el Casto, Alfonso el Sabio and Jaime I.

Since 1200, the monastery has maintained a cultural center where the nuns copy and decorate books. They also teach grammar, liturgy, calligraphy and music. Over the centuries, the complex was enlarged resulting in a mix of architectural styles. The Gothic church most likely dates from the 14th century and safeguards several precious tombs including that of Queen Violante of Hungary. It was the queen's request to be buried in the church in a tomb devoid of ornamentation. The tomb of Princess Sancha, the queen's daughter, is contained within the church as well. The 14th century statue of the Virgin Mary by Guillem Seqauer distinguishes the choir.

The first four centuries of the monastery's existence are reflected by several architectural styles: Cistercian, Romanesque and Renaissance. The design of the chapter hall is quite simple and adorned with the 15th century statue of the Virgen de la Misericordia. The modern chapel conserves the renowned Virgin of the Cloister, perhaps one of the first images venerated in the monastery. The antique pharmacy preserves ancient tools and molds once used to make pills. For a small fee, guided tours can be arranged every day except Monday.

Monasterio de Santa María

Monestir de Poblet

Santes Creus

To complete what is known as the Cistercian Triangle, the nuns suggest a visit to the Monestir de Poblet and Santes Creus. The first and most important of the three sister monasteries, Poblet is in a sequestered valley, the environs imbued with a sense of peace and tranquility. During the 1835 Carlist revolution, the monastery was damaged by fire and theft. Restoration was begun in 1930 and a decade later, the monks returned. The compound harbors the royal tombs. Begun in the 14th century, they were later redone by sculptor Frederic Marés. The evocative cloisters are late Romanesque style; the capitals are decorated with carved scroll work. Alabaster reredos rendered by Damiá Forment dominate the apse.

Santes Creus is enclosed by ancient walls amidst a landscape of poplar and hazelnut trees and is considered the loveliest of the three monasteries. Founded in 1150 by Ramon Berenguer IV during his reconquest of Catalonia, the Gothic cloisters are embellished by figurative sculptures. The tomb of Jaime II lies within the 12th century church, a somber affair offset by a splendid rose window.

Somewhat further afield is the town of Tarragona. Perched atop a rocky hill which gradually slopes down towards the sea, the city is known as the balcony of the Mediterranean. From a geographical and climatological point of view, it can be divided into two sections: the coastal area and the inland area. The coastal region, known as the Costa Daurada, encompasses a succession of fine, sandy beaches with calm, blue water, impressive cliffs, a pine-covered headland and small cove. The landscape of the inland area is one of carob trees, vineyards and hazel, almond and olive groves, its beauty magnified by the intense brightness of the sun.

The medieval cathedral is the town's most representative monument. Begun in 1170, it was completed towards the middle of the 14th and comprises a tasteful mix of Romanesque and Gothic including a rose window and handsome sculptures. The interior has an outstanding reredos above the main altar. The work of sculptor Pere Joan, it depicts scenes from the life of Santa Tecla.

Tarragona

Tarragona was founded by Publius Cornelius Scipio during the Second Punic War (218 BC) and preserves the characteristics of a great Roman city. Reminders of its heritage are evident in the amphitheater, aqueduct, forum, walls and towers. The former Roman roads are the town's present day streets and squares. The Plaza de la Font stands over part of what was the Roman circus while the port is the continuation of a breakwater built by the Romans.

Accommodations
20 single and double rooms (35 beds), most with private bath. Both men and women are welcome. Refugio de San Bernardo is a large dormitory (24 beds) for groups of youths seeking spiritual retreats.

Amenities

Towels and linens are provided. There are two large rooms, one is a library for meetings and study, the other a chapel reserved for guests.

Meals

All meals can be included with the lodging except on Christmas and Easter when the restaurant is closed.

Cost of lodging

Prices are arranged according to visitor's needs and abilities.

Products of the institution

The nuns create elaborate original music by computer and print it for sale. They produce and sell pottery and prints for various occasions. One of the nuns is a painter and her paintings are sold in the monastery.

Special rules

The nuns host all guests, but preference is given to those seeking peace and meditation. Curfew will be arranged upon arrival.
Note: All services are held in Catalan.

Directions

By car: From Barcelona follow directions to Lérida, taking highway A7 and then A2. Exit at Montblanc and follow C240 north for 24 kms to Vallbona.

By train: Get off at Montblanc and take a taxi to the monastery or get off at Lérida and take the local bus to Vallbona. There is only one bus that leaves about 1:00 pm. The bus does not run on Sundays or holidays.

Contact

Madre Hospedera
Monasterio de Santa María de Vallbona
25268 Vallbona de Las Monjas (Lérida), Spain
Tel: 973/330266
Fax: 973/330491
Email: vallbona@archired.es
Website: www.vallbona.com

MONASTERIO CLARISAS DE VILA-SACRA
Clarisse Nuns

The monastery is in a peaceful locale in Alto Ampurdán, a fertile area of Catalonia stretching between the Gulf of Roses and the inland pre-Pyrenean hills. Well located for touring some of the most interesting sites of Catalonia, the complex is less than a mile from the small town of Vila-Sacra and the Costa Brava.

The community inhabiting the monastery was founded in 1267 in Castelló d'Empuries but moved to this location in 1973 and settled in a farm donated to the Franciscan Order by a wealthy woman. With the exception of *Virgin Mary with the Child*, a statue dating from the 16th/17th century, the monastery does not possess any works of art.

"Most people, especially those who live nearby and already know of the monastery, come because of the absolute peace and quiet. They can retreat, study, meditate and take walks to reach the river in only ten minutes," said one of the nuns.

Costa Brava

The monastery is not far from the heart of *Costa Brava*, the wild coast. A realm of sunny beaches, rocky shorelines and memorable landscapes, it stretches from Portbou near the French border and skirts the Mediterranean before ending at Blanes. The region is blessed with great natural beauty characterized by steep cliffs and romantic coves. Its allure inspired the surreal settings of Salvador Dalí's art including the stark sea-lashed and sun-baked headlands of Cabo de Creus where the artist spent many summers. Lying at the tip of Cape Creus is Cadaqués, a whitewashed waterfront town with jewel-like beaches. The atmospheric resort is overlooked by the massive Baroque Església de Santa María. The Centre d'Art Perrot-Moore houses examples of Dalí's work. Picasso and other contemporary artists are also represented. At the head of the sweeping bay, the nearby town of Roses, originally founded by the Greeks, claims the longest sand beach of the entire coast.

Ancient Empúries is on the south shore of the gulf. Also founded by the Greeks around 600 BC, it then became an important Roman port. The extensive ruins of the pine-fringed Greco-Roman town include the *agorá* (meeting place), streets, temples and cisterns. An amphitheater, floor mosaics and two villas have also been discovered in a partially excavated Roman town, ca. 3rd century BC.

Teatro-Museo Dalí

Heading inland from the monastery is Figueras, hometown of Salvador Dalí. The Teatro-Museo Dalí is a remarkable edifice, recognizable from afar by its glass dome. Composed of honeycomb-like features, the dome crowns the old theater and displays an enormous concentration of the artist's works. Dalí's tomb is under the museum's dome. In keeping with his unusual artistic perception, the tomb includes a representation of a Cadillac with Dali at the wheel.

Accommodations

7 single, double and triple rooms (12 beds) with private bath. Both men and women are welcome in groups of men only, women only or married couples.

Amenities

Towels and linens are supplied.

Meals

No meals are supplied. Guests may use the kitchen facilities.

Cost of lodging

Voluntary contribution (in winter, please consider the extra cost of heat).

Special rules

Curfew at 10:00 pm. Maximum stay one week. Open year round.

Directions

By car: From Barcelona or Girona take the Autopista (route A7) and exit at Figueras. Go east on the Figueras-Roses route (route C260). The monastery is located at Km 33 on the left-hand side (opposite a gas station).

By train: Get off at Figueras and take a bus to Vila-Sacra. The bus stops 2 kms from the monastery. Or take a taxi from Figueras.

Contact

Anyone who answers the phone
(Call in advance)
Monasterio Clarisas de Vila-Sacra
Ctra de Roses s/n
17485 Vila-Sacra (Girona), Spain
Tel: 972/507595
Fax: 972/507595

EXTREMADURA

CASA DE EJERCICIOS NUESTRA SEÑORA DE LA MONTAÑA

Instituto Secular de Obreras de la Cruz
(Secular Institute of the Workers of the Cross Nuns)

Casa de Ejercicios Nuestra Señora de la Montaña

About a mile from the center of Cáceres, the Casa de Ejercicios occupies a lofty perch. From its terrace, guests can enjoy a splendid view of the city. The casa sits beside the famous Santuario de Nuestra Señora de la Montaña which houses a statue of the Virgin Mary, patron saint of the city. The Casa de Ejercicios is independent from the sanctuary. It hosts guests seeking rest and relaxation, groups seeking spiritual retreats or pilgrims to the sanctuary.

The devotion of the statue can be traced to the 17th century. At that time, a hermit safeguarded the statue with the exception of one week each year when he carried it to Cáceres for the people to worship. In 1668, the statue was declared patron saint of the city and the church was erected. It contains a Baroque retablo and is visited by pilgrims who often stop when journeying to the more famous Monasterio de Guadalupe.

The Tagus River flows westward through scenic countryside before reaching Cáceres, capital of Upper Extremadura. A two thousand year old city, it has been occupied and ruled in turn by Romans, Moors and Christians. Its Roman heritage is exemplified by the Bridge of Alcántara. Built over the Tagus River in the days of Trajan, it is ranked among the most important bridges of the Roman Empire and one of the few Roman works to bear the name of its maker, Caius Julius Lacer. When the Moors controlled the city, they called it Quarzi and built the walls which stand today. Twelve of the thirteen towers protecting the old city remain. Especially outstanding is the square-shaped Redonda.

Declared a World Heritage city by UNESCO in 1986, Cáceres is considered one of the best-conserved medieval stonemasonry collections in Europe; a city whose historic center, Ciudad Monumental, seems to be entirely composed of palaces. Many of the noble houses are still used as family residences and a few are open to visitors. The 15th century Palace of the Golfines de Abajo is considered the most beautiful. The structure combines Gothic, Mudéjar and Plateresque elements and includes battlements along the façade as well as medallions and coats of arms of the Catholic kings, the Golfines and Alvarez families.

Porticoed Plaza Mayor, heart of the old town, is home to the Tower of Bujaco. The Arco de Estrella is a low-arched gateway flanked by a 15th century watchtower, the work of Manuel Churriguera, an architect of the famous family of architects. It is the starting point of a journey along the cobblestone streets of town, an excursion that offers a glimpse of life during the Middle Ages.

Cuesta de Aldana allows access to the highest part of the enclosed walls and leads to the Museo de Bellas Artes, the only Mudéjar house (14th century) in the city. The Church of San Mateo was erected in the

16th century over a mosque. It has a fine classic façade flanked by the towers of Los Plata.

The Barrio de San Antonio is the old Jewish Quarter, a place of narrow streets edged with whitewashed houses. Outside the walls is the Church of Santiago, a Romanesque-Gothic affair with a main altarpiece by Berruguete and several noteworthy buildings including the Palaces of Godoy, Jusatic and la Isla. The Convento de San Pablo is known for its biscuits or *yemas* (candied egg yolks), a specialty made and sold by the nuns.

In the late winter months, hundreds of storks migrate from Africa to Cáceres to build large nests on the towers and belfries of medieval Cáceres, filling the air with their singular clacking sound.

Accommodations
16 single and 21 double rooms with private bath. Both men and women are welcome. The casa books early, reserve well in advance.

Amenities
Towels and linens are supplied.

Meals
Meals are supplied only to groups of 15 and more. Other guests may dine at the restaurant beside the shrine.

Cost of lodging
To be arranged depending on the size of the group, length of stay, etc.

Special rules
Curfew at 11:30 pm. Open year round.

Directions
By car: From Cáceres follow the signs to Santuario Nuestra Señora de la Montaña.
By train: Get off at Cáceres and take a taxi to Nuestra Señora de la Montaña (there is no public transportation).

Contact
Anyone who answers the phone
Casa de Ejercicios Nuestra Señora de la Montaña
Ctra. De la Montaña, s/n
10003 Cáceres (Cáceres), Spain
Tel: 927/220512

MONASTERIO DE SAN JERÓNIMO DE YUSTE
Jerónimos Monks

Monasterio de San Jerónimo de Yuste

Founded in 1408 by the monks of San Jerónimo, the monastery is nestled in a wooded region and looks today as it did centuries ago. The same order has inhabited the monastery from its inception, living in seclusion as they have always done. The Jerónimos monks are a small religious community intrinsic to Spain. There are only two monasteries inhabited by the order: San Jerónimo and Santa María del El Parral in Segovia.

The fame of the monastery can be traced to the fact that Carlo V, Holy Roman Emperor lived on the monastery grounds for nearly two years after he abdicated the throne in 1556. Although he died in the monastery in 1558, his remains were later moved to the Escorial in Madrid. Among the most interesting features of the monastery are the apartments built by the king and the place where he spent the final years of his life. The rooms were designed so that the king, ill with gout, could remain seated while attending mass or enjoying the view of the nearby pond. The original furnishings have been preserved. Opera lovers will be intrigued by the fact that the king's residence was the setting of the first scene of *Don Carlos* by Giuseppe Verdi. The apartments can be visited from 9:00 am to 1:00 pm and from 3:00 pm to 7:00 pm.

Like many other religious institutions, the monastery suffered during the Napoleonic invasion and was nearly destroyed during the War of Independence. It was later rebuilt and in 1958 returned to the order of Jerónimos. The Gothic church dates from the 15th century and shelters two cloisters, one Gothic, the other Plateresque, (an architectural and decorative style which originated in Spain towards the middle of

Monasterio de San Jerónimo de Yuste

the 16th century). The design is characterized by a profusion of ornamental components resembling silver work.

The monastery is on the outskirts of Cuacos de Yuste, an old village
in the wooded valley of La Vera. Its houses are characterized by red
peppers which flank the doorways; the peppers are hung to dry before
being used to make paprika. Every September 30th, a festival is held to
honor San Jerónimo.

Nearby Trujillo is a medieval hilltop town accentuated by a massive
Arab castle and encircling battlements. During the reconquest, the
Islamic fortress defended the town against the Christian advance.
Trujillo was home to many conquistadores including several notable
explorers instrumental in the history of the Americas: Francisco
Pizarro who conquered Peru, Orellana who discovered the Amazon
and Diego García Paredes who founded Trujillo in Venezuela. An
equestrian statue of Pizarro stands in the center of the Plaza Mayor,
twin of the statue in Lima.

The Plateresque Palacio de la Conquista is the most imposing palace
in the square. Built by Hernán Pizarro, the corner windows feature

busts of Francisco Pizarro and his wife, the Inca princess Yupanqui. Flanked by two towers, the Renaissance Palacio de Orellana-Pizarro was built by Orellana and is graced with a fine Plateresque patio.

Accommodations

Outside the monastery: 8 single rooms, each with private bath. Both men and women are welcome.

Inside the monastery: 5 single rooms, each with private bath. Open exclusively to men willing to share the religious life of the monks.

Cost of lodging

To be determined.

Amenities

Towels and linens are supplied.

Meals

All meals are included with the lodging.

Special rules

Curfew is 9:00 pm when dinner is served. Lodging is offered to everyone. The monks invite guests to share the atmosphere of the site.

Directions

By car: From Madrid take E90 east to Navalmoral de la Mata (approximately 165 kms). At exit 178 (on E90) go north on route EX119 to Jarandilla de la Vera and follow the signs to Cuacos de Yuste. The monastery is about 2 kms outside of town.

By train: Get off at Navalmoral and take the bus to Cuacos de Yuste. From there, walk or take a taxi to the monastery.

Contact

Padre Hospedero
Monasterio de San Jerónimo
10430, Cuacos de Yuste (Cáceres), Spain
Tel/Fax: 927/172130

Casa de Oración Nuestra Señora de Guadalupe
Esclavas de Cristo Rey Nuns

The casa is quartered at the entrance to a tiny village just outside the city of Badajoz, a couple of miles from the Portuguese border. The nuns built the house twenty years ago. "The casa is a beautiful building, full of light," said one of the sisters. A large garden envelopes the premises. It is filled with orange and lemon trees that create a peaceful and relaxing atmosphere while adding a sweet fragrance to the air.

The casa is quite large and capable of hosting many groups at the same time. "There are four separate dining rooms where excellent meals are offered. I am not saying this to promote our house," the sister explained. "We have more than enough guests. But I can assure you that good food is guaranteed."

The lands of Extremadura are steeped in history. The paintings in the region's Maltravieso Cave represent man in the earliest stages. During the first century, the capital city of Cáceres was inhabited by the Celts and ranked as one of the five most important colonies of ancient Lusitania. Dolmens can be seen throughout the countryside. Relics of the New Stone Age period. The Neolithic monuments consist of a large, flat stone laid across upright stones.

A tableland bordering Portugal, Extremadura is crossed by mountains and by the Tagus and Guadiana rivers and comprises the provinces of Badajoz and Cáceres. Its finest monuments are the remarkably well-preserved ruins of ancient settlements. Reconquered from the Moors in the 12th and 13th centuries, the region was frequently a battlefield in the Spanish wars with Portugal. This legacy is evidenced by numerous fortresses scattered over the terrain.

Badajoz is the provincial capital of the southern half of Extremadura. Known in Roman times as Colonia Pacensis, the center of the old town revolves around the Plaza de España and the encom-

passing pedestrianized streets. The plaza is home to the medieval Catedral de San Juan. Built in the 13th century on the site of a mosque, the structure has Plateresque windows in the tower, a tiled cloister and ornate interior. Although the cathedral is predominantly Gothic in design, it reflects a touch of Romanesque, both in its proportions and construction elements.

Other interesting sites include the ancient town walls, watchtowers and Moorish Alcázaba, now the Museo Arqueológico. The museum houses a collection of more than 15,000 artifacts, some dating from Paleolithic times. The Museo de Bellas Artes shelters more than 1,200 paintings and sculptures including works by Picasso and Dalí. The granite Puente de Palmas is the town's finest structure. Built in 1596, it leads over the Río Guadiana to a monumental gateway with round towers, part of the ancient fortifications.

A number of historic towns are nearby. Zafra was a Moorish settlement once known as Zafar. Nicknamed *Sevilla la Chica* (little Seville) because of its Andalusian ambience, the graceful city boasts a 15th century castle built over the former Alcázar. The fortress is remarkable for its massive towers and pyramidical merlons (the solid part of the battlement between two openings). The arcaded Plazas Grande and Chica are at the heart of town and are joined by a column on which a measuring rod is sculpted. The rod was used during the cattle fairs once held in the square.

Olivenza was formerly a Portuguese enclave. Its stout walls shelter a medieval castle housing the Museo Municipal. The museum's interior is one of ribbed vaulting and spiraling columns; exhibits depict rural life in Extremadura. The church of Santa María Magdalena represents a rare example of 16th century Portuguese Manueline style. Named after Manual I of Portugal, the design combines Moorish and Gothic components with Renaissance features. The 16th century Santa Casa de Misericordia has Portuguese azulejos in blue and white.

Alburquerque is an old-world town situated on a hill overlooked by a massive 13th century castle. Traces of the ancient battlements can still be seen. The fortified tower of the Gothic church of Santa María del Mercada reflects the history of this often conflicted frontier town.

Accommodations
90 beds in 52 single and double rooms with private bath. Both men and women are welcome.

Amenities
Towels and linens are supplied. 11 meeting rooms, 4 dining rooms and a garden.

Meals
All meals are supplied with the lodging.

Cost of lodging
Provisional cost per person/per night full pension: $24.00.

Special rules
Punctuality is required at meals. Curfew at 11:00 pm. Open year round.

Directions
By car: From Badajoz take EX 100 to Cáceres. Travel about 5 kms to Gévora del Caudillo and the casa.
By train: Get off in Badajoz and take a bus to Gévora. Buses do not run on weekends.

Contact
Anyone who answers the phone
(Write a letter in advance of your call)
Casa de Oración Nuestra Señora de Guadalupe
Nuestra Señora de Guadalupe, s/n
06180 Gévora del Caudillo (Badajoz), Spain
Tel: 924/430045

REAL MONASTERIO DE SANTA MARÍA DE GUADALUPE

Franciscan Monks

Real Monasterio de Santa María de Guadalupe

Real Monasterio de Santa María de Guadalupe

Guadalupe is a picturesque village of narrow streets and ancient houses that grew up around the monastery, one of the most famous in Spain. From its central location, the monastery's turreted towers and crenelations rise dramatically over the town and surrounding wooded valley. Founded in 1340, the architecture is a combination of Gothic, Mudéjar and Plateresque components of unusual grandeur. In many ways, the monastery closely resembles a medieval castle. The west front of its church is delineated by two square flanking towers. Originally inhabited by Jerónimos monks, the monastery flourished under the Catholic kings and became an important cultural center acquiring schools of grammar and medicine, three hospitals, a pharmacy and a valuable library. In 1402, the first Spanish anatomical dissection was performed in the medical facility.

The monastery's church is entered through double bronze doors which depict scenes from the lives of Christ and the Virgin. The sculptural adornment of the Baroque retablo was the work of Giraldo de Merió. The paintings were done by Vincent Carducho and Eugenio Caxás.

Behind the Capilla Mayor and reached by a stairway of extraordinary red jasper steps is the Rococo Camarin. The aisles are separated from the nave by wrought iron grilles partially forged from the chains of freed slaves. The Baroque choir stalls and organs are by Churriguera, a highly regarded architect. Beyond the church is the two-story Mudéjar cloister, ca. 14th century.

Guided visits of the complex are available and include three museums. The Museo de Bordados displays embroidered vestments and altar cloths from the 14th to 18th centuries, most made in convents. Among the treasures of the Museo de Libros Miniados are illuminated books of hours and missals produced in the monastery. The Museo de Pintura y Escultura showcases paintings by El Greco and Goya and a small ivory crucifixion attributed to Michelangelo. Also included on the tour is the Baroque Sacristy known as the Spanish "Sistine Chapel" because of the portraits of eight monks which hang from its walls. The paintings were done by Francisco Zurbarán (1598-1664).

When the Romans came to Spain, they built a roadway which came to be known as the Silver Way, or *La Ruta de la Plata*. Centuries after its construction, portions of the route can still be traced across Asturias, Castilla - León, Extremadura and Andalusia. Carefully engineered, the roads were built in layers. The first level was comprised of boulders fixed in place with soil; the second consisted of gravel; the third of hewn stone. On the base rested the *summa crest*, large, smooth stone slabs. Every twenty kilometers along all Roman roads, *mansios* (places to spend the night), were established. The Romans also laid down milestones and landmarks that credited the emperor under whom construction had taken place and indicated the distance in kilometers from the city of origin.

Monastery gardens

Nearby Mérida was founded in 25 BC by Augustus. The town enjoyed the rank of colony and possessed one of the largest territories in Hispania. Rich in Roman architecture and relics, it was one of the towns along the Silver Way. The road entered from the north, crossed the Roman bridge over the Albarregas, went under the Arch of Trajan and ended at the Forum. Views from the massive Puente de Guadiana encompass the walls of the Alcázaba, one of Spain's oldest Moorish structures.

The western part of the city boasts exceptional Roman monuments including a theater, amphitheater and circus, reminders of life during Roman times. Mérida's theater is one of the most accomplished Roman constructions of its kind. There are thirty-two, two-story Corinthian marble columns lavishly adorned with statues. The semicircular orchestra was paved with blue and white marble tiles. The amphitheater was built in 8 AD and could accommodate 15,000 spectators. Elliptical in shape, the center held a *naumachia* (a huge tank filled with water) and was used for the celebration of sea battles. Fights between gladiators and lions also took place in the amphitheater.

The Casa Romana is embellished with a Pompeiian-style mosaic pavement and fresco paintings. The Circus Maximus is outside the town walls. Dating from the first century AD, the enormous edifice was capable of holding 30,000 spectators and was the venue for chariot races.

Accommodations
46 double, triple and quadruple rooms and 1 suite, each with private bath. Both men and women are welcome.

Amenities
Towels and linens are supplied.

Meals
All meals can be supplied on request but only to large groups. Individuals and small groups must dine outside of the hospedería.

Cost of lodging
Basic price per double room/per night (no meals included) $48.00 + 7% VAT. Closed from mid-January until mid-February.

Directions
By car: From Madrid take highway 5 and exit at Talavera de la Reina. From there follow the signs to Guadalupe on N502 and C411.
By train: Get off at Madrid and take a bus to Guadalupe.

Contact
Anyone who answers the phone
Real Monasterio de Santa María de Guadalupe
Plaza Juan Carlos 1, s/n
10140 Guadalupe (Cáceres), Spain
Tel: 927/367000 / Fax: 927/367177

MONASTERIO SAN JOSÉ DEL MONTE DE LAS BATUECAS
Carmelite Monks

Las Mestas is at the border of Extremadura and Castilla - León. Although it officially belongs to the province of Cáceres, it is closer to Salamanca and considered part of its province. The monastery, named after the Batuecas River, was founded in 1599 by Padre Tomas de Jesus. An Andalusian monk, he chose the site because of its natural beauty. "The surroundings are splendid," said Padre Emilio. "The environs are ideal for relaxation and meditation. The ruins of the ancient monastery are an archaeological treasure," he added. The monastery is in a deep green valley of the Sierra de Francia, a chain of hills and mountains whose peak is occupied by the famous Santuario de Nuestra Señora de la Peña de Francia (see listing in Castilla - León).

The monks can trace a glorious 400-year history but perhaps the monastery's most famous personality was Padre José María del Monte Carmelo, also known as *El Cadete* (the Cadet). A soldier, he abandoned military life and retreated from the world. Whenever time allowed, he would seclude himself in the trunk of a hollow tree that he had fashioned into a small room and spend hours in solitary meditation. The tree no longer exists. "We have planted a new one," explained the monk. "Hopefully it will grow if the goats don't eat it!"

During the religious suppressions, the monks were forced to leave the institution and the buildings were abandoned for 80 years. When the monks returned, they could no longer live in the original facility and had to build a new one. Part of the old church has been restored and turned into a small chapel. The monks manage the small guest house. "We host agnostics and atheists too," the monk said humorously. "We don't ask them to take part in the liturgy if they don't want to. Guests are invited to dine with us and 'breath' the atmosphere. We eat in silence and listen to the Gospel or to sacred or classical music," he explained.

Throughout the verdant countryside, small towns and hamlets offer a glimpse into the country's past. Baños de Montamayor is the first town along the *Ruta de la Plata* (Silver Route) in Extremadura. The route continues amidst a captivating landscape to Hervás. Sprawled atop the grand Valle del Ambroz, the small town harbors an atmospheric Jewish Quarter. Its whitewashed, two-story trellis and adobe houses date from the 13th and 14th centuries.

Lying on the banks of the Río Jerte, Plasencia is a town of inviting streets and aristocratic palaces. Behind a double circuit of golden gray walls, dozens of towers, noble mansions and handsome manors are reminders of the conquistadores and colonists who returned from America as rich men. A town of monumental sights, heraldic signs adorn many of the buildings and attest to past glories.

Plasencia

The Romanesque Catedral Vieja features a "Door of Forgiveness," a dome with Byzantine style flakes and a museum with works by Ribera. The Catedral Nueva dates to the 15th century; its Plateresque façade was designed by Diego de Siloé and Juan de Álava. The church has an altarpiece by Gregorio Fernández, a Baroque organ and carved wooden choir stalls.

A walkway on the battlements offers views in every direction. A market is held every Tuesday in the main square, a ritual unbroken since the 12th century.

Accommodations
13 single rooms with private bath. The monastery is for men only.

Amenities
Towels and linens are supplied.

Meals
All meals are supplied.

Cost of lodging
$21.00 per person/per night (all meals included).

Special rules
Punctuality at meal times. Minimum stay three days, maximum one month.

Directions
By car: From Salamanca reach La Alberca by route C512 and SA210. From there follow the sign to Las Batuecas.

By train: Get off at Salamanca. Take a bus to La Alberca and from there take a taxi to Las Batuecas, approximately 3 kms.

Contact
Padre Hospedero
Monasterio San José del Monte de Las Batuecas
10624 Las Mestas (Cáceres), Spain
Tel/Fax: 923/161099

GALICIA

MONASTERIO DE SANTA MARÍA DE ARMENTEIRA

Cistercian Nuns

Monasterio de Santa María de Armenteira

The monastery was founded in the 12th century by the Knights of Don Ero de Armenteira. The Don came from an aristocratic family and accompanied Alphonso VII on his battles against Hispanic Islam in the south of Spain. In 1150, he retreated to his estate and founded the monastery, adopting the austere spiritual life inspired by St. Bernard of Clairvaux and the newly created Cistercian Order. According to legend, during one of Ero's meditations in the nearby woods, he became engrossed listening to the sweet song of a bird for what seemed like a few minutes. When he returned to the monastery, centuries, not minutes, had passed. He was the first Abbot of Armenteira and as a result of his devotion and piety eventually became St. Ero.

Although the complex is still being restored, it is possible to visit the 12th century church, one of the loveliest Cistercian-style Galician churches of medieval Europe. Built with Cistercian simplicity and decorated with a beautiful Mudéjar dome, the structure has a bell tower and cloister from the 18th century. The ceiling is a pointed barrel vault above the center aisle with sections separated by broad-framed arches.

The main façade of the church is graced by a rose window which diffuses the interior with light. It was thought to be a mandala for meditation, particularly important in Tibetan Buddhism. The mandala occurs as a basic pattern in religious art and ritual. The four corners of a mandala represent the four corners of the world.

Six archivolts are worked around the main entrance. An inscription indicates that it was completed in 1212 and attributed to master builder Petrus Froya. The carved moldings around the door are Mudéjar inspired. According to one of the nuns, "The portal is lovely. It has engraved archivolts and is considered one of the most beautiful in the whole country."

The cloister was renewed around 1576 in a Renaissance design by another master builder, Bartolomé de Hermosa. The design is a square base with six arched, semi-circular galleries and stellated vaults. At a later date, the upper floor was built in Baroque style.

About 12 miles from the monastery, the town of Pontevedra is set in a countryside dotted with *pazos* (traditional stone manor houses). The provincial capital, its origins date to the time of the Romans. It is situated along the Rías Baixas, an area known as "the land of the 1,000 rivers."

Backdropped by verdant hillsides, the old quarter manifests an archetypically granite Galician atmosphere portrayed by fine examples of urban architecture. A romantic aura permeates the cobbled alleys and intimate squares. Along with many other cities, Pontevedra claims Columbus as a native son. A statue dedicated to the explorer faces towards the ocean and the Americas.

Pontevedra is a bustling place with a fine monumental heritage. The churches of San Francisco, Santa Clara and Santo Domingo represent Galician-Gothic architecture from the late 14th and early 16th centuries. Other monuments include the Basilica of Santa María. Paid for by the powerful Seamen's Guild, the church is an harmonious blend of late-Gothic Manueline and Plateresque styles, delineated by an intricate Plateresque façade. The 18th century shrine of La Virgen Peregrina has a distinctive curved façade and tall, slender twin towers. It was designed by Antonio Souto in the shape of a scallop, a motif common to the region and one that suggests a Portuguese influence.

On the shaded Praza de Leña, two 18th century mansions form the Museo Provincial. Exhibits include Celtic Bronze Age relics evocative of Galicia's origins and a collection of work by Alfonso Castelao, a modern-day Galician artist. The museum also conserves documentary graphic archives with nearly 100,000 photographs and a library of over 75,000 books.

The ivy-covered Convento de Santo Domingo and adjacent Jardines de Vincenti are popular spots for the *paseo*, a traditional evening stroll. Just outside of town is the 16th century Iglesia de Santa María la Mayor. The church is accented by a Plateresque façade with carved figures of seamen.

The nearby enclave of Cambados is earmarked by a granite paved square, the Plaza de Fefiñanes. Lined with arcaded houses, the seaside town is bordered by a grand 17th century mansion and the 18th century Iglesia de San Benito. The neighboring vineyards produce the fruity Albariño wine.

Accommodations

The guest house has just been completed and has 2 single and 11 double rooms, each with private bath. Both men and women are welcome.

Amenities

Towels and linens are provided.

Cost of lodging

To be determined upon arrival, (pProvisional cost, $18 per person).

Products of the institution

The nuns produce honey which is sold in the shop of the convent. They also make and repair religious ornaments.

Special rules

Maximum stay 8 days. Punctuality is required at meals. Curfew is at 10:00 pm. The monastery is open year round, however, due to the cold temperatures of the region and the high cost of heating, only large groups are allowed during the winter. Priority is given to guests seeking spiritual retreats.

Directions

By car: From Pontevedra take A9 or route 550 north, exit at Meis and follow the signs to Armenteira.
By train: Get off at Pontevedra and take the local bus to Armenteira.

Contact

Madre Hospedera
(In addition to Spanish, the nuns speak French and a little English)
Monasterio de Santa María de Armenteira
36192 Armenteira - Meis
(Pontevedra), Spain
Tel: 986/718300
Fax: 986/710595
Email: ocsoponte@planalfa.es

SANTUARIO DE NUESTRA SEÑORA DE LOS MILAGROS

Paules Fathers

Santuario de Nuestra Señora de Los Milagros

Isolated on a mountain of the Sierra de Queija, the sanctuary lies amidst a milieu of pine trees with views over the valley. According to the rector, Eladio Gomez, "The place is wonderful... beautiful, a hill in the middle of a valley full of trees and meadows."

The sanctuary was founded after a miraculous apparition of the Virgin Mary to a local shepherdess and is dedicated to the Virgin of the Miracles. When the chapel proved insufficient to contain the pilgrims, a large shrine was erected in the 18th century. It is the largest sanctuary of the province and one of the most important of Galicia and Portugal. About a century ago, upon the invitation of the bishopric of Orense, the present religious community took up residence. The complex faces a large square. It is flanked on one side by the domicile of the fathers and the Casa Spiritual and on the other by the hospedería, restaurant and cafeteria.

The Baroque-neoclassical church contains a statue of the Virgin and paintings representing the miracles performed by her. Its façade resembles the exterior of the cathedral of Santiago of Compostela. "The church is very pretty and many people come here to get married," said the manager of the guest house. "From April onwards, we are very, very busy!" he exclaimed. In addition, an important ethnological museum has recently been opened.

Within the province of Orense, the small town of Baños de Molgas is renowned for its thermal springs. Orense is the only Galician province without a coastline but it possesses fresh, navigable waters that support a fertile landscape including the well-known vineyards of Ribero.

Santuario de Nuestra Señora de Los Milagros

Famous for its healing sulphur springs, Orense, main town of the province, is believed to have Celtic and Roman origins. Archeological remains representing these periods are preserved in the Provincial Museum. North of town, the landmark Puente Romano crosses the wooded banks of the Miño. The seven-arched structure is one of the most beautiful and oldest in Europe.

The historic core of the city has been declared a National Artistic and Historical Site and incorporates the Cathedral de San Martin, principal monument of Orense. Sitting beside the arcaded plaza, the cathedral was built in the second half of the 12th century and is highlighted by the Romanesque sculpture of the *Portico del Paraíso* (Porch of Paradise), modeled on the Portico de la Gloria in Santiago. The interior conserves an equestrian statue of the namesake saint and a Plateresque screen. The Church of the Santisima Trinidad has an ogival portico and two cylindrical towers flanking the façade. The transition from Romanesque to Gothic can be seen in the cloister of San Francisco, a convent rebuilt at the beginning of the 16th century.

The monastery is convenient to many interesting cities. The southern route incorporates Allariz, Xinzo de Limia and Verin. Approached through an upland region of woodlands, Allariz retains traces of a long circuit of walls. Among the town's ancient mansions, Casa de Armoeiro is particularly noteworthy. Composed of two parts, it is linked by an arch which crosses the street. Allariz also preserves a few Romanesque churches and an ancient Jewish Quarter marked by narrow streets.

Known for its thermal springs, the small town of Verin lies in a valley of vineyards overlooked by Monterrei Castle, a fortress dating to the 8th century. It was built during the wars with Portugal to guard the frontier. Over the centuries, the castle developed into a fortified town enclosed by three rings of walls which seclude a 13th century church and several historic monuments.

Another route comprises the villages of Ribadavia, Celanova and Bande. Located on the Miño riverside, the history of Ribadavia is portrayed by its grand manors, castles, Romanesque churches and ancient Jewish Quarter. Although the inquisition expelled all Jews in 1492, many who converted to Christianity or fled to Portugal, returned years later. The old town is a medley of cobbled squares lined with stone arcades. Its architecture represents a range of styles including the ogival Santo Domingo and La Huerta del Castillo, an assemblage of walls, towers and tombs carved into the rock. Ribadavia is the heart of Ribeiro wine country, acclaimed for its dry white and port-like red wines.

The vistas from Celanova embrace a good portion of Galicia. The town's 10th century San Miguel chapel reflects Mozarabic style, a design not often seen in the region. Constructed of granite with a cannon vault, the chapel is in the garden of the Benedictine Monastery of San Salvador. Once an important monastery, it harbors 16th century cloisters and a Baroque church with a carved, Gothic-styled choir.

The small village of Bande was known to the Romans as Aquis Querquinnis. Set in a scenic milieu, Bande is home to the church of Santa Comba o San Torcuato de Bande, a Visigothic edifice believed to date to the 7th century. It is highlighted by a lantern turret and an arch with carved marble pillars.

Accommodations

There are two types:

1) Hospedería: The property of the sanctuary, it is managed by lay personnel. There are 8 single and 22 double rooms with private bath. Both men and women are welcome.

2) Inside the convent: Casa Spiritual has 13 beds in single and double rooms reserved for guests seeking spiritual retreats. Both men and women are welcome.

Amenities

Towels and linens are supplied in all accommodations.

Meals

1) Hospedería: All meals can be supplied. There is a large restaurant with 3 dining rooms (approximately 500 people can be seated).

2) Inside the convent: All meals are supplied with the lodging.

Cost of lodging

Hospedería: Provisional price per person/per night in a single room is $30.00 (full pension). Casa Spiritual: To be arranged upon arrival.

Directions

By car: From Orense take route C536 east towards Ponferrada. After about 20 kms, turn right following the signs to Maceda and the sanctuary. By train: Get off at Orense and take the bus to Baños de Molgas. It stops near the sanctuary.

Contact

1) Hospedería: Anyone who answers the phone. For reservations in spring and summer, call at least 2 months prior.

2) For the Casa Spiritual: Anyone at the sanctuary

Santuario de Nuestra Señora de Los Milagros

32705 Baños de Molgas (Orense), Spain

Hospedería phone: 988/463127

Sanctuary phone: 988/463176

Sanctuary fax: 988/463249

CONVENTO DE LOS PADRES FRANCISCANOS
Franciscan Friars

Convento de Los Padres Franciscanos

The convent was founded in the 13th century by Saint Francis. When the saint visited Santiago de Compostela, he established a convent there. After visiting Louro, he created a small hermitage which was later enlarged and became a convent in the 14th century. The Franciscan friars inhabited the institution until 1835 at which time they were forced to leave due to the suppression of religious orders. Some time later, a wealthy man from Santiago de Compostela bought the property and returned it to the Franciscan Order. After an absence of thirty-five years, the friars returned.

"The convent is a very simple stone structure. It is not full of works of art as many other places in the area. What we have here though are beautiful views and surroundings," said one of the friars. Once a boarding school, the convent has served as a guest house for more than twenty-five years. "We receive many guests every year. Our guest house is very popular and we are almost always booked," the friar commented.

The convent lies in the most tranquil part of the Rias Baixes, along the western coast of Galicia, between Santiago de Compostela and Finisterre. Composed of four rias that are also estuaries of rivers, it is a place of rocky bays in a hilly milieu. The convent is very close to the beach of Louro on the tip of the cape.

Scattered on a hill, nearby Muros is marked by well-preserved granite buildings emblematic of the region. Founded in the 10th century, the tiny port boasts the engaging quarters of A Cerca and A Xesta where arcaded lanes are crowded with old Galician houses with glazed balconies.

A pistache of inviting towns and sites populate the immediate area including Noia and Padrón. Between Muros and Noia lies a beautiful open coast, bare and rocky and backdropped by hills. Noia is a small port with a big legend; it is believed to be one of the three cities founded in Spain by Tubal, grandson of Noah. During the 12th century, it was encircled by stone walls; evidence of the ancient structure remains. Possessing a somewhat medieval flavor, Noia is home to several old churches and mansions. Gothic San Martin has a sculpted façade and rose window. Santa María La Nova dates to the 14th century; its cemetery is a coterie of ancient carved headstones.

Hórreos

Lying at the mouth of the Río Ulla, Padrón traces its name to the mooring stone or pedrón associated with the Apostle Saint James. It is believed that the boat bearing the remains of the saint was anchored to the pedrón and so began the origin of the pilgrimage to Santiago de Compostela. The environs are known for *hórreos*, granaries commonly made of granite. Rectangular in design, the structures are raised on stone stilts. Some are extremely long and often reflect the wealth of the owner.

Accommodations

24 single and double rooms with private bath. Some doubles can be turned into triples for families with children. There also is a campsite for tents and RVs. Both men and women are welcome.

Amenities

Towels and linens are supplied. Meeting room, TV room and garden are available to guests.

Meals

All meals can be supplied on request.

Cost of lodging

$31.00 per person, full pension. Other prices vary depending on number of meals.

Special rules

Guests are provided with a key. Open from May until the end of September.

Directions

By car: From Santiago de Compostela take C543 (becomes C550) towards Noia and Muros. From Muros follow the signs to Playa de San Francisco or Convento de Los Padres Franciscanos.

By train: Get off in Santiago or La Coruña and take a bus to Muros and then a taxi to the convent.

Contact

Padre Hospedero
Convento de Los Padres Franciscanos
15291 Louro-Muros (La Coruña), Spain
Tel: 981/826146

MONASTERIO DE SAN JUAN DE POIO
Mercedarios Fathers

Monasterio de San Juan de Poio

The monastery is situated along the coast of Galicia. Waterways criss-cross the region from the mountainous inland and form characteristic rías; narrow, wedge-shaped inlets that flow between pine-covered hills, uniformly widening and deepening toward the sea.

Monasterio de San Juan de Poio

It is believed that the large complex was originally founded in the 7th century in light of the religious communities established by St. Fructuoso, a member of the Visigothic royal family. Tradition holds that the saint caused a sensation by walking across the water to the islet of Tambo to rescue a sinking boat. The oldest part of the church contains the tomb of another Galician saint, Santa Trahamunda. According to legend, her body floated to Galicia in a stone boat from Córdoba clutching an Andalusian palm tree. It was believed that she could cure deafness.

The Monastery of Poio dates to the high Middle Ages when it was in the hands of the Benedictine Order. Documents dated 942 reveal that a Benedictine monastery existed at Poio at the time the countryside was being resettled in the 10th century.

During the 12th and 13th centuries, under the protection of the Spanish monarchs, the monastery flourished and grew in importance. Endowments of estates and rural manors greatly increased and were entrusted to the Benedictine monks. The monastery reached its acme in the 16th and 17th centuries when it was enlarged and enriched by many works of art.

In 1548, it became a Colegio Mayor De Teologia and remained as such until 1835 when it was abandoned during the suppression of the religious orders. In 1890, it was once again inhabited, this time by friars of the Order of La Merced who have continued in residence since that time. The Mercedarios became quite famous because of the Schola Cantorum (1890-1968), a school where they taught Gregorian Chant.

During the course of the 20th century, the Mercedarios fathers have enhanced the transcendental spirit of life. Cultural activities have been revived including seminars and specialized colleges organized during the summer months by the Universidad de l'Atlantico. The community maintains its own archives and reference library which contains the extraordinary legacy of the poet Rey Soto.

The complex is an assemblage of artistic styles: Gothic, Renaissance, Romanesque and Baroque, testimony to the monastery's diverse history. The church's stone façade (ca. 1600) is divided into two sections: the lower is reminiscent of Greek Doric, the upper is Corinthian, flanked by Baroque towers. The most impressive works of art include the Baroque retablo of the main altar and the sacristy, called the Gothic Christ's Chapel because of its 16th century cross.

Claustro de las Procesiones and Claustro del Crucero combine Gothic and Baroque elements. At the center of the former stands a Baroque fountain whose water comes directly from Mount Castrove. The latter reveals a large mosaic of the Camino de Santiago by Czech artist, Antoine Machourek.

During the Renaissance period in Galicia, the monastery was one of the first buildings remodeled by Portuguese architect Mateo Lopez. In 1580, he redid the exterior of the cloister with columns of the Ionic order. In later years, he designed St. Martiño Pinario in Compostela for the Benedictine monks.

The monastery's new church was built between the 17th and 18th centuries by Friar Gabriel de Casas, a monk from St. Martiño Pinario. It is considered one of the finest creations of Baroque style in Galicia. Its magnificent granite façade is the work of architect Pedro Monteagudo. The main nave is graced by an archway of columns inspired by those at Santiago Cathedral. It is distinguished by a slightly undulating entablature and a vaulted niche with scrolled buttresses which portray the figure of St. John the Baptist, patron saint of the monastery.

Poio lies within the densely populated Morrazo Peninsula, home to the small towns and villages of Marin, Bueu, Cangas, Mouña and Vilaboa. The peninsula has a rich archeological legacy encompassing remains from the Megalithic period: the Chan de Armada Dolmen near Marin and Vilaboa; the Chan de Arquiña Dolmen at Moaña; Bronze Age sites known as O Fixon and Lavapés; and the Mogor rock drawings at Marin.

From an architectural point of view, there is a fine selection of Romanesque churches throughout the region. Undoubtedly though, the most outstanding structure on the Morrazo Peninsula is the Collegiate Church of Santiago at Cangas. Its history is interwoven with the powerful Seamen's Guild and constitutes one of the great Galician creations of the 16th century.

The Island of Toja, among the most stylish resorts in Galicia, is across the sea from the monastery. A tiny, pine-covered gem, it is joined to the mainland by a bridge. Luxurious villas, a Belle Epoque palace and a small church covered in scallop shells add to the island's allure.

Not far from the monastery is the small fishing village of Combarro where the streets, houses and buildings have adapted themselves to both the demands of the sea and that of the land. The complete ensemble is one of the most interesting sites in the region. Combarro also claims the largest collection of *hórreos* (raised granaries) in Galicia.

Accommodations

The hospedería can host up to 400 guests in 237 single and double rooms. Most rooms have private baths, the remainder are shared.

Amenities

Towels and linens are supplied. Conference rooms, cafeteria, restaurant, TV room and chapel are available for guest use. The monastery organizes exhibitions, concerts and courses during the summer months.

Meals

All meals can be included with the lodging.

Cost of lodging

$29.00 for a double room with private bath plus 7% VAT.
$22.00 for a double room with shared bath plus 7% VAT.

Special rules

Curfew to be arranged upon arrival. The guest house is closed from the end of October until Easter week.

Directions

By car: From Pontevedra heading west take the route along the coast (G41). After approximately 2 kms there will be signs to the monastery.
By train: Get off at Pontevedra and take a bus or taxi to the monastery.

Contact

Anyone who answers the phone
Monasterio de San Juan de Poio
Apartado 205
36995 Poio (Pontevedra), Spain
Tel: 986/770000 or 986/770258
Fax: 986/770202

MONASTERIO DE SAN PELAYO

Benedictine Nuns

Situated in front of the Cathedral of Santiago de Compostela, at the end of the Camino de Santiago, the monastery was founded in the 9th century, the same time as the city. It was established by a community of Benedictine monks who were later replaced by the present female community.

The life of the monastery has always been tied to that of the city. Apart from being a very famous pilgrimage site, Santiago is also a university town. In that regard, the monastery hosts female students of the University of Santiago. Since the nuns live in seclusion, only a portion of the complex can be visited. An attractive Romanesque church is open to the public as well as a small museum exhibiting objects of the monastery: paintings, religious ornaments and antique parchments.

According to legend, the tomb of St. James the Apostle (son of Zebedee and brother of John the Divine), was discovered in Santiago. King Alfonso II of Asturias had a sanctuary built on the site. The discovery was instrumental in the birth of pilgrimages along the Camino de Santiago which, in turn, brought prosperity to the region. It also provided the groundwork for the development of Romanesque art, the new art of the Christian world. Typical architectural segments include massive walls, few windows, round, heavy arches and barrel vaulting. Many examples of Spanish Romanesque architecture can be seen along the pilgrimage route linking the cathedrals of Jaca and Santiago.

The medieval city of Santiago is one of the chief shrines of Christiandom. At the height of its popularity in the 11th and 12th centuries, the city grew around the shrine and continues to thrive as a pilgrimage and tourist center. Its most remarkable building is the monumentally opulent cathedral, a sanctuary of international importance.

Santiago cathedral

Constructed of warm, golden granite, the building is a mix of domes, statues and pyramids flanked by immense bell towers. Of Romanesque design, it is characterized by a Baroque façade on its western flank and Baroque and Plateresque additions. The cathedral is the magnum opus of Spanish Romanesque art and represents an unparalleled specimen of the architectural style. (The original sanctuary was a much smaller structure destroyed by the Moors in the 10th century.)

The interior of the cathedral contains El Pórtico de la Gloria, a masterpiece of medieval art designed by Master Mateo in the 12th century. Covered by early cross vaults, the portico is dedicated to a condensed version of Christian theology. The elaborate arches support a series of beautifully carved figures. Presiding over the entire setting is the imposing figure of St. James, resting his feet on two young lions. One of the most memorable features of the cathedral involves an elaborate pulley system. Located in front of the

El Pórtico de la Gloria

altar, the pulley is used for moving an immense incense burner. Operated by eight priests, it is swung in a vast ceiling-to-ceiling arc across the transept. A singular custom, it only takes place at special services.

Santiago de Compostela is home to many monasteries and convents including the enormous Benedictine San Martin whose interior shelters an altarpiece depicting the patron saint riding alongside St. James. Just north of the city is Santo Domingo. The structure is highlighted by a prodigious triple spiral stairway, each leading to different levels of a single tower.

Galicia is situated in the northwest corner of the Iberian peninsula. It is surrounded by mountains and embraced by a sea that has filled it with fjord-like rías, beaches and islands. Often shrouded in a fine mist, the region's small villages dwell in a landscape largely unchanged for centuries. The lush land is divided into four provinces: La Coruña, Lugo, Orense and Pontevedra. Of the four, Orense is the only land-locked province. The symbols of Galicia include the *cruceiro*, an elabo-rately carved stone cross on a tall column used for praying and the *hórreo*, a granary raised on stilts and made of stone or wood.

The medieval town of Betanzos is a short distance from the monastery. Set in a fertile valley, the town's streets are lined with multi-storied houses with wrought iron balconies. The ancient core lays claim to the Gothic churches of Santa María do Azogue and San Francisco. Separated by a small square, the latter was inspired by the basilica in Assisi, Italy. The heart of town is centered around the mon-umental Praza de García Hermanos. The buildings that encircle the square date to the 18th century and include a neoclassical palace and the Iglesia de Santiago which showcases an equestrian statue of St. James.

miradores

Nearby La Coruña is a busy Atlantic port with windswept beaches and a sheltered harbor. Often referred to as the "City of Glass," it is highlighted by emblematic glazed galleries or *miradores*. The old part of town, Ciudad Vieja, is a warren of atmospheric streets. Its heart is represented by the elegant Plaza de María Pita, home to the arcaded town hall. The square was named after a local heroine credited with saving the town during an attack by Sir Francis Drake.

Standing just outside of La Coruña on the northernmost tip of the peninsula is the Torre de Hércules, La Coruña's proudest symbol. Built in the 2nd century AD, it is the oldest continuous working Roman lighthouse. Nearly 250 steps lead to the top and panoramic views.

Accommodations
5 beds in 1 single and 2 double rooms with private bath. Women and married couples are welcome.

Amenities
Towels and linens are provided.

Meals
All meals can be included with the lodging.

Cost of lodging
$30.00 per person, full pension. Other arrangements are available and will be determined upon arrival.

Products of the institution
The nuns are adept in the preparation of Tartas de Compostela, a specialty of Santiago. The original recipe for the sweet pastries called for almonds. "Today, they are made with many different ingredients and variations," said one of the sisters. "We make them in the classic style," she added.

Special rules
Curfew at 10:00 pm. Minimum stay 3 days, maximum 8 days.

Directions
By car: In Santiago de Compostela, the monastery is next to the cathedral.

By train: Get off in Santiago and take the bus to the cathedral.

Contact
Madre Hospedera
Monasterio de San Pelayo
San Pelayo de Ante-Altares, 23
15704 Santiago de Compostela (La Coruña), Spain
Tel: 981/583127
Fax: 981/560623

Monasterio Transfiguración del Señor
Benedictine Nuns

Monasterio Transfiguración del Señor

The monastery sits on a small mountain in a verdant landscape typical of coastal Galicia. The structure was completed in 1984 on a site chosen for its exceptional natural beauty. "I think the monastery occupies one of the most picturesque locales in all of Spain," one sister offered.

The nuns who inhabit the monastery came from a small town near the sea. They decided to move to the present location because the once quiet atmosphere of their lives had been effected by an increasing number of residences built near their former monastery. "We did what Saint Benedict would have done; we chose a little mountain, isolated, but not too far from people," the nun commented. The building is new and doesn't contain any works of art. "We are the works of art since we are God's works of art," the mother added.

Vigo, Galicia's largest town and Spain's biggest fishing port, is five miles from the monastery. In a setting near the mouth of a deep ría, the town combines the beauty of coastal scenery with the lushness of wooded hillsides. Two ancient forts, Castillo de San Sebastián and Castillo del Castro offer far-reaching views.

The newer part of town is a mixture of broad avenues and parks. Once the sailors' quarters, an old-world sensibility permeates the unusually steep cobbled streets of the Barrio del Berbes. The bronze equestrian statue in the Plaza de España was sculpted by local artist Juan José Oliveira. Monte del Castro, a notable archeological site, dates to between the second century BC and the third or fourth century AD. On the outskirts of town, the Parque Quiñones de León is celebrated for its geometric gardens.

From Vigo, it isn't far to the frontier town of Tui, one of the seven ancient capitals of Galicia. Picturesquely piled upon its acropolis above the Río Miño, legend holds that it was founded by Greeks after the Trojan War. Spain's main border town with Portugal, Tui's graceful, curving granite lanes ascend to a district of stone houses.

The twin-towered Cathedral de San Telmo dominates the small medieval center. A handsome structure dating to the 13th century, it shelters the remains of San Telmo, patron saint of Spanish sailors. Since Spain and Portugal were often at war during the Middle Ages, the style of the church resembles that of a fortress, complete with towers and battlements. It has a Romanesque porch and portal adorned with the Gothic-style *Adoration of the Magi*. Many religious objects are showcased in the cathedral's museum. The cloisters were built in the latter half of the 13th century and restored in the 15th.

The Portuguese walled city of Valença do Minho is reached by crossing an iron bridge built in 1884 by Gustave Eiffel. Gothic Iglesia de Santo Domingo occupies a space beside the Parque de la Alameda. Its cloisters and tombs are ivy covered and enhanced with carved effigies. Nearby Monte Aloia was the first site in Galicia to be declared a nature park. It offers an excellent scenic lookout of the Ría de Vigo and the valley of the Loura River.

Farther south along the coast, Baiona is one of Galicia's loveliest resort towns. Offset by the walls of the medieval Castillo de Monterreal, soft sand beaches are strung along the shoreline. Baiona was an important fortified hill settlement in Spain and the first to hear of the discovery of America when the Pinta sailed into port after its historic voyage.

The small fishing port of A Guarda is also very close. Remnants of a Celtic settlement of one hundred round stone dwellings, ca. 600-200 BC, pepper the slopes of Monte de Santa Tecda.

Accommodations
12 single and 4 double rooms, each with private bath. Both men and women are welcome.

Amenities
Towels and lines are supplied.

Meals
Breakfast, lunch and dinner are provided with the lodging.

Cost of lodging
Voluntary contribution.

Products of the institution
The nuns' main activity is making and selling pastries.

Special rules
Curfew: 10:00 pm summer; 8:00 pm winter. Maximum stay 8 days. Due to extreme winter temperatures, the guest house is only open continuously from the beginning of June until September 15th and during weekends and festivities in the winter.

Directions
By car: From Vigo or Redondela head north following the signs to San Vicente de Trasmaño and the monastery.
By train/bus: Get off at Redondela and take a taxi to the monastery.

Contact
Madre Hospedera
Monasterio Transfiguracíon del Señor
36811 San Vicente de Trasmaño (Pontevedra), Spain
Tel: 986/452903
Fax: 986/450909
Email: benidictinassvtr@planalfa.es

LA RIOJA

SAN JOSÈ
Discalced Carmelite Nuns

San Josè

The monastery is in Calahorra, capital of Rioja Baja. Situated on the Cidacos River in Old Castile, Calahorra is more than two thousand years old. Known in ancient times as Calagurris, it has been inhabited since Paleolithic times. Surrounding the town are the remains of once mighty walls. The alleys of the old quarter comprise a quaint picture accented by many Mudéjar-inspired buildings. A number of sites reflect the town's diverse history, including its Roman heritage as evidenced in the ruins of the Arco del Planillo, the only gateway remaining from the Roman walls.

San Josè

The monastery was founded in 1598 by a group of nuns who came from various Carmelite monasteries established by Santa Teresa de Ávila. The Calahorran townspeople wanted a symbolic presence of the saint in their town and the nuns honored their request. The community was begun without the patronage of a noble or wealthy family. During the early years of their residency, the nuns lived in absolute poverty, supported solely by the local populace. At one point, Don José Gonzales de la Uzqueta (uncle of one of the nuns) proposed building a monastery and church if the nuns declared him their *Patrono*. They did. The structures were built and occupied by the nuns.

"Since that time, we have lived a serene and joyful life typical of our order. Today we earn our living by making pastries," said the Madre Portera. During the suppressions of the 19th century, the sisters were not forced to leave. "We lost most of our works of art," she added.

The nuns live in strict seclusion and only the church can be visited. Classicist in style, the structure dates to the first half of the 17th century. The retablo of the main altar is organized in three different sections and arrayed with paintings and sculptures representing the life of Saint Teresa, Christ, the Holy Family and various saints. The most interesting images are the *Cristo at the Column* and the *Sagrada Familia*, both attributed to Gregorio Fernandez. The painting of Saint Teresa was done by Angelo Nardi.

The monastery sits beside a cathedral enriched by a Plateresque cloister. The edifice dates to the 5th century but was restored in the 15th. Home to the Museo Diocesano, it is highlighted by a 12th century bible and a 15th century Custodia made of gold and silver that was donated to the museum by Henry IV.

Nearby Alfaro was once an important frontier town between Castile and the Kingdom of Navarra. Poised on a high hill, it overlooks a plain of cornfields and vineyards. The monumental architecture of the twin-towered Collegiate Church of San Miguel is strongly influenced by the artistic forms of Aragón. The church is known for the stork nests on its roof which house nearly 250 birds.

Accommodations
16 beds in double rooms located on three floors. Baths are shared, one per floor. Both men and women are welcome, together only if married.

Amenities
Towels and linens are supplied. There is a kitchen, dining room and meeting room that guests may use.

Meals
Meals are not supplied with the lodging.

Cost of lodging
$9.00 per person per night.

Products of the institution
A selection of pastries is sold at the monastery.

Special rules
On the day of their arrival, guests must check in before 7:00 pm. They are provided with a key to the guest house.

Directions
By car: From Zaragoza take A68 or route N232 north and exit at Calahorra.
By train: Get off at Calahorra. There also are buses to Calahorra from Soria, Vitoria and Zaragoza.

Contact
Madre Portera
San Josè
Tenerías, 18
26500 Calahorra (La Rioja), Spain
Tel/Fax: 941/131787
Email: mmcarmelitascalahorra@portalmix.zzn.com

SAN MILLÁN DE SUSO Y YUSO
Augustinian Monks

San Millán de Suso

San Millán de Yuso

San Millán de la Cogolla is a small town that developed around two monasteries, now national monuments: San Millán de Suso and San Millán de Yuso. The town's name is derived from a hermit who died in the 6th century. It is believed that like St. James the Apostle, the holy hermit appeared on a white horse to defend the Christians from the Moors.

San Millán de Suso (upper monastery) is located about half a mile above town on the Distercios mountains. The complex enjoys views of the landscape including snow-covered Mount San Lorenzo. Founded in 537 by the hermit San Millán, it is where he lived and died (574). The church and two chapels were originally carved out of the pink sandstone mountain; they are distinguished by Romanesque and Mozarabic features and delineated by horseshoe arches. In 923, a formal building was erected on the same site and entrusted to Mozarabic monks (the caves are still preserved in the interior).

San Millán de Suso

The monastery of Suso enjoys a vista of the Cárdenas Valley River. The Romanesque church contains various tombs and a carved alabaster monument to San Millán. Gonzalo de Berceo, an important Spanish poet and writer of the 13th century, was one of the monks of the order. He is the first known poet in the Castilian language.

San Millán de Yuso

The body of San Millán is not contained here. Legend holds that in 1053 when the entourage carrying the saint's remains reached the valley on its way to Nájera, the oxen pulling the cart stopped and refused to move. The refusal was taken as a miraculous sign of the will of the saint and his wish to remain near his monastery. To honor him, King García de Nájera built a second monastery called Yuso on the very site the oxen had stopped.

The institution was inhabited by Benedictine monks until 1878 when the Augustinian Order took up residence. The original building was reconstructed in the 16th and 17th centuries in the style of Herrera and is known as the *Escorial de la Rioja* because of its remarkable size and outstanding walls. The 16th century church is partly Renaissance with Baroque golden doors. It has a retablo and Baroque sacristy. The original tomb of San Millán was destroyed in 1809 by the French army. All that remains are two plaques that belonged to the reliquary of San Millán and San Felices.

The library of Yuso is among the most important sites of the monastery. San Millán is considered the *Cuna de la Lengua Castellana y Euskera* (Cradle of the Castilian and Basque language). In the 10th century when Latin was the dominant language, a monk reported some comments about a work by Saint Augustin in the new language known as Castilian Romance. The monk did something similar for the *Euskera* (Basque) language of which he wrote a few words. A copy of the manuscript, *Codex Aemilianensis* or *Glosas Emilianenses*, can be seen at Yuso. This first use of Castilian is engraved on stone in the Salón de Reyes. The library also has an archive of manuscripts and incunabula from the 10th to the 16th centuries.

The environs are rich with tiny hamlets and villages offering unique diversions and historic sites. Saint Magdalen Festival in nearby Anguiano is characterized by stilt dancers. The *Route of Monasteries* includes those of Nájera, Cañas and Valvanera. The *Route of Wines* takes in the centennial wine cellars of Cenicero and the modern ones of Badarán.

Beginning in Nájera, another scenic itinerary is the *Route of the Valley* of the Najerilla River. Just east of Nájera, evocative Alesón reveals tumbling ruins of the Convent of San Antón. In Navarette, traditional potters' workshops are open to visitors. A glimpse of the town's past can be seen in the ruins of a Romanesque shrine and a statue of St. James on horseback which sits in a niche of an old mansion.

Accommodations

Located inside the monastery of Yuso, the hostería is a 4-star hotel. The property of the monastery, it is managed by lay personnel and contains 22 doubles, 2 suites and 1 royal suite. Both men and women are welcome.

Amenities

Towels and linens are supplied.

Meals

All meals are supplied in the San Augustin Restaurant.

Cost of lodging

Doubles: $93.00.
Suites: $108.00.
Royal suite: $150.00.
Breakfast: $6.00. Cost of other meals at the restaurant: $13.00.

Products of the institution

Although not produced by the monastery, a selection of *D.O.C.* wines of La Rioja are available in the restaurant. Closed January 8th-24th.

Directions

By car: From Logroño take N120 west to Nájera and then south on C113 following the signs to San Millán.
By train: Getting to San Millán by public transportation can be difficult. Get off in Logroño and take a local bus to San Millán (there is also a bus from Nájera).

Contact

1) Hostería San Millán de la Cogolla
Anyone who answers the phone
Plaza del Convento, s/n
26226 San Millán de la Cogolla (La Rioja), Spain
Tel: 941/373277
Fax: 941/373266
Email: hosteria@sanmillan.com
Website: www.sanmillan.com
2) Monasterio San Millán de la Cogolla
Plaza del Convento s/n
26226 San Millán de la Cogolla (La Rioja), Spain
Tel: 941/373049

MONASTERIO DE NUESTRA SEÑORA DE LA ANUNCIACIÓN

Cistercian Nuns

The monastery and its hospedería are sited beside the walls of the city. The institution was founded in 1621 by an order of nuns through the authority of the monastery of Las Huelgas in Burgos. The community became independent in 1873, but continued its original mission of hosting pilgrims to Santiago. Both the church and monastery are Romanesque in style. The church possesses a Renaissance retablo with seven niches and is decorated with *conchas* (shells), one of the symbols of the Camino de Santiago.

The last and perhaps most important stage on the "Way to Santiago" (in La Rioja) is the picturesque walled town of Santo Domingo de la Calzada. Founded in the second half of the 11th century, its streets are graced with a number of handsome old manors.

Santo Domingo de la Calzada

A holy man and hermit, Santo Domingo made his home on the bank of the Oja River, not far from the place where the pilgrims crossed. According to legend, the saint observed the difficulties the pilgrims endured and decided to help them. He built *calzadas* (roads) and bridges including a 24-arched stone bridge. In addition, he installed a hospice in his former hermitage.

In the 14th century, Pedro the Cruel, King of Castile, surrounded the town with ramparts. Earmarked by a Baroque bell tower, the Cathedral of La Rioja is a Romanesque-Gothic structure which shelters the saint's tomb. It is embellished with carvings reflecting miracles performed by the saint. The church is accented by a 16th century carved walnut reredos, last work of artist Damián Forment.

Perhaps the best known feature of the cathedral is the *Cock and Hen of Santo Domingo*. As a tribute to the saint's miraculous powers, a live cock and hen are kept in the church in their own Gothic-style henhouse. Another noteworthy structure is the Convent of San Francisco which represents the loveliness of Herrera style. Its interior features a carved stone retablo dating to the 16th century.

Cock and Hen of Santo Domingo

The nearby town of Haro is the heart of the La Rioja Alta wine producing region, a scenic area of gently rolling hills. Haro is on the Río Ebro and crowned by the hilltop Iglesia de Santo Tomás. A Flamboyant Gothic building, the church is highlighted by a Baroque reredos and Plateresque façade. The town grew around a large arcaded square in the old quarter. The Museo del Vino has a detailed display on how wine is made. A well-known folk event is the annual "Battle of the Wine."

Not far from the monastery, the village of Belorado is a place that owes its existence to Castilians on one side, Frank settlers on the other. The Churches of Santa María and San Pedro contain figures of St. James in the guise of a wayfarer and warrior. The small town has been an important urban center since the Middle Ages. Its Plaza Mayor is arcaded in typically Castilian style.

Accommodations
There are 70 single and double rooms (104 beds), most with private bath. Rooms without baths have sinks. Both men and women are welcome.

Amenities
Towels and linens are provided.

Meals
All meals can be included with the lodging.

Cost of lodging
$33.00 per double room + 7% VAT.

Products of the institution

The nuns specialize in making pastries, cakes and *polvorones,* a typical Spanish sweet named after its texture which is reminiscent of *polvoron* (powder/dust). They also have a bookbinding laboratory and they decorate ceramics.

Special rules

Curfew 11:00 pm in winter, midnight in summer.

Directions

By car: From Burgos (heading west) or Logroño (heading east) take route 120. Santo Domingo de la Calzada is located between the two towns.

By train: Get off in Logroño and take a bus to Santo Domingo de la Calzada.

Contact

Madre Hospedera
Monasterio de Nuestra Señora de la Anunciación
Mayor, 31
26250 Santo Domingo de la Calzada (La Rioja), Spain
Tel: 941/340860 - 941/340700
Fax: 941/343304

ABADÍA NUESTRA SEÑORA DE VALVANERA
Benedictine Monks

Abadía Nuestra Señora de Valvanera

Occupying a lofty and somewhat isolated site 4000' above sea level, the monastery sits in a wooded, mountainous terrain on the edge of the Sierra de la Demanda Nature Reserve. Founded more than a thousand years ago by the Benedictine Order, the monks have continued in residence since that time. In the Middle Ages, the monastery was famous and powerful and once hosted Queen Isabel.

During the Napoleonic invasions, the structure was partially destroyed in a fire. It was later rebuilt in an austere style; little remains of the antique architecture. The Gothic church is highly regarded and preserves the Visigothic wooden statue of Mary, patron saint of the region of La Rioja. Throughout the year, pilgrims travel to the monastery to worship the miraculous statue. Not far from the abbey is a holy fountain whose waters are believed to have healing powers. "But you have to have faith," said the Father Hospedero.

Abadía Nuestra Señora de Valvanera

The monastery produces liqueurs and honey. In addition, the monks are actively involved in recycling in order to maintain the purity of the surrounding woodlands. Gregorian Chant is sung on Sundays, celebrations and festivals.

Nearby Nájera, stationed along the pilgrims' road to Santiago de Compostela, is the historical capital of La Rioja and ancient court of the Kings of Castile. According to tradition, King García Sánchez discovered a hidden cave containing an altar dedicated to the Virgin. The discovery led to the founding of the monastery of Santa María la Real beside the sandstone cliff and cave. Gothic in style, it was built at the beginning of the 15th century on the site of an earlier church. The Panteón of the Kings contains the tombs of the kings of Navarra, Castilla and León, the finest of which is the Romanesque stone sarcophagus of Queen Doña Blanca of Navarra. The choir is Isabeline Gothic and displays painted kings and queens.

Accommodations

There are two types:
1) Outside the monastery:
There is a 2-star hotel where
both men and women are
welcome. The hotel contains
28 single and double rooms,
each with private bath.
2) Inside the monastery:
Only men are allowed in the
13 single cells reserved exclusively for spiritual retreats.
All accommodations are
closed from December 22nd
until January 7th.

Amenities

Towels and linens are provided.

Meals

Meals are prepared by the monks and can be included with lodging.

Cost of lodging

$40.00 per double room, meals excluded.

Products of the institution

The monks produce and sell liqueurs (*Licor de Valvanera* and *Pachagin*),
honey and honey products.

Directions

By car only, there is no public transportation: From Logroño take route
120 west towards Burgos - Nájera. Just before entering Nájera, go south
on route LR 113 following the signs to Anguiano. Continue south to
LR 435 and then head west to the monastery.

Contact

Padre Hospedero, Frail Martin
Abadía Nuestra Señora de Valvanera
26323 Valvanera (La Rioja), Spain
Tel: 941/377044 (Frail Martin prefers to be contacted by phone. He
does not speak English, but he speaks German.)

MONASTERIO DE NUESTRA SEÑORA DE VICO
Cistercian Nuns

Monasterio de Nuestra Señora de Vico

The monastery occupies a solitary position in a variegated panorama of verdant pine trees, rolling hills and dramatic mountains. It is very close to Arnedo, chief town of a judicial district.

"We are far from the noise and the crowds because this is how we like to live," said Sister Carmen. "We don't ask our guests to pray with us because we host anyone, no matter their creed. This is a spiritual place where visitors can enjoy relaxing walks along the river and meditate."

The history of the monastery began in 1142 when a group of Franciscan friars founded a convent. They occupied the convent until 1835 when the *Desamortización* (suppression) forced them to leave. They returned a few years later and remained until the 1970s. At that time, their declining numbers forced them to leave again and join another institution. Sometime later, a couple from Arnedo bought the complex and then sold it to the Cistercian Order. It has been their residence since October 1977.

The monastery is a modern, functional building. Ruins of the partly Gothic, partly Baroque ancient church can be visited. "Don't misunderstand me," one of the sisters commented, "they are mostly ruins, but those who know art find them most interesting."

The monastery preserves a copy of *Nuestra Señora de Vico*, an image of the Virgin Mary. "Although the original copy resides in a church in Arnedo, the people of Arnedo care very deeply about Vico and consider it the original pilgrimage site," the sister added. The monastery's church is defined by opulent Baroque ornamentation. Throughout the area, festivities and pilgrimages of Our Lady of Vico have a longstanding custom.

The history of the monastery's site reflects both tradition and research. According to legend, the first hermit to inhabit the site was an Arab who had a vision of the Virgin of Vico. She appeared in order to convert him to Christianity. Most historians maintain that the first foundation took place in 1456 by Friar Lope de Salinas. According to this view, the friar strongly wanted to repristinate the original spirituality of the Franciscan rule as established by Saint Francis. In 1635, fire destroyed the institution. Another fire in 1766 caused the relocation of the sacred image to Arnedo where it is presently preserved.

The region of La Rioja lies on the western side of the Ebro Valley. The Upper Rioja is mountainous; the Lower Rioja is a flat area with an almost Mediterranean climate. A crossroads of cultures, the towns and villages mirror a diverse history. The people of La Rioja have lived in the company of Basques, Romans, Arabs, Navarrese and Castilians. Until four hundred years after the reconquest, the Moorish population in Cervera del Río Alhama (south of Arnedo) was more numerous than Christians or Jews.

Nearby Logroño is closely associated with Santiago de Compostela, once a main artery of Europe's religious and cultural life. Beginning in the 10th century, the Kings of Navarra and Castile fought over Logroño until its final annexation to Castile. A farming center, the town is renowned for its wines. Predominantly modern, the city is bisected by wide boulevards filled with tasteful shopping districts.

Logroño sits on the banks of the Ebro and seems to rise out of the river. Two bridges, one iron, the other stone, span the waterway. The old quarter retains the aura of a medieval borough, exemplified by an arrangement of towers and buildings encircling the noble 18th century Santa María la Redonda and its handsome Baroque towers.

Among the most interesting sights is the Imperial Church of Santa María del Palacio. Founded in the 11th century by Emperor Constantine the Great, its pyramidal tower stands 146' tall. The Iglesia de Santiago el Real has a Renaissance reredos, a nave without aisles and six columns. It showcases a Baroque equestrian statue of St. James (patron saint of Spain) as Moorslayer. The Iglesia de San Bartolomé is noteworthy for its portal and an array of Gothic sculpture.

Accommodations

14 double rooms, each with private bath. Both men and women are welcome. According to Sister Carmen, "it is a spiritual institution and guests should behave as such."

Amenities

Towels and linens are supplied.

Meals

All meals are supplied with the lodging.

Cost of lodging

The provisional cost per person/per night is $21.00. (The nuns do not want make money from the hospedería; the rate indicated covers only their operating expenses. Additional donations would be appreciated.)

Products of the institution

The sisters decorate pottery sold in a small shop. They also make a large variety of pastries.

Special rules

Rules are posted in each room. The nuns clean the rooms before guests arrive, but request that guests clean their rooms before leaving. Sometimes guests lend a hand in cleaning after the meals. Punctuality is required at meal times. Open year round.

Directions

By car: From Zaragoza take highway A68 west exiting at Calahorra and follow the signs heading south to Arnedo. From Arnedo continue south following the signs to Vico-Arnedo and the monastery.
By train/bus: Get off at Calahorra and take the bus to Arnedo. From Arnedo take a taxi to the monastery.

Contact

Madre Hospedera
Monasterio de Nuestra Señora de Vico
Carretera de Prejano
26589 Vico-Arnedo (La Rioja), Spain
Tel: 941/380295
Fax: 941/381274

MONASTERIO LA INMACULADA CONCEPCIÓN
Capuchin Clarisse Nuns

Monasterio La Inmaculada Concepción

In a verdant countryside locale on the outskirts of Alcobendas, a small town just north of Madrid, the monastery is backdropped by the Sierra de Guadarrama. "At night you hear the crickets, during the day, sweet bird songs. It is such serene isolation!" exclaimed one of the sisters.

The city of Madrid can trace its origins to the times of Arab Emir Mohamed I (9th century). The heart of Old Madrid stretches from the medieval Plaza de la Villa to the Puerta del Sol and the porticoed Plaza Mayor. Castilian in character, the three-storied, stone-paved square is delineated by its arcades, dormer windows and slate roofs. Until the last century, it served as a marketplace and the scene of popular events including bullfights. At one time it was also the setting for trials of the inquisition and public executions. The plaza's most striking building is the Casa de la Panadería, a bakery house with a colorful, fresco-adorned façade.

Madrid

Shaped like a half moon, the Puerta del Sol and its sign for Tio Pepe, a brand of sherry, have become Madrid landmarks. Once a 15th century defensive bulwark, it was part of a wall which enclosed the town; today it is filled with shops and cafes. Located on one corner of the square is the symbol of Madrid, a bronze bear reaching for the fruit of a *madroño,*(strawberry tree).

The Plaza de la Villa is home to the 15th century Torre de los Lujanes. Delineated by a Gothic portal and Mudéjar-style horseshoe arches, it is the oldest building on the square. The façade of the Casa de Cisneros is Plateresque in style. From the casa, town hall can be reached through an enclosed bridge. Designed by Juan Gómez de la Mora, the architect responsible for the Plaza Mayor, the brick and stone Ayuntamiento has the same interesting combination of steep roofs with dormer windows and steeple-like towers.

Not far from the Plaza de la Villa is the Plaza del Conde de Miranda, an area that forms the framework of what was once a medieval town. The design of the Basílica de San Miguel was inspired by Italian Baroque and is offset by a curved façade. The Iglesia de San Pedro el Viejo was built in the 15th century, its Mudéjar tower erected over the minaret of a former mosque.

The Museo del Prado is in a neoclassical building designed in 1785 by architect Juan de Villanueva. Planned as a museum of natural history, it has been an art museum since 1818. It

The Last Supper by Juan de Juanes

contains the most important collection of Spanish art through the 19th century and exhibits masterpieces by Velázquez, Goya, Murillo, Ribera and Zurbarán as well as *The Last Supper* by Juan de Juanes

The Salamanca District is an elegant, stately neighborhood and home to many of Madrid's art galleries and boutiques. The grid-like design of the district was the initiative of the Marquis of Salamanca.

The Palacio Real and adjacent gardens were built on the site of a Moorish fortress destroyed by fire in 1734. They were designed by Italian architects Juan Bautista Sacchetti and Francisco Sabatini. Views of the palace and gardens can be had from Puente de Segovia, the city's oldest bridge.

Outside of the city center, Puerta de Toledo was built between 1817 and 1827 as a project of King José Bonaparte. Sited in La Latina, a neighborhood of working class Madrileños, it is personified by streets lined with tall, narrow houses. Close by is the landmark Basílica de San Francisco el Grande. Goya was one of the artists commissioned to decorate the interior.

The nearby town of Aranjuez was built by King Fernando VI and based on the ideas of the Enlightenment Movement. It is remarkable for its Royal Palace of brick and white stone. Although plagued by fires and restorations, the palace maintains an authentic architectural harmony. Its interior reveals Baroque rooms modeled on the Alhambra in Granada. More than 700 acres of the complex are dedicated to gardens: Jardin del Parterre features fountains and trees from the

Americas, Jardin de la Isla boasts numerous fountains, Jardin del Principe reflects a formal English layout.

A short distance away is the town of Chinchón. At its heart is the Plaza Mayor. A typically Castilian square, it is surrounded on three sides by two-and three-story houses with wooden balconies. In August, bullfights are held in the square. The parish church harbors an altar painting by Goya. Views of the countryside and of picturesque Chinchón can be had from the ruins of a 15th century hilltop castle just west of town.

Accommodations
32 beds in double, triple and quadruple rooms with shared baths. Both men and women are welcome. Groups seeking spiritual retreats have priority. These groups usually come for weekend stays. Weekdays are more readily available. Call at least one month in advance.

Amenities
Towels and linens are supplied. Meeting room and chapel may be used by guests.

Meals
All meals can be provided on request.

Cost of lodging
To be arranged depending on the combination of meals provided.

Special rules
Curfew at 9:00 pm.

Directions
By car: From Madrid take route 1 and exit at Alcobendas. From Alcobendas follow the signs to Monasterios Madres Capuchinas.
By train: Get off at Madrid. From Plaza de Castilla take the bus to Alcobendas and change buses to the monastery.

Contact
Madre Superiora or Madre Economa
Monasterio La Inmaculada Concepción
Carretera El Goloso, km 3.3
Apartado 36
26100 Alcobendas (Madrid), Spain
Tel: 91/6624622Fax: 91/6624690

REAL MONASTERIO DE SANTA MARÌA DE EL PAULAR

Benedictine Monks

Real Monasterio de Santa Marìa

Ensconced atop the Sierra de Guadarrama, a scenic mountainous region with numerous ski resorts, Real Monasterio de Santa Marìa de El Paular is believed to be Castile's first monastery. Enveloped by the beautiful valley of the Río Lozoya, it was founded by Juan I in 1390 and built on the site of a medieval royal hunting lodge. Although the structure is mainly Gothic in design, Romanesque and Plateresque traits are evident. During the 15th and 16th centuries, the monastery achieved a certain degree of importance and remained a renowned spiritual center until it was closed during the religious suppression of 1836. Abandoned until 1954, the monastery was then given to the Benedictine Order. In 1976, it was declared a national monument.

The monastery has a Gothic cloister with vaults in Mudéjar, a highly decorative Christian-Islamic style. The dominant Oriental character is reflected in the ceramics, brickwork, ornamental metals and wood carvings. The pulpit in the refectory also mirrors the Mudéjar style. There is a bas-relief representing the crucifixion from the life of Jesus. An elaborate Baroque chamber designed by Francisco de Hurtado in 1718 is behind the altar. The alabaster altarpiece is attributed to Flemish craftsmen. The vaults of the library are emblazoned with 16th century frescoes. Although the facts remain obscure, it is believed that many of the monastery's precious works of art were lost during an earthquake in 1700. As an aside, the innovative shutters were invented by the monks as protection against severe winters.

The complex is comprised of a working Benedictine monastery, a church and private hotel for the lodging of guests. A guided tour of the monastery is offered by the monks. It does not include the monks' residence. Every Sunday, services are sung in Gregorian Chant.

Nearby La Granja de San Ildefonso is a sumptuous palace backdropped by the Sierra de Guadarrama. Erected by Enrique IV, it displays a collection of Spanish and French tapestries and cut-glass chandeliers. Its church exemplifies the finest in Baroque design; the royal mausoleum shelters the tomb of Felipe V and his queen. The hedgerowed gardens are shaded by elegant chestnut trees and highlight several unusual pools. Guided tours are available.

The walled village of Pedraza de la Sierra is not far off. Dominated by a grand medieval castle which overlooks the town from its barren, rocky roost, Pedraza preserves a medieval ambience as if time had come to a standstill at the entrance gate. Ancient walls encompass a characteristic main square. Surrounded by cobblestone streets, the porticoed plaza serves as a bullring for the September corridas. At the heart of town is a medley of stone mansions with coats of arms. Every July the town hosts an international music festival.

The Castle of Pedraza is famous for having been one of the most impregnable castles in the country. Completely inaccessible from three sides, the fourth side offered limited access. The fortress' plan is polygonal and irregular with a wide esplanade separating the building from the houses of the village. The entrance gate is topped by a Gothic arch and the coat of arms of the Velasco family who lived in the town in the 16th century and who contributed to the castle's preservation.

Accommodations
There is a 4-star hotel within the complex containing 47 double rooms and 7 suites, each with private bath.

Note: The monastery is divided into two parts; one is occupied by the Sheraton Hotel, the other by the monastery's hospedería. At the present time, the guest house is under renovation. Lodging is available only at the Hotel Santa María de El Paular Sheraton Hotel, 28741 Rascafría (Madrid), Spain.

Amenities
Two restaurants, the Don Lope and the Mesòn Trastamara. 4-star amenities include a bar, summer terrace, reception and meeting halls, heated outdoor pool, tennis court, gardens and nursery. During the winter, the hotel offers packages for skiers. For further information: www.sierranorte.com/paular and www.valdesqui.com

Cost of lodging
To be determined when reservations are made.

Products of the institution
There is a shop that sells cheese and spirits made by the monks.

Directions
By car: From Madrid take Highway M607 north. Exit at Navacerrada and continue north following signs to Rascafría and the monastery.
By train: Get off in Madrid and take the local bus to Rascafría.

Contact
Anyone who answers the phone
Real Monasterio de Santa Maria
28741 Rascafría (Madrid), Spain
Monastery
Tel: 91/8691425
Fax: 91/8691015
Hotel
Tel: (Spain) 91/8691011, (US): 800.325.3535
Fax: (Spain) 91/8691006
Email: reservas@paular.palace-hotel-madrid.es
Website: www.sheraton.com

ABADÍA DE SANTA CRUZ DEL VALLE DE LOS CAÍDOS

Benedictine Monks

Abadía de Santa Cruz del Valle de los Caídos

Loftily situated, the abbey is enclosed by a woodland that has been declared a protected area. Founded by General Franco in 1958 to commemorate the dead (*Caídos*) of the Spanish Civil War, it was entrusted to a group of twenty-six monks who originally resided in Abadía de Santo Domingo. A large and simple structure, the abbey's architecture is reminiscent of Renaissance style; arcades surround a square containing two fountains.

Abadía de Santa Cruz del Valle de los Caídos

Dominating the hilly countryside, the church's immense cross was built as a memorial to those who died in the Civil War. The cross is considered gloomy by many. The fact that it was built by prisoners of war does little to erase that image. Nearly 500' high, it soars above a cave-like basilica carved into the rock. The tomb of Franco sits beside the basilica's high altar. Untold soldiers from both sides of the Civil War are also buried at the site. The church has a vast nave and circular altar with modern bronze sculptures and Flemish tapestries. An elevator climbs to the arms of the cross and provides excellent views over the monastery and pine-clad hills and valleys.

Nearby El Escorial is one of the most famous monuments in Spain. Poised against the foothills of the Sierra de Guadarrama, the complex was designed by architects Juan Bautista de Toledo and Juan de Herrera. Felipe II ordered construction of the austere, albeit grandiose

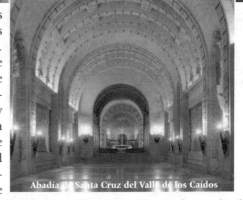

Abadía de Santa Cruz del Valle de los Caídos

granite structures in the 16th century. The decoration is the work of Spanish and Italian artists including Luca Giordano and Pellegrino Tibaldi and sculptors Pompeo and Leone Leoni. The ensemble is distinguished by a framework of courtyards, corridors and rooms that form a rectangular block crowned by four towers. The somber basilica is topped by a grand dome. Paintings on the vaults are by Lucas Jordán; the walls contain forty-three altars with painted altarpieces.

The monastery portion of Escorial was founded in 1567 and is inhabited by Augustinian monks. It is closed to the public. The monks sing their daily service in Gregorian Chant and organize concerts and musical events throughout the year. Beneath the church is the Panteón de los Reyes where nearly all of Spain's monarchs and spouses (since Carlos I) are interred. The royal corpses lie in gilded marble coffins which reflect elaborate Baroque design elements.

The Patio de los Reyes is a solemn courtyard where the bareness of the walls contrasts with the royal grandeur of the front façade. It houses statues of the six kings of Judah. The rooms once belonged to the Bourbons and are bedecked with luxurious tapestries and Pompeian ceilings. Paintings from the 16th century Venetian School in addition to works by El Greco, Velázquez, Ribera, Titian and Bosch can be seen in the Salas Capitulares.

The biblioteca has more than 40,000 volumes and manuscripts dating to the 9th century as well as the 11th century Codex Aureus of the Gospels. Its art museum houses works by Titian, Veronese, Zurbarán and Tintoretto among others. Another museum has documents pertaining to the construction of the monastery. Just outside the complex are two palaces. Casita del Principe was built by Carlos II. Casita del Infante was built for Prince Gabriel, brother of Carlos IV. Both were designed by Juan de Villanueva.

Northeast of the monastery is the scenic town of Manzanares el Real, a summer haven for Madrileños. Its 15th century castle is a jewel of civil architecture. Below it stands a 16th century church complete with Renaissance portico and capitals. In the foothills, La Pedriza, a jumble of granite screes and ravines, is popular with mountain climbers.

Accommodations
There are two types:
1) Outside the monastery: Open to all guests, a large hospedería has 110 rooms, mostly doubles with private baths. Rooms without private baths have a private sink and shower. The hospedería is closed from December 15th until January 15th.
2) Inside the monastery: Only men are allowed (preferably religious representatives) for spiritual retreats. There are 16 single rooms. For reservations contact, "Encargado de la Hospedería Interna."

Amenities
Towels and linens are provided.

Meals
There is a restaurant on the premises. All meals can be included with the lodging.

Cost of lodging
Full pension in single or double room: $31.00-$36.00 per person depending on the type of room, season and number of meals.

Products of the institution
The monks sell a liqueur called *Fray Alkuino*. They don't personally make it, but it is formulated according to their special recipe. They also sell CDs and cassettes of Gregorian Chant recorded by the Escolaria.

Special rules
External hospedería: There is no curfew, however, the reception closes at 10:00 pm. Guests cannot be received after that hour.
Note: The Abadía is closed on Mondays but the church can be visited every day.

Directions
By car: From Madrid take highway A6 north (changes to M505) and exit at the second exit for El Escorial (at Guadarrama). Continue north on M600 following the signs to the Abadía.

By train: Get off at Madrid and take a bus to El Escorial and then another to Valle de los Caídos; or get off at El Escorial and take the bus to Valle de los Caídos. There is only one bus from El Escorial. It leaves daily at 3:00 pm (except Monday).

Contact
Encargado de la Hospedería Externa or call the hospedería directly
Abadía de Santa Cruz del Valle de los Caídos
28209 Valle de los Caídos (Madrid), Spain
Abadía - Tel: 91/8905411, Fax: 91/8905594
Hospedería - Tel: 91/8905511 - 8905494, Fax: 91/8961542

NAVARRA

MONASTERIO DE LA OLIVA

Cistercian Monks

Monasterio de la Oliva

The monastery was founded around 1140 by French Cistercian monks who built the structure according to the rules dictated by Saint Bernard of Clairvaux, hence its similarity to the French and Italian complexes of the same order. It lies in a remote plain surrounded by vineyards and fields, some of which belong to the order. Thanks to the protection of the kings of Navarra, the monastery grew to importance in the Middle Ages. During the religious suppressions of the 19th century, the monastery was abandoned and nearly destroyed. It remained closed for almost a century until 1927 at which time it was restored and reopened. The restoration paid strict attention to detail and maintained the integrity of the architecture, insuring that the monastery's diverse history would remain clearly visible.

Monasterio de la Oliva

Characteristic of the Cistercian Order, the compound's design is quite simple. The cloister adjoins a 13th century chapter house and can be reached through the church. An artful structure, the large arcades are decorated with traceries. The cloister imparts a sense of serenity, its architecture enriched by carved columns and a mosaic floor. The Sala Capitular is one of the most interesting sections of the monastery because it has preserved the original 12th century structure. It leads to the outdoors where a kitchen and refectory once stood. This area is now an open, green space offering vistas of the entire complex. There are also views of the farm worked by the monks. Products sold by the monastery include honey, cheese and wine.

Cistercian ideology places a good deal of importance upon nature and plays in important role in determining placement of a Cistercian structure. As with all monasteries of this order, it was built near a river with the church facing east. Between March 21st and September 21st, sunlight illuminates the façade until 6:00 pm. As the light passes through the rose window, it is projected directly on the altar.

Nearby Tafalla is anchored by its Plaza Mayor. The church of Santa María is an architecturally simple structure with an illustrious retablo by Basque artist Juan de Ancheta. West of Tafalla, the village of Artajona is defined by medieval walls and crenelated towers. Originally built by the Templars in the late 11th and early 12th centuries, the fortifications were rebuilt in the 13th.

Just south of Tafalla is the town of Olite where traces of ancient battlements are still evident. Although founded by the Romans, the town's main heritage is Gothic. Within the walled city is a patchwork of steep, narrow lanes and tiny squares.

The kings of Navarra decided upon Olite as a royal residence and in the 15th century, Carlos III built the Palacio Real de Olite. The building is noteworthy for its Mudéjar ceramic tiles and marquetry ceilings. Its history, including that of its royal residents, is rife with violence and intrigue as evidenced by the former lion pit and dungeons.

Although much of the palace was laid to waste in the 19th century, restoration has reinstated some of its former glory. The castle is an elaborate, if somewhat foreboding structure comprised of steep stairs, massive halls, royal apartments, towers, turrets and courtyards. During the summer months, it becomes a backdrop for the performances of the Festival of Navarra. The Iglesia de Santa María la Real, once the royal chapel, adjoins the castle. Its façade is graced with a carved Gothic portal; its interior reveals a 16th century reredos.

Accommodations
Preference is given to men and women seeking spiritual retreats. However, guests seeking rest, relaxation and meditation are also welcomed. There are 11 single and 11 double rooms, each with a private bath.

Amenities
Towels and linens are supplied.

Meals
All meals can be included with the lodging.

Cost of lodging
To be arranged upon arrival.

Products of the institution
Cheese, honey and wines are produced from the monastery's vineyards.

Directions
By car: From Pamplona take route 121 south to route 124 (Caparroso). Go east on 124 towards Carcastillo following the signs to the monastery.
By train: Get off at Pamplona and take the bus of the Tafallesa lines to Carcastillo; buses leave at noon and 5:30 pm. From Zaragoza take the local bus of the Tafallesa lines and get off at Carcastillo. The bus leaves at 6:00 pm.

Contact
Padre Hospedero (Mobile phone: 676/783864)
Monasterio de la Oliva
31310 Carcastillo (Navarra), Spain
Tel: 948/725006
Fax: 948/715055
Email: oxolaoliva@planalfa.es

MONASTERIO DE SAN BENITO
Benedictine Nuns

The original name of the monastery was Santa María de la Horta. It has always been inhabited by the Benedictine Order. The first document regarding the monastery is dated 1268. In the 17th century, the monastery underwent a total restoration and its name was changed to Monasterio de San Benito. Whatever works of art that existed at that time did not survive the renovation. However, as the nuns are quick to point out, what the monastery lacks in artwork is made up for by its generous hospitality. "The Benedictine Order is renowned for its hospitality. Here at San Benito, we have always tried to preserve this attitude and treat our guests with affection," said the Madre Hospedera.

Estella

The monastery is near the Shrine of Nuestra Señora in Estella, a town based on a miracle. According to tradition, centuries ago showers of shooting stars rained on the identical place. This occurrence intrigued a group of shepherds who investigated and found a cave which sheltered a statue of the Virgin. The site is now marked by the Basílica de Nuestra Señora de Puy.

Occupying a tree-shaded niche on the Río Ega, ancient Estella (also known as Lizarra) is among the most engaging small towns on the Santiago de Compostela Route. It acquired its Castilian name in 1090 when it was founded by King Sancho Ramirez on the site of an earlier Roman settlement. In the Middle Ages, it was known as Estella la Bella for the beauty of its setting and was the center of the royal court of Navarra.

The town's heritage included Jews and Franks who were invited by the kings to settle in Estella. They occupied separate quarters and their numerous contributions are substantiated by the towers, palaces and structures they built including the 12th century Santa María de Jus del Castilio, once a synagogue.

The bridge across the Río Ega leads to the arcaded Plaza de San Martín, site of the Palacio de los Reyes de Navarra, a rare example of civil Romanesque architecture. Its towers were added in the 16th century. The palace features a gallery of Navarrese art. From the plaza, steps climb to the clifftop Iglesia de San Pedro de la Rúa, one of Estella's most important monuments. The landmark tower was built in the 12th century and is embellished with a Mudéjar-style doorway. At one time, the church contained a Romanesque cloister. All that remains of the structure are carved capitals depicting a variety of biblical scenes. The interior has three apses and a column in the central apse composed of intertwined snakes. The Baroque Capilla de San Andrés conserves a silver shrine containing a relic of San Andrés.

Calle de la Rúa, Estella's main street, is bordered by the Plateresque Casa Fray Diego, Palacio del Gobernador and the former synagogue. The Iglesia de San Miguel sits in the town center. Although the exterior of the church is quite simple, the north doorway represents an elaborate example of Romanesque sculpture.

Nearby Monasterio de Nuestra Señora de Irache was built by Cistercian monks who offered shelter to pilgrims traveling to Santiago. Its Romanesque church reposes under a Renaissance dome. The cloisters are Plateresque in design. The monastery is presently inhabited by the Benedictine Order. There is a small wine museum and bodega run by the order which continues Irache's centuries-old tradition of providing free wine to pilgrims.

Puente la Reina is quite close to Estella. Once the meeting point of the two main roads which ran from the Pyrenean passes of Ibañeta and Somport, it takes its name from the five-arched, medieval bridge built in the 11th century by order of Doña Mayor. The Church of Santiago is a fine example of Romanesque architecture. It is enhanced by a gilded carving of the apostle dressed as a pilgrim.

Monasterio de Nuestra Señora de Irache

Nestled in the countryside about three miles from Puente la Reina is the 12th century Iglesia de Santa María de Eunate. Octagonal in shape, it is believed to have been a cemetery church for pilgrims. West of Puenta la Reina is Ciraqui, a quaint hilltop village. Balconied houses fringe the twisting alleys that are linked by steps. On the hill is the 13th century Iglesia de San Román, highlighted by a sculpted west door.

Accommodations
15 singles, each with private bath. Only women are allowed.

Amenities
Towels and linens are supplied.

Meals
All meals are included with the lodging.

Special rules
Guests are required to be punctual at meal times and are required to be quiet when in the guest quarters.

Cost of lodging
$21.00 per person, full board.

Products of the institution
The nuns work for a local textile factory and are famous for their embroidery. A few years ago, they recorded a music cassette of their chants.

Directions
By car: From Pamplona go west on route N111 about 50 kms to Estella.
By train: Get off in Pamplona and take the local bus to Estella.

Contact
Madre Hospedera
Monasterio de San Benito
31200 Estella (Navarra), Spain
Tel: 948/550882

MONASTERIO DE IRANZU
Teatinos Monks

Monasterio de Iranzu

The monastery is blessed with a magnificent mountainside position. "It is beautiful around here. We have guests year round. During the fall and winter, mountaineers come for excursions; in the spring, the pilgrims arrive; in the summer, many spend their holidays with us and then... we start all over again," said the woman in charge of the hospedería.

Reached through a wooded gorge, the Monasterio de Iranzu was built in the 12th century. As befitting a Cistercian institution, the church and its cloisters reflect an austere but graceful simplicity. The first information about the monastery dates to the 11th century when it was a Benedictine institution, founded by Saint Adrián.

Within the next hundred years, the monastery had just about disappeared; the church was the only evidence of its previous existence. The institution was rebuilt in 1176 by the Cistercian Order with funds supplied by Don Pedro de Paris, Bishop of Pamplona.

Monasterio de Iranzu

Unlike many other institutions, Iranzu did not have a royal foundation, nevertheless, it was supported by such kings as Sancho el Sabio, Sancho el Fuerte, Teobaldo I and II. Their aegis allowed the monastery to flourish over the course of the ensuing centuries until 1839 when it was abandoned and became the property of the state. After some time, the Prince of Viana Institute financed the restoration and reconstruction which was completed in 1945. At that time, the present order of the Teatinos established residence.

Monasterio de Iranzu

Monasterio de Iranzu

Iranzu is a paragon of Cistercian design, having respected the austere decorative rules of the order of Saint Bernard. The architectural tenets are most visible in the church which is divided into three naves and lighted by a rose window. Over time, the once pure Roman cloister developed into Gothic. Other interesting elements include the chapter hall, a monumental kitchen with a large fireplace and the church dedicated to Saint Adrián.

Accommodations

There are two types of accommodations which operate independently, but both belong to the monastery.

1) Hospedería Iranzu: 19 beds in 4 large rooms with private bath. Both men and women are welcome.

2) Inside the monastery: 21 single rooms with shared bath and a large dormitory with shared bath. Both men and women are welcome, but only in groups of 20 or more.

Amenities

1) Hospedería Iranzu: Towels and linens are supplied.

2) Inside the monastery: Towels and linens are supplied only in the single rooms.

Meals
All meals can be supplied on request in the hospedería and within the monastery.

Cost of lodging
1) Hospedería Iranzu: $12.00 per person/per night, no meals included; $30.00, full pension.
2) Inside the monastery: To be arranged when reservations are made.

Special rules
1) Hospedería Iranzu: Guests are provided with a key to the guest quarters.
2) Inside the monastery: Winter curfew is 9:00 pm; summer 10:00 pm. Open year round.

Directions
By car: From Pamplona take route N111 southwest to Estella and then follow the signs taking NA120 north towards Abárzuza/Iranzu and the monastery.
By train: Get off at Pamplona and take a bus to Estella. From Estella take a taxi to Iranzu.

Contact
1) Hospedería Iranzu: Anyone who answers the phone
2) Inside the monastery: Señor Vicente
Monasterio de Iranzu
31178 Iranzu - Abárzuza (Navarra), Spain
Hospedería: 948/520150
Monastery: 948/520012
Fax: 948/520048

COLEGIATA DE RONCESVALLES

Canonicos

Colegiata de Roncesvalles

Originally founded by Sancho de la Rosa, Bishop of Pamplona, the 13th century colegiata offered shelter to millions of pilgrims traveling the "Road to Santiago" and crossing the Pyrenees at Roncesvalles. Following custom, the pilgrims were often dressed in the traditional garb of cape, long staff and curling felt hat adorned with scallop shells (a symbol of the saint they came to honor).

The complex has been enlarged and enriched throughout the years. The church exemplifies French-style early Gothic (1212). The Santuario of the Holy Spirit was supposedly built by Charlemagne to contain the tomb of his nephew Roland. Roncesvalles is traditionally regarded as the place where the army of Charlemagne, led by Roland, was slaughtered by the Basques in 778. Although no evidence exists of the battle, the 12th century epic poem, *Chanson de Roland*, praised Roland's heroism and presented Charlemagne as the savior of Christendom.

The colegiata's interior contains a silverplated *Virgin and Child* below a high canopy. The white tomb of Sancho VII and his wife are contained in the elegant chapter house. The tombs repose under a stained glass window depicting the *Battle of Las Navas de Tolosa* (ca. 1212), the victory that led to Moorish Spain's decline. Golden retablos and a 13th century wooden statue of the Virgin Mary are conserved within the structure. According to legend, the statue appeared miraculously at a place indicated by a red stag with a star shining between its antlers.

The museum shelters a Gospel book which belonged to the kings of Navarra, several reliquaries in precious materials, a collection of weapons believed to have belonged to Sancho VII and a cache of valuable paintings. It is possible to visit the entire complex with or without a guide. For information, contact the Central de Visitas Guiadas (Tel: 948/790480).

Pilgrim's cross

Roncesvalles is located on the Spanish side of a pass through the Pyrenees, the mountain range between Spain and France. It is the starting point of the Santiago de Compostela. It is believed that this was the route taken when the body of James, Christ's apostle, was brought to Galicia. In 813, the relics were discovered and gave rise to the construction of the cathedral. The Pyrenean Roncal Valley is among the most scenic in Navarra and is favored by mountaineers who climb the Mesa de los Tres Reyes.

Accommodations

Hostal La Posada functions as a small hotel. It has 12 double and 6 quadruple rooms with private bath.

Amenities

Towels and linens are provided. All meals can be included with the lodging at an additional cost (to be determined).

Cost of lodging

Double room: $42.00 (no meals included).
Quadruple room: $57.00 (no meals included).

Directions

By car: From Pamplona take route 135 north to Roncesvalles.
By train: Get off in Pamplona and take the bus to Roncesvalles. There is only one bus per day; it leaves Pamplona at 6:00 pm.

Contact

For lodging reservations, contact the Hostal La Posada
Tel/Fax: 948/760225
Colegiata only (not for reservations)
Colegiata de Roncesvalles
31650 Roncesvalles (Navarra), Spain
Tel/Fax: 948/760000

Santuario de Codés
Brotherhood of Nuestra Señora de Codés

Santuario de Codés

In a region of rolling countryside, the Santuario de Codés sits in a solitary, peaceful spot on the beautiful mountains of the Sierra de Codés. "We guarantee serenity and a good night's sleep," said Señor Álvaro, the man in charge of the hospedería.

The sanctuary traces it roots to the 13th century when a local shepherd, Juan de Codés, found the image of Mary in this secluded locale. According to legend, the image had been hidden some 200 years earlier by the inhabitants of Cantabria, a city that had been destroyed because its population shared atheist beliefs. Initially the shrine was housed in a small hermitage but over the centuries, as devotion to the Virgin grew, the structure was enlarged. The main retablo of the church sustains the original image of the Virgin found by the shepherd.

Santuario de Codés

In the 17th century, the Bishop of Calahorra built his summer residence in this sector. He wished to enjoy the fine mountain air as well as the tranquility of the Sierra de Codés. "We know that during those years, the church always chose the best places," added Señor Álvaro.

Codés, along with the majority of religious institutions, suffered from the anti-religious events of the 19th century. It was plundered by the French army and endured the Spanish and French troops who inhabited the shrine. It was eventually set on fire. After some time, it was restored by the Brotherhood of Codés.

Until a century ago, both facilities were the property of the Church of Navarra. When maintenance (and restoration) costs became too dear for the church, the local populace arranged to have the Brotherhood of Codés assume management of the institution. The old summer palace of the bishop now serves as a hospedería and restaurant. Restoration was completed about ten years ago. The facility is managed by lay personnel.

The Province of Navarra is surrounded by Spain's northern provinces and shares its border with France. As such, its architecture is directly linked with that country. It has often been described as a miniature continent; within its relatively small borders resides a rich tableau of scenery and people.

Not far from the sanctuary is the town of Vitoria, seat of the Basque government. Situated on a hill at the province's highest point, Vitoria, also known as Gasteiz, is one of Spain's modern industrial centers. During the Middle Ages, the kingdoms of Navarra and Castile fought for control of the region. In 1181, King Alfonso VI founded a fortress and town but soon lost it to the Castilians. The old part of town is composed of a concentric ring of narrow streets. At its heart is the Plaza de la Virgen Blanca and a monument to a battle fought in 1813. The square is edged by tall houses with *miradores*, (glazed balconies). Nearby Plaza de España is a porticoed neoclassical structure.

A patchwork of old alleys linked by steps surrounds the 16th century Palacio de Escoriaza-Esquivel. A Plateresque façade and a Renaissance courtyard with a marble loggia are among the palace's outstanding architectural elements. Fortress-like Torre de Doña Otxanta dates from the 15th-16th centuries and is reminiscent of early Italian Renaissance cities. El Portalón is a series of timber and brick-built structures representing some of the oldest buildings in town. Another construction standout is Los Arquillos, an arcaded street which adjoins the Plaza de Espana. West of town, Roman ruins include a 13-arched bridge at Trespuentes (near the remains of a town) and the oppidum of Iruna.

Vitoria is renowned for the August *Fiesta de la Virgen Blanca*, a time when everything else takes second billing and festivities reign supreme. The celebration includes fireworks and parties which continue until the wee hours.

Accommodations

8 double rooms with private bath. Both men and women are welcome.

Amenities

Towels and linens are supplied.

Meals

All meals can be supplied by the restaurant.

Cost of lodging

Double room/per night: $24.00 with full pension: $36.00.

Special rules

Minimum stay 2 days. Open year round.

Directions

By car: From Pamplona or Logroño take N111 to Torres del Río. Once there head west on route NA720 and follow the signs to Torralba del Río and the santuario.

By train: Get off in Pamplona and take the bus to Torres del Río and contact the santuario. Small groups can be picked up. Larger groups must take the bus to Los Arcos and then take a taxi to the shrine.

Contact

Señor Álvaro (he speaks English)
Santuario de Codés
31228 Torralba del Río (Navarra), Spain
Tel: 948/657082
Website: www.mundofree.com/richiski/codes/codes.html

Monasterio Santa María de la Caridad
Cistercian Nuns

Monasterio Santa María de la Caridad

Santa María de la Caridad is the oldest female Cistercian monastery in Spain. Founded in 1147 by García Ramirez, King of Navarra, it is credited with starting the Cistercian diffusion in the country. Over the ensuing centuries, the monastery became a center of

Monasterio Santa María de la Caridad

reference and education for the entire Cistercian Order. Unlike the majority of other monasteries and convents, it resisted the expulsion begun during the Napoleonic invasion in the 19th century. In fact, the nuns, depredated of all their possessions, refused to leave the monastery. Instead they chose to live in complete and abject poverty. "With an admirable display of endurance and strength that only women can show in similar tragic situations," added one of the sisters.

"The village of Tulebras is very small. There are only about 100 inhabitants including us nuns," she stated. Located on a plain near the Ebro River, the terrain features vineyards and fruit and olive trees typical of the Mediterranean landscape.

Although numerous works of art were lost in 1800, most of the complex remains intact. The church, cloister and chapter hall are Romanesque in style. In the 16th century, the original Romanesque vault of the church was rebuilt in Renaissance style. The museum contains the remaining works of art once housed in the monastery. During the summer months, it is open every day except Mondays. In the winter, it is only open Saturdays and Sundays. Arrangements can be made for special visits.

Tudela is just a few miles from the monastery. A prosperous agricultural center, it is the second largest town of Navarra and capital of La Ribera region. Founded by the Moors, for several centuries it was also home to a large community of Jews. The town had always been a haven for diverse groups and was the last place in Navarra to finally submit to Fernando the Catholic and evict its non-Christian citizens.

The lingering Muslim/Judeo heritage is apparent in the winding streets and alleys of the ancient core. The well-preserved Mudéjar and Jewish districts are centered around the 17th century Plaza de los Fueros. Delineated by ancient houses with wrought iron balconies, the façades portray bullfighting scenes, reminders of the plaza's former use as a bullring.

The Gothic cathedral was built in the 12th century and much of its artistry exemplified the religious open-mindedness of the town's citizenry. The capitals in the north and south portals depict New Testament scenes while the Puerta del Juicio portrays 114 different scenes from the *Last Judgement*. The Romanesque cloister encloses the ruins of a 9th century mosque and Mudéjar chapel thought to have once been a synagogue. It has an octagonal bell tower and a smaller tower with a helm roof.

The town is highlighted by several noteworthy structures: the Palace of the Marqués de San Adrián; a 13th century bridge characterized by seventeen irregular arches; and the 18th century Chapel of Santa Ana. Not far off, Bárdenas Reales is a dramatic milieu of craggy hills and rocks perched upon pyramids and limestone cliffs suggestive of mesas in the American West.

Another nearby town, Tarazona is distinguished by Mudéjar-style architecture as reflected in its maze of narrow, hilly streets and in the extraordinary towers which hang over the cliffs of the ancient town. One of the most memorable structures is Plaza de Toros, the former bullring. Dating from the 18th century, the octagonal space is enclosed by a complex of houses.

South of Tarazona in the province of Aragón is the Monasterio de Veruela, considered one of the greatest monasteries of the province. An isolated Cistercian retreat, the imposing complex is quartered in the verdant Huecha Valley near the Sierra de Moncayo. Protected by a battlemented wall, it was founded in the 12th century by French monks. Its vast abbey church is a mixture of Gothic and Romanesque details. Green and blue Aragónese tiles line the floor of the triple nave.

Accommodations

There are two guest houses. One is older, the other a recent construction. The older hospedería has 15 single and double rooms, some with private bath. The new facility has 4 double and 14 single rooms, each with private bath.

Amenities

Towels and linens are provided.

Meals

All meals are included with the lodging.

Cost of lodging

$21.00 per person, all meals included.

Products of the institution

The nuns specialize in the preparation of sweet pastries and honey as well as a number of beauty products. According to one of the sisters, "There is no proper shop, it is all very homey. Just inquire at the entrance."

Special rules

Guests are required to be punctual at meal times and to be quiet when in their rooms. The older guest house is closed in the winter.

Directions

By car: From Pamplona take route 121 south to Tudela and continue towards Tarazona. Tulebras is between Tudela and Tarazona.

From Zaragoza take highway A68, exit at Tarazona and continue north on 121 to Tulebras.

By train: Get off at Tudela and take the local bus to Tulebras. Buses run infrequently.

Contact

Anyone who answers the phone
Monasterio Santa María de la Caridad
31522 Tulebras (Navarra), Spain
Tel: 948/851475
Fax: 948/850012

Santuario de San Miguel de Aralar
Property of the Archidiocese of Pamplona

Santuario de San Miguel de Aralar

The shrine occupies an isolated setting at 4,000' on the Sierra de Aralar. "On clear days there is a marvelous vista," said Padre Inocencio, the father in charge of the shrine and its hospedería. "With numerous peaks over 4,000', the Sierra de Aralar is the paradise of mountaineers," he added.

The church is dedicated to St. Michael, the archangel. The local population has always been particularly devoted to the saint who has been credited with several miracles during centuries past. Studies indicate that the sanctuary was founded in 1074 and was originally inhabited by a group of friars, however, many legends exist that relate different tales about its history.

The most famous tale dates the shrine to 707 after a miraculous apparition of St. Michael. It is believed that the saint helped Don Teodosio de Goñi kill a dragon who threatened the people of Aralar. Don Teodosio had mistakenly killed his parents. To expiate his crime, he had traveled to Rome where he was told to carry heavy metal chains. Upon his return to Spain, he climbed to Aralar as a pilgrim and encountered the dragon. He killed the beast while invoking the saint who appeared holding a cross above his head.

The legend of the dragon became very popular. Beginning in the 16th century, people started to believe that the interior of the chapel had once been the cave of the dragon. The believers made a hole in the wall and put their head in the hole while praying, a practice which continues today. Another rite tied to the legend is that of turning around three times under the chains which hang near the entrance. The chains are believed to be the same ones that Don Teodosio carried for seven years.

Church detail

Church detail

Although it has been restored and remodeled over the centuries, the Romanesque stone church remains quite austere. The most interesting works of art include the Baroque statue of St. Michael and the retablo; studies date it between the end of the 12th century and the beginning of the 13th.

The fortress city of Pamplona is not far from the sanctuary. An ancient city of the Basques known as Iruña, it was repeatedly captured by the Visigoths, Franks and Moors. Capital of Navarra, it is regarded as the most important town in the Spanish Pyrenees. It combines the redolence of its medieval quarters with the universal attraction of the annual running of the bulls during the *Fiesta de San Fermin*. Every morning of the week-long July celebration, fighting bulls are driven through the streets while hordes of young men confront the animals, racing ahead of them to the Plaza de Toros. This event is described by Ernest Hemingway in his novel *The Sun Also Rises.*

Pamplona is midway between the Pyrenees and the Ebro. It was named after the Roman general Pompey who encamped on a hill beside the Arga River in the winter years of 75-74 BC. The hill is believed to be the site of a primitive Basque village and it was from this village that the city of Pamplona emerged. The central part of town is defined by the porticoed Plaza del Castillo where bullfights were held until the middle of the 19th century.

The city's massive cathedral was built of ocher-colored stone on the site of an ancient Romanesque cathedral that has long since disappeared. Built by order of Philip II in the latter part of the 16th century, its interior has been restored and consists of a nave and two aisles in the form of a Roman cross. The French style cloister is enhanced by tall, graceful arches with beautiful tracery. The structure is considered one of the finest examples of its kind in medieval European architecture.

Accommodations
25 double rooms with bath. Both men and women are welcome.

Amenities
Towels and linens are supplied. There is a restaurant and bar.

Meals
All meals are supplied with the lodging.

Cost of lodging
Provisional cost $30.00 per person/per day with full pension.

Special rules
Curfew at 12:00 midnight. Maximum stay 9 days. Closed during the Christmas holidays.

Directions
By car: From Pamplona take highway A15 west to Irurzun and continue west on N240 until Uharte-Arakil. Follow the signs to the shrine (the road is narrow). Alternate route from Pamplona: Take A15 northwest to Lekunberri and from there head southwest following the signs to the shrine (the road is longer but wider and in better condition).
By train: There is no public transportation to the shrine nor are there taxis from Uharte-Arakil or Lekunberri.

Contact
Padre Inocencio Ayerbe Irañeta
(or anyone who answers the phone)
Santuario de San Miguel de Aralar
31840 Uharte-Arakil (Navarra), Spain
Tel/Fax: 948/396028

ABADÌA DE SAN SALVADOR DE LEYRE
Benedictine Monks

The Abadìa de San Salvador de Leyre was founded in the 11th century and quickly became an illustrious spiritual center. It occupies a commanding hilltop site in an isolated yet inviting landscape. Installed high above the artificial lake of Yesa, it is backdropped by limestone cliffs. Sancho III and his successors made it the royal pantheon of Navarra. The 11th century crypt ranks among the country's finest instances of early Romanesque design and is underscored by squat columns supporting massive capitals. A three-nave structure with a low roof, its unusually shaped arches are peculiar to the monastery.

Abadìa de San Salvador de Leyre

Abadìa

The first religious community of hermits settled here in the 12th century. The abbey was later inhabited by the Benedictine Order of Cluny followed by the Cistercian Order. During the 17th century, the importance of the monastery increased due in large measure to its position along the Santiago de Compostela Route. The monastery was the last addition to the original complex. At the time of the religious suppressions in 1836, the monks were forced to abandon the institution.

Continuing its centuries-old tradition, a portion of the monastery has been turned into a two-star hotel; a small section is reserved for the three dozen monks who live in seclusion. All masses are celebrated in Gregorian Chant performed by the monks; recordings are available for sale. Every morning and afternoon, tours of the monastery are conducted by the monks.

Nearby is the fortified town of Sangüesa. Since medieval times, it has been a stop on the Aragónese pilgrimage route to Santiago. The arcaded Rue Mayor is lined with palaces possessing architectural elements ranging from austere 12th century designs to ornate Plateresque and Gothic. During the 15th and 16th centuries, many fine mansions were built including the Palacio Vallesantoro (now the Casa de Cultural), a structure noted for its dramatic doorway and lavishly carved canopy.

The Castle of Olite is about 25 miles southwest of Sangüesa. The extraordinary castle/royal palace was built between the 13th and 15th centuries and restored in 1940. Burning red sandstone walls and limestone white combine with marble to create a stunning contrast. Many of the castle's large towers and walls have survived through the years and form one of the most picturesque complexes of Spanish military architecture. Underground passages, isolated towers, galleries with hidden exits and secret doors add to the mystique.

Accommodations

There are two types:

1) Outside the monastery: Hotel Hospedería de Leyre (property of the monks, but managed by lay personnel) contains 13 single, 17 double and 8 triple rooms each with private bath.

2) Inside the monastery: 8 single rooms with private bath. Only men on religious retreat are allowed.

Amenities

Towels and linens provided. All meals are included with the lodging.

Cost of lodging

To be determined.

Products of the institution

The monks produce cheese and a liqueur called *Leyre*. Both products are sold in the shop on the premises. There are also CDs of Gregorian Chant.

Directions

By car: From Pamplona take route 240 east towards Huesca. Exit at Yesa and follow the signs to the monastery.

By train: Get off at Pamplona or Jaca and take the local bus to Yesa.

Contact

Outside the monastery:
Hotel Hospedería de Leyre
31410 Yesa (Navarra), Spain
Hotel numbers:
Tel: 948/884100
Fax: 948/884137
Email: info@monasterioguion.deguion.com
         hotel@monasteriodeleyre.com
Website: www.monasteriodeleyre.com

Inside the monastery:
Padre Hospedero
Abadìa de San Salvador de Leyre
31410 Yesa (Navarra), Spain
Monastery numbers:
Tel: 948/884011 / Fax: 948/884137

VALENCIA

STELLA MARIS
Missionaries of Jesus, Mary and Joseph Sisters

Stella Maris is a social center located on the hills above Alicante, one of the most popular resorts of Spain and the principal city of the Costa Blanca. "Although we are in Alicante, our facility is away from the noise of the city. It is very peaceful here, that's why people like it."

The order of the Missionaries of Jesus, Mary and Joseph has been in Alicante for thirty years and has numerous missions throughout the world. During the winter months, the order hosts mainly older people traveling from the northern regions of Spain to escape the cold weather. In the summer, individuals and families come to spend their summer holidays. "As part of our mission, we have very reasonable prices in order to offer enjoyable summer holidays to all. Although we have many guests, we have preserved the taste of homemade Spanish cuisine served amid a very familiar atmosphere," the sister added.

Esplanada de España

Alicante is a busy summer resort, easier to navigate on foot than by auto; a city where palms and sea are everpresent companions. Principal town of the Costa Blanca, it was called the white fortress by the Carthaginians, Greeks and Romans and is underscored by the Esplanada de España, a marine promenade alongside a yacht-filled harbor. Palm shaded and paved in colorful mosaic patterns, the Esplanada is the focus of city life and the venue for outdoor concerts.

The urban development of the city flourished in the first quarter of the 20th century but the modern layout has not obliterated the narrow, steep streets of the Santa Cruz Quarter, setting of the Baroque Church of Santa María. Built by the Catholic monarchs atop a former mosque, it has a Rococo doorway and an elaborate interior; its façade is a fine example of Valencia Baroque.

Dedicated to the town's patron saint, the Concatedral of San Nicolás was built in Herrerian style. The 18th century Ayuntamiento displays a striking Churrigueresque façade. The cathedral's Salón Azul is distinguished by a mirrored gallery. (A metal disk on the marble staircase is a reference point in measuring the sea level throughout Spain.)

Castillo de Santa Bárbara

From its perch 500' above the port, Castillo de Santa Bárbara dominates the landscape and offers views in every direction. Sprawled on the summit of Mount Benacantil, the fortress is the oldest structure in town.

Excursions from Alicante uncover inviting towns and small villages. Coastal Santa Pola is home to a traditional and noisy wharfside auction. The ancient stones of its 16th century fort recall times when the city faced the imminent menace of Barbary pirates. Linked to Alicante and Santa Pola by a ferry service, Tabarca is a small islet of coves and inlets in a milieu of crystal clear water.

Continuing south, the road traverses salt pans and endless beaches. The salt pans are defined by their shimmering, pool-stippled surface and by the blinding whiteness of the salt mountains. Jutting out over a long strip of beach, the town of Guardamar is surrounded by dunes and dotted with pine and eucalyptus trees, shrubs and liquor-ice plants.

Inland, along what is called the *Route of the Palms*, is the town of Elche, notable for its Baroque Basilica de Santa María. La Calahorra is a surviving remnant of the wall that once guarded the city. The town's parkland embraces orchards enclosed by tall, mast-like palms. In the

Huerto del Cura (Priest's Garden), a palm in the form of a seven-armed candelabra occupies center stage.

The town of Orihuela preserves a complement of monumental buildings. The old Universidad de Santo Domingo has two cloisters, one Renaissance, the other Baroque. The Cathedral of the Saviour is accented by Gothic and Renaissance elements and houses the Diocesan Museum.

Accommodations
30 double and triple rooms, some with private bath. Both men and women are welcome.

Amenities
Towels and linens are supplied. Swimming pool, TV, living room, laundry room and garden.

Meals
All meals are provided with the lodging.

Cost of lodging
Provisional cost: $30.00 per person including full board.

Special rules
Curfew at midnight. Punctuality at meal times (9:00 am, 2:00 pm and 9:00 pm). Silence during siesta (3:00-5:00 pm) and after dinner. During the summer (July-September), maximum stay is 15 days. Closed in October.

Directions
By car: Stella Maris is located near the Centro Comercial (Mall) Gran Via, between the restaurants Juan XXIII and Pollastre.
By train: Get off at Alicante and take a bus to the Centro Commercial Gran Vía and then walk 5 minutes to Stella Maris.

Contact
Responsable de la residencia
Stella Maris
Antonio Ramos Carratalà, 29
03015 Alicante (Alicante), Spain
Tel: 96/5266737
Fax: 96/5266736

MONASTERIO NUESTRA SEÑORA DE MIRAMBEL
Augustinian Nuns

Situated along the Costa del Azahar, the monastery overlooks the sea. The resident community of Augustinian nuns was founded in 1580. Due to the deteriorating condition of their previous facility, the sisters relocated to this institution in 1980.

"Today we live in a modern, functional building which looks more like a small villa than a monastery," said the Mother Superior. The nuns once did sewing for a local company. Today, however, they earn their living through the hospedería which has been recently renewed and enlarged.

Set amid palm plantations, Benicasím has been a popular summer retreat with wealthy Valencian families since the 19th century. The mountain range that backdrops Benicasím is the Desierto de las Palmas. In 1694, the Order of Barefooted Carmelites bought the mountain range and built a monastery. Now a natural park, the area offers views of the coast.

The region of Valencia is considered the garden of Spain. Initially inhabited by the Iberians, it was later colonized by Greek and Carthaginian traders and passed to the Moors in the 8th century. Its system of cultivation can be traced to the latter.

The *Costa del Azahar* (Orange Blossom Coast) is named after the fragrant and plentiful citrus groves of the coastal plain. A lovely stretch of beach, it extends in a wide arc along the shores of the provinces of Castellón and Valencia. Vinarós and Benicarló are nearby fishing ports. The beach town of Oropesa sits on a hill crowned by a castle dating from Moorish times.

Peñiscola, a fortified town built around a castle, is on a rocky promontory surrounded on three sides by the sea. The enclave is ringed by enormous ramparts, its old town a tight cluster of narrow cobblestone streets lined with whitewashed houses. The Castell del Papa Luna was erected on the foundation of an Arab fortress in the late 13th century by the Knights Templar.

Like the Knights Hospitalers and Teutonic Knights, the fabled Templars were recruited to protect pilgrims in the Holy Land during the Crusades. At one time their reach extended from Syria to Scotland but their main concentration was in France where the order was conceived and eventually eliminated. Bernard of Clairvaux, a powerful monk, drew up the Templar rules and championed their formation into the most powerful military religious order in Europe. By combining monastic privilege with chivalrous adventure, the Knights Templar attracted many nobles and answered only to the pope. With their long beards, shorn hair and white mantles emblazoned with red crosses, they were feared by Muslims and Christians alike.

Although they had taken vows of poverty, the gifts of estates and money they received changed the character of the order. Their power and wealth aroused the hostility, fear and jealousy of secular rulers and the secular clergy. When the Crusades failed, the Templars grew more decadent and more despised. After years of unprecedented power, Pope Clement V ordered the mass arrest of the knights on October 13, 1307, a day now memorialized as Friday the 13th. After years of trials and torture to extract confessions of sacrilegious practices, the order was completely destroyed by 1314, the knights sentenced to life imprisonment. After denouncing their confessions, many were burned at the stake.

Nearby Castelló de la Plana is the capital of Castellón province. Originally founded on high ground, the attractive city was reconquered from the Moors in 1233 by James I of Aragón and in 1251 was moved from its hilltop locale to a plain closer to the coast, hence "de la Plana." The heart of the city center is the 16th century Fadri, an octagonal bell tower. Paintings by native son Francisco Ribalta are preserved within the building.

In addition to exhibits on holography and minerals, El Planetario offers views of the night sky, solar system and nearest stars. The Museo Provincial de Bellas Artes is housed in an 18th century structure and contains artifacts dating from the middle Paleolithic era, regional ceramics and paintings from the 15th to the 20th centuries.

Accommodations
10 beds in 5 single and 5 double rooms, each with private bath. Both men and women are welcome. Make reservations at least 15 days in advance.

Amenities
Towels and linens are supplied. There is a refrigerator and microwave for guest use.

Meals
All meals can be supplied with the lodging.

Cost of lodging
Voluntary contribution.

Special rules
Maximum stay is 15 days; punctuality at meals is required. Guests are provided with their own key. Open year round.

Directions
By car: From Castelló de la Plana (going north) or Barcelona (going south), take highway A7 and exit at Benicasím. Take N340 (Carretera General) north towards Barcelona. After a few kms there will be signs to "Urbanización Las Palmas," (not to be confused with "Desierto de Las Palmas") and the monastery.

By train: Get off at Benicasím and take a bus to the monastery. The nuns suggest taking a taxi.

Contact
Madre Superiora
Monasterio Nuestra Señora de Mirambel
Urbanizacion Las Palmas
Avenida Barranquet, 262/B
12560 Benicasím (Castellón), Spain
Tel:/Fax: 964/398224
Note: There is only one phone/fax line, call before sending a fax.

CASA DE ESPIRITUALIDAD OBRERAS DE LA CRUZ
Workers of the Cross Nuns

Casa de Espiritualidad Obreras de La Cruz

In a peaceful and isolated setting surrounded by pine trees, the institution is just minutes from the small town of Castalla. Through the generosity of a local wealthy man, it was founded about thirty years ago by the present order. The sisters maintain a private school in Castalla but their residence is in the institution. They host groups seeking spiritual retreats and others simply on holiday. According to one of the sisters, "Visitors can avoid the crowds of Alicante but still be close enough to enjoy its beaches." The town of Castalla holds colorful celebrations during Easter week, a very popular time of year for the institution.

For day trips, an itinerary can comprise a sampling of coastal towns. Altea's old quarter sits on a hill with panoramic views. At every turn, at every new tier, the ascent to the top along staired streets and alleyways presents an ever-widening horizon of the entire La Marina District including the silhouettes of Peñon de Ifach and Helada Range. Orange orchards and almond groves stretch to the south, backdropped by the massif of the Puig Campana. At the zenith of town, a small parish church is offset by a glazed tile dome, one of Altea's most symbolic emblems.

The nearby town of Benidorm is delineated by the sum and substance of its old alleyways. The Balcón de Mediterráneo is a terrace standing on a site once occupied by a fortress. It offers commanding views of the Levante and Poniente beaches. A popular resort destination, the area is thronged with visitors in the summer months.

In the small fishing port of Villajoyosa, the lower part of town has a palm-shaded esplanade lined by old façades painted in vivid ocher, red, yellow and indigo blue. These colorways are repeated in the houses (which seem to hang as though suspended over the dry riverbed) and create an image synonymous with Villajoyosa.

The Route of the Castles is another itinerary. Heading south towards Novelda, the first castle is La Mola. A Moorish fort, it was razed and rebuilt by turns throughout the Middle Ages. Its most distinguishing feature is the triangular-based keep which dates from the Christian era. The town of Sax harbors one of the best-preserved strongholds. Pressed against the base of the unscalable walls, the town seems to huddle there seeking protection.

Casa de Espiritualidad Obreras de La Cruz

Northwest of Castalla, Biar is dominated by a Moorish fortress with a 12th century Almohad keep. The focal point of the interior is a room roofed by caliphal-type vaulting. Conserved within the town are arches which, in the Middle Ages, sealed off the streets at night and during times of siege.

Nearby Villena is home to the Atalaya Castle, an excellent example of medieval architecture. Of Muslim and Christian heritage, its dungeon is topped by a beading of turrets and shelters traces of a Moorish castle. The churches of Santiago and Santa María date from the 15th and 16th centuries. Together with the Renaissance edifice, they are among the finest monumental sights in the province. The Archaeological Museum showcases a valuable collection of prehistoric gold and silver work.

Accommodations

22 single and double rooms, some with private bath. Both men and women are welcome.

Note: During Easter week the institution is usually fully booked. Make reservations at least one month in advance.

Amenities

Towels and linens are supplied. There is a meeting hall and garden.

Meals

All meals can be supplied with the lodging.

Cost of lodging

Single room with private bath: $33.00 per person, full pension. Single room with shared bath: $27.00 per person, full pension. Double room with private bath: $31 per person, full pension. Double room with shared bath: $25 per person, full pension.

Special rules

Punctuality at meal times. Curfew at midnight. Open year round.

Directions

By car: From Alicante take highway N330, exit at Sax and follow the signs to Castalla on A211. Once in Castalla ask for "los pinitos," the local name for the site where San Leonardo is located.

By train: Get off at Valencia or Alicante and take a bus to Castalla. Once there call San Leonardo and they will provide transportation.

Contact

Directora
Casa de Espiritualidad Obreras de La Cruz
Partida de Confiters, s/n
03420 Castalla (Alicante), Spain
Tel: 96/5560998

Convento Santos Abdon y Senen y de la Divina Pastora

Franciscan Capuchin Friars

Convento Santos Abdon y Senen y de la Divina Pastora

Lying at the foot of a mountain, the convent is less than a mile from L'Olleria, a small town in the province of Valencia. According to the friar, "there is a perfect silence here and visitors like it very much because it is so pretty and welcoming."

Founded in 1401 by the Franciscan Order, the monks have inhabited the complex almost uninterruptedly since that time. On two occasions they were forced to leave: in 1835 during the Desamortización and again in 1936 during the Spanish Civil War. During their absence, the buildings were ransacked and vandalized. The church was partially set afire during the Civil War but was restored a few years ago. The restoration of the complex has not been totally completed. Construction is currently underway to enlarge and improve the guest house. In past centuries, the convent was an important spiritual center, hosting a noviciate for the education of new Franciscan friars. Due to advancing age and attrition, only four friars remain in residence.

Convento Santos Abdon y Senen y de la Divina Pastora

It is possible to visit the church and convent, both built in simple Franciscan style. The interior of the restored church has relics of the original structure as well as paintings from the 1940s.

The institution is well situated for tours of the region including the Costa Blanca, an area of sharply different coastal scenery. To the north, a wall of mountains closely parallels the sea, dropping away here and there to form sheer cliffs and secluded pebbled coves; to the south lies a vast plain of dunes, palm groves and salt pans.

At the northern end of the Costa Blanca, Dénia is dominated by a castle with seascape views. Despite its urban feel, a fishing village atmosphere can be sensed in the old quarters of Baix el Mar and Les Roques. The 18th century Church of the Assumption is the city's most noteworthy structure.

Continuing south to Cape San Antonia, the shoreline is characterized by beautiful Mediterranean scenery backdropped by the mountain range of Sierra del Montgó. The road twists along cliffs, mountains, coves and the sea until Cape La Nau. Between the two capes is
Jávea or Xábia, whose original town center is accentuated by a fortified
church with a Gothic façade.

Jávea is one of the most provocative places in the Valencia
Community. The old part of town steeply descends from the foot of a
buttressed hill. Palaces and convents in the area around Moncada
Street represent various architectural periods. Pope Alexander VI was
born and baptized in the nearby Church of San Pedro. Views can be
had from the castle and the Hermitage of San Félix. The latter is an
example of East Coast Gothic from the 13th century. It harbors a valuable collection of Gothic paintings.

At the far end of Jávea's sweep of bay is the jutting, rocky profile of
the coastline leading to Cape La Nau and the tiny islet of Porticholl.
The seaside cliffs are pockmarked by natural cave formations. The
town's ancient core is set off by San Bartolomé, a late-Gothic structure
which closely resembles a fortress, a reminder of the once frequent
incursion of pirates.

The coast from Jávea to Moraira passes a series of rocky coves and
beaches made all the more striking by the luminous blue mountains
in the background. The old fishing harbor of Moraira is overlooked by
a castle and watchtower. A little further along the coast is Calp, a village at the foot of Peñon de Ifach. A Gibraltar-style rock, the Peñon is
joined to the mainland by a narrow isthmus, a landmark along the
Costa Blanca. A Gothic-Mudéjar church and 16th century tower, a relic
from the former fortifications, are at the heart of the old town. Telltale
signs of the Roman baths are also evident.

Altea is a typically Mediterranean village whose ancient district
clings to a hill topped by a parish church. The combined effect of the
church's glazed tile dome, whitewashed houses, palm trees and sea cre-
ates a provocative picture.

Heading inland, the landscape assumes a different quality, one of
vineyards, orchards and market gardens as well as the intrinsic *riurau*,

whitewashed dwellings fronted by an arcaded porch-like section. The
route travels through pretty scenery passing one quaint village after
another before reaching Callosa d'En Sarriá. The ensuing town of
Guadalest was constructed within the core of a castle hewn from rock.
Its setting presents an unusual and compelling sight. Unspoiled
Confrides and Peñáguila offer glimpses of typical mountain towns.
The latter contains the elements of a Morosco village and is home to a
Moorish castle.

Alcoi is one of the oldest cloth-weaving centers in mainland Spain.
Plunging ravines and steep slopes lend the town a peculiar profile. Its
architecture runs the gamut from Baroque to ramshackle to once glorious manor homes of the 19th century. Another tour meanders through
mountain scenery past tiny hamlets indelibly stamped by a Moorish
influence. In the 13th century, al-Azraq was born in this locale. A figure of legendary proportions, he besieged and then battled the troops
of James I before the walls of Alcoi. This region is perhaps the least
known yet most representative of all the inland districts. The enfolding
hillsides are mantled in fig and cherry orchards, almond groves and
vineyards, interrupted every so often by a ruined keep or crumbling
stronghold.

The journey south to Agres encompasses an area popular with hikers
and outdoor enthusiasts, a place filled with caves that once preserved
snow until summer. Agres sits in the foothills of the Mariola Range
and is close to *El Fratre*, (the Friar of Agres), an unusually shaped rock
beside the waters of a thermal spring. The town's calvary commands a
fine view of the countryside. At the very top is the Mare de Deu
d'Agres, a small convent. According to tradition, it stands on the site
miraculously indicated by the figure housed within.

Planes is crouched on a hill under the watchful protection of a castle
and is a faithful likeness of a medieval burg. A smattering of noble
mansions and small tile retables comprises the Vía Crucis and are the
most idiosyncratic traits of Planes. Bordering the town and forming a
delightful environment is an ogival-arched aqueduct in a shaded landscape. Just outside of town, the road runs beside the beautiful *Barranco
de la Encantada* (Enchanted Ravine).

Accommodations
12 single, double and triple rooms, some with private bath. Both men
and women are welcome.

Amenities
Towels and linens are supplied.

Meals
All meals can be supplied on request.

Cost of lodging
Prices will be determined when reservations are made.

Special rules
Small groups only. Open year round.

Directions
By car: From Valencia take route 340 south and exit at CV40. From
there follow the signs to L'Olleria and then ask for the "Convento del
los Capuchinos."
By train: Get off at Xátiva and take a bus to L'Olleria. The bus stop is
close to the convent.

Contact
Director
Convento Santos Abdon y Senen y de la Divina Pastora
Camino de Capuchinos
46850 L'Olleria (Valencia), Spain
Tel: 96/2200063

SECTION TWO

Monasteries Offering
Hospitality for Spiritual Endeavors

Belalcazar

Monasterio Santa Clara de la Columna
Clarisse Nuns

The monastery is a monumental building of over 25,000 square yards. "Once the current restoration is completed, it will be the second largest historical building in the province of Cordoba," according to the sister. It is located in the countryside in Belalcazar, a small town 60 miles from Cordoba. Founded in 1400, it flourished through the centuries. During World War II it was occupied by the army and all the art disappeared during the occupation. Only the frescoes remain. They have been restored and can be visited.

Accommodations

32 beds in large dorms and 3 single rooms. Baths are shared. Both men and women are welcome, but only in a group and exclusively for spiritual retreats.

Amenities

Towels and linens are not supplied. Guests must provide sleeping bags or linens (covers are supplied). Kitchen, chapel, garden.

Meals

Meals are not supplied, guests may use the kitchen at their disposal.

Cost of lodging

To be arranged depending on the size of the group and length of stay.

Special rules

Open year round. There is no central heating, only a stove.

Contact

Hermana Hospedera
Monasterio Santa Clara de la Columna
Villeta de Santa Clara, s/n
14280 Belalcazar, Spain
Tel/Fax: 957/146124

Estepona

Monasterio Santa María del Monte Carmen y San Elias Profeta
Carmelite Nuns

The monastery occupies an enchanting spot on the outskirts of Estepona. It has a magnificent view of the sea and the mountains of the Sierra de Ronda. "It is wonderful, the sea on one side and the 'sierra' on the other; an ideal place for those who come for spiritual retreats," said the Mother Superior. The monastery was founded 11 years ago by a small group of nuns from Canete la Real. The institution was previously a clinic for medical studies. Since its foundation, the nuns have been working to embellish the institution. On June 30, 2000, they inaugurated the church. They are now completing the construction of the Casa de Oración, which will host groups coming for spiritual retreats.

Accommodations

The guesthouse is being constructed at his time.. Both men and women are welcome, but only in groups seeking spiritual retreat, preferably accompanied by a religious representative. Open year round.

Amenities

Towels and linens are not supplied, guests must provide sleeping bags or linens. Chapel, kitchen.

Meals

Meals are not supplied. Guests can hire a cook to prepare and serve meals.

Cost of lodging
To be determined.
Contact
Madre Superiora
Finca Fatima
Monasterio Santa María del Monte Carmen y San Elias Profeta
Apartado de Correo 256
29680 Estepona, Spain
Tel: 95/279947

Puerto de Santa María
Monasterio San Miguel Arcangel
Clarisse Nuns

The institution is on the outskirts of Puerto de Santa María, one of the most popular towns of the Costa de la Luz. It lies inland about 2 miles from the beach. The community was founded in 1730 in a large building in the center of Puerto de Santa María. Twenty-five years ago, the nuns moved. "We moved because the old building was falling apart, and we didn't have the money to restore it, so we decided to build a new one." On the low hills along the coast, the order runs an egg farm with 1,200 chickens. Additionally, they are very busy washing and ironing delicate garments. "We also decorate tablecloths and other items with fine embroidery'" said the sister. The new construction does not contain any works of art except a rather impressive cross. "It is unique, there are no others like this in Spain. I think it is beautiful and many people come from all over Spain to see it," said the Mother Superior.
Accommodations
1 single room and 7 beds in 3 double rooms with private bath. Both men and women are welcome, but only for religious purposes. Open year round.
Amenities
Towels and linens are supplied. There are 2 large halls for meetings. Guests can participate in the services with the nuns, who are separated by a grating.
Meals
All meals can be supplied on request for small groups up to 4 people
Cost of lodging
Provisional cost per person $18 (full pension).
Products of the institution
Farm products are for sale and embroidery can be commissioned.
Contact
Finca de la Caridad
Monasterio San Miguel Arcangel
11500 Puerto de Santa María, Spain
Tel/Fax: 956/871894
Note: Write or call the Madre Superiora (well in advance).

Sevilla

Monasterio San Clemente
Cistercian Nuns

The monastery is in Sevilla near the bridge, "Puente de la Barqueta," on the river Guadalquivir. It is in front of the Isle of the Cartuja and the Monasterio de Santa María de las Cuevas (site of the Expo 1992). The monastery has been declared a National Monument but cannot be visited because the nuns live in seclusion. It was founded in 1248 and the Cistercian nuns have lived here almost uninterruptedly since that time. The 15th century Baroque church can be visited on request. It shelters Baroque decorations, a Baroque retablo and 15th centuries paintings representing the story of the Cistercian Order painted by a nun with the help of her father.

Accommodations

6 single rooms with private bath. Both men and women are welcome, but only for spiritual retreats.

Amenities

Towels and linens are supplied.

Meals

Meals are not supplied with the lodging.

Cost of lodging

2,500 pesetas per person/per night.

Special rules

Curfew 9.00 pm. Maximum stay 1 week. Guests are required to participate in the liturgy. Closed at Christmas and Easter Week.

Contact

Madre Hospedera (Madre Soledad)
Monasterio San Clemente
Reposo, 9
41002 Sevilla, Spain
Tel: 95/4378040
Fax: 95/4378801

Barbastro

Monasterio Nuestra Señora de Pueyo
Salesian Monks

Contact
Padre Juan
Monasterio Nuestra Señora de Pueyo
22300 Barbastro (Huesca), Spain
Tel/Fax: 974/310934
Note: Single men and women for spiritual retreats only. Open year round.

Tarazona

Monasterio de Santa Ana
Discalced Carmelite Nuns

Contact
Madre Superiora
San Anton, 51
50500 Tarazona (Zaragoza) - Spain
Tel: 976/641988
Note: Small groups of men and women (max 12) for spiritual retreats, only if accompanied by a religious representative. Open year round.

Zaragoza

Monasterio La Encarnacion
Carmelite Nuns

The monastery is in the center of Zaragoza, near the Puerta del Carmen. Zaragoza is one of the historical cities of Spain. Its name derives from the Roman "cesaraugusta." Although it was severely damaged during the War of Independence, some interesting antique buildings have been preserved. One of the most important is the "Basilica de Nuestra Señora del Pilar" (hence the name Pilar of many Spanish women). The church is impressive and features 11 domes. The Santa Capilla preserves the highly venerated image of the Virgen del Pilar. It rests upon a pillar, surrounded by rich adornments and flowers. The clothes of the statue are changed everyday. The monastery was founded in 1615, but a new branch was built in 1965 and is the nun's present residence. Although the monastery is situated in the center of the city, "it is surrounded by a wonderful garden. It is a very comfortable place. What strikes our guests the most is the silence and the peace we enjoy," the sister added.

Accommodations

8 beds in 1 double room and 7 single rooms with private bath. Both men and women are welcome, but for spiritual retreats or pilgrimage.

Amenities

Towels and linens are supplied. Kitchen, meeting room, garden, terrace, chapel.

Meals

Meals are not supplied with the lodging. Guests may use the kitchen.

Cost of lodging

$9 per person/per night.

Special rules

Guests are required to participate in the liturgy when possible and respect the silence of the monastery. Open year round.

Contact

Madre Superiora

Monasterio La Encarnacion

Avenida Cesar Augusto, 1 - 50004 Zaragoza, Spain

Tel: 976/439868

Fax: 976/439399

Email: materunitatis@wanadoo.es

Lugones

Santa María de Los Angels
Cistercian Nuns

Contact
Madre Superiora
Santa María de Los Angels
Pico del Cueto
33420 Lugones (Oviedo), Spain
Tel: 98/5264995
Note: 3 beds reserved for religious representatives of the Cistercian Order.

Oviedo

Monasterio de San Pelayo
Benedictine Nuns

Contact
Madre Hospedera (they speak English and French)
Monasterio de San Pelayo
Calle San Vicente, 11
33003 Oviedo, Spain
Tel: 98/5218981 / e.mail mspelayo@las.es
Note: There is a small guest house (6 single and double rooms with private bath) for spiritual retreats. Men and women are welcome. Closed July and August.

Nuestra Santisima Madre del Carmen
Discalced Carmelites

The monastery is in Oviedo, an historical university town and the cultural center of Asturias. The monastery is a modern building settled by the nuns in 1981. The original congregation was founded in 1884 and previously lived in a building in the center of the city. Today they sustain themselves making pastries and decorating linens with embroidery.. The monastery is near Santa María de Naranco, one of the finest Romanesque churches of Oviedo.

Accommodations
3 double rooms, each with a bathroom. Showers are shared. Both men and women are welcome.

Amenities
Towels and linens are supplied on request. Kitchen and living room.

Meals
Meals are not supplied with the lodging. Guests may use the kitchen.

Cost of lodging
Voluntary contribution.

Products of the institution
Homemade pastries are sold at the monastery.

Contact
Madre Superiora
Nuestra Santisima Madre del Carmen
Fitoria de Arriba, 16
33011 Oviedo, Spain
Tel: 985/285604
Fax: 985/283272
Note: In June, July and August, the hospedería is reserved to the relatives of the nuns.

Ciutadela de Menorca
Reial Monestir de Santa Clara
Clarisse Nuns

Contact
Madre Hospedera
Reial Monestir de Santa Clara
Portal de la Font, 2
07760 Ciutadela de Menorca (Baleares), Spain
Tel/Fax: 98/382778
Note: Small groups (8) of men and women and religious representatives, for spiritual retreats. Open year round.

Manacor
Monasterio de la Santa Familia
Benedictine Nuns

Contact
Madre Hospedera
Monasterio de la Santa Familia
Afueras, s/n
07500 Manacor (Baleares), Spain
Tel: 971/551484
Note: 6 rooms open to men and women in small groups of 2-4 people, exclusively for spiritual purposes. Open all year. Summer months are very busy.

Mao
Monasterio Purisima Concepción
Concepciónistas Franciscanas

Contact
Anyone who answers the phone. Write or call well in advance.
Monasterio Purisima Concepción
Placa Constitucio, 20
07701 Mao (Baleares), Spain
Tel/Fax: 971/362606
Note: Small groups or singles for spiritual retreats; reference of a religious representative mandatory. Open year round.

Mercadal
Santuario de Monte Toro
Franciscan Nuns

Contact
Madre Superiora
Santuario de Monte Toro
07740 Mercadal (Baleares), Spain
Tel: 971/375060
Note: 30 beds for organized groups of men and women for spiritual retreats. Open year round.

Soller (Baleares)

Canonica de Santa Marida de l'Olivar
Regular Canon Nuns

The institution is located on the island of Palma, about 20 miles from Palma de Mallorca. "It is the most beautiful valley of Soller." A picturesque town surrounded by vineyards and orchards, it is sprawled on the mountains of Sierra Tramuntana. Santa María de l'Olivar is a 1980 construction built in order to assist and host the pilgrims to a chapel which commemorates the apparition of the Virgin in Lourdes. There are three nuns and they like to say that "we host people as if we were family; they eat and pray with us. If anyone needs silence and isolation, we respect that too."

Accommodations
1 single and 3 double rooms. Only one of the rooms has a private bath; the rest are shared. Both men and women are welcome, but only for spiritual retreats.

Amenities
Towels and linens are supplied.

Meals
All meals are supplied with the lodging.

Cost of lodging
Voluntary contribution.

Special rules
Maximum stay 8 days. Open all year.

Directions
By car: From Palma de Mallorca take C711 to Lluc and exit at Soller. Follow the signs to Monasterio Santa María de l'Olivar.
By train: Get off at Soller and take a taxi or walk (4 km) to the Monastery.

Contact
Responsable de la Canonica (preferably accompanying request with a reference from a religious representative).
Canonica de Santa Marida de l'Olivar
Apartado 154
07100 Soller (Baleares), Spain
Tel/Fax: 971/631870

Bilbao

Monasterio de Santa Monica
Augustinian Nuns

Contact
Madre Superiora
Monasterio de Santa Monica
Zabalbide, 61
48006 Bilbao (Vizcaya), Spain
Tel: 94/4458730
Note: 18 beds in a large dorm open to groups of only women or only men for days of spiritual activities. Open all year.

Donostia/San Sebastián

Monasterio Santa Teresa
Discalced Carmelite Nuns

The monastery is in the old section of San Sebastian. It was founded in 1663; the church was built about 20 years later. The antique facade of the church is all that remains of the original building. The interior has been completely modified. "Neither the church or the monastery have much artistic value, but they in good condition and are comfortable," the sister said.

Accommodations
2 single rooms with shared bath. Only female religious representatives or women seeking spiritual retreats.

Amenities
Towels and linens are supplied.

Meals
All meals are supplied to religious representatives.

Cost of lodging
To be arranged upon arrival.

Special rules
To be arranged upon arrival. Open all year.

Directions
By car: Donostia/San Sebastian is on the coast and is connected by Highway A8. Exit at Donostia and ask for the Convento Santa Teresa (as a reference, it is near the Basilica Santa María).
By train: Get off at Donostia/San Sebastian and take a bus to the monastery.

Contact
Madre Priora
Monasterio Santa Teresa
Elvira Cipitria (or Zipitria), 3
20003 Donostia/San Sebastian (Guipuzcoa) - Spain
Tel: 943/424043

Hondarribia-Fuentearribía
Monasterio de la Sagrada Familia
Carmelite Nuns

The monastery is in the outskirts of Fuentearribía, an interesting historical town of the Basque Country. It was founded in 1962 and is inhabited by 15 nuns. It does not contain any works of art.

Accommodations

The small and simple hospedería is reserved to the relatives of the nuns and people seeking spiritual retreats. 1 single and 2 double rooms, baths are shared. Both men and women are welcome, together only if married.

Amenities

Towels and linens are supplied.

Meals

Meals are not supplied. Guests may cook their own meals in the kitchen.

Cost of lodging

Voluntary contribution.

Special rules

Guests must accompany their request with references from a parish or a religious representative. Closed in July and August, Christmas and Easter week.

Directions

By car: From Irun, follow the signs to Hondarribia. Before reaching it, turn left following the signs to Carmelitas (in Euskera Carmel Darrak).

By train: Get off in Fuentearribía and take a taxi or a bus to the monastery. The bus stop is on the main road, approximately 1 km from the monastery.

Contact

Madre Superiora
Monasterio de la Sagrada Familia
Barrio Mendelu s/n
20280 Hondarribia-Fuentearribía (Guipúzcoa), Spain
Tel: 943/541973

Lujiua
Monasterio de San José
Mercederias Nuns of the Monastery of San José

Contact

Madre Superiora
Monasterio de San José
Barrio Lanomendi
480180 Lujiua (Vizcaya), Spain
Tel/Fax: 94/4541366

Note: 15 beds. Open to religious representatives, men and women but only for spiritual retreats. Guests must accompany their request with a reference from a religious representative or parish. Closed in July and August.

Oñati

Monasterio de Santa Ana
Clarisse Nuns

The monastery is above the center of the town of Oñati, an historical city of the Basque Country. The community was founded in 1500 and once inhabited a monastery in the heart of Oñati. In 1982 they left the building because restoration would have been too costly. The Ayuntamiento took charge of the antique building, turning it into a school. The new monastery is a modern, functional building. "We enjoy a great vista of the city," said the Mother Superior.

Accommodations

3 double rooms and 1 dorm with 6 beds, Two of the rooms have private bath, the remaining room and dorm are in a small apartment with 1 bath. Both men and women are welcome, but only for spiritual retreats. Guests should include a reference from a parish. Open all year. Make reservations well in advance.

Amenities

Towels and linens are supplied.

Meals

Meals are not supplied. Guests may use the kitchen at their disposal.

Cost of lodging

Voluntary contribution to be used for charity donation. The nuns consider hosting groups as part of their mission.

Special rules

Curfew at 10 pm.

Directions

By car: From Vitoria take route 240 North, then take C6213 following the signs to Oñati. Before entering the city there are signs to Santa Ana.

By train: Get off at Vitoria-Gasteiz and take a bus to Oñati. Once in Oñati, walk to the monastery (about a 10-minute uphill walk from the center).

Contact
Madre Superiora
Monasterio de Santa Ana
Barrio Garagaltza, 13
20569 Oñati (Guipúzcoa), Spain
Tel/Fax: 943/781695
Note: The liturgy is held in Euskera.

Salvatierra - Augurain

San Pedro Apostol
Clarisse Nuns

Contact
Anyone answering the phone
San Pedro Apostol
Plaza de Santa Clara
01200 Salvatierra - Augurain (Alava), Spain
Tel: 945/300062
Fax: 945/312449
Note: Open to groups and singles, only for spiritual retreats. Open all year.

Garachico

Monasterio Inmaculada Concepción
Franciscan Nuns

The monastery is on the sea in the small town of Garachico. "It is very peaceful here, ideal for retreats," said Sor Inmaculada. The institution was founded in 1643 and the Franciscan nuns have inhabited it ever since. The nuns do embroidery and make clothing for sacred images.

Accommodations

5 beds in 1 single room and 2 double rooms, baths are shared. Both men and women are welcome, for spiritual retreats only. Make arrangements well in advance.

Amenities

Towels and linens are supplied. Meeting room and refrigerator are available for guests.

Meals

All meals are supplied by the nuns.

Cost of lodging

Provisional cost: $15 per person/per night (meals not included).

Products of the institution

Embroidery of linens and clothes on request.

Special rules

To be arranged upon arrival. Open all year except during the nuns' spiritual practice (the date varies).

Directions

By car: From Santa Cruz de Tenerife take TF5 and then route 820 until Garachico. Once there ask for the monastery.

By plane or ferry: From Santa Cruz there are buses to Garachico.

Contact

Madre Abadesa
Monasterio Inmaculada Concepción
San Diego, 15
38450 Garachico (Tenerife), Spain
Tel: 922/830273

Santa Brigida

Monasterio Benidictino de la Santisima Trinidad
Benedictine Monks

Contact

Padre Hospedero
Monasterio Benidictino de la Santisima Trinidad
Camino al Monasterio, 79
35300 Santa Brigida (Gran Canaria), Spain
Tel/Fax: 928/641141

Note: Both men and women are welcome. They are expected to participate in the liturgy of the monastery. Maximum stay 15 days. Closed 10 days during the spiritual retreat of the monks, which usually takes place in September (dates vary).

Hoz de Anero

Monasterio Desierto de San José
Carmelitas Fathers

Contact
Padre Superior
Monasterio Desierto de San José
39794 Hoz de Anero (Cantabria), Spain
Tel: 942/507185
Note: Inside the monastery: Only religious men are welcome for spiritual retreats or to learn Spanish (guests come from many countries). Outside the monastery: Small groups, both men and women for spiritual retreats are welcome.

Ruiloba

Monasterio de San José
Discalced Carmelite Nuns

Located on a rise above the small town of Ruiloba, the monastery enjoys a splendid view of the sea and the mountains of the Picos de Europa. Comillas, famous for the modern Catalan architecture of its buildings (designed by Antoni Gaudí and Joan Martorell), is only 3 km from the monastery. The institution was founded in 1877 by the Carmelite nuns, but suffered the tragic events of the Civil War and the World War II, which resulted in the loss of all the monastery's artwork. Now "the work of art is the nature which surrounds us," the sister said.

Accommodations
20 beds in single and double rooms, some with private bath. Both men and women are welcome, but only for spiritual retreats. Make reservations well in advance.

Amenities
Towels and linens are supplied on request. Meeting rooms and 2 kitchens.

Meals
Meals are not supplied. Guests may use the kitchen at their disposal.

Cost of lodging
Provisional cost per person/per night: groups of 10 or more: $3 per person; individuals or smaller groups: $10 per person.

Products of the institution
The nuns decorate pottery to order. Some may be purchased at the monastery.

Special rules
Curfew at 11 pm. Maximum stay 15 days. Open year round.

Directions
By car: From Santander take E70 West until Cabezon de la Sal. Turn right following the signs to Ruiloba and Comillas. Once in Ruiloba ask directions for the monastery.
By train: Get off at Santander and take the bus to Comillas, then walk or take a taxi to San José. The bus stop is 1 km from the monastery.

Contact
Hermana Hospedera
Monasterio de San José
Fuente del Carmelo, 10
39527 Ruiloba (Cantabria) - Spain
Tel/Fax: 942/721085

Madridejos

Convento Santa Ana
Clarisse Nuns

Contact
Madre Hospedera
Convento Santa Ana
De Las Monjas, 25
45710 Madridejos (Toledo), Spain
Tel: 925/460965
Note: Men and women for spiritual retreats only. Guests must have a reference from a religious representative or a parish. Closed during Christmas and Easter week.

Villarubia de los Ojos

Monasterio Nuestra Señora de la Soledad
Clarisse Nuns

Contact
Madre Abadesa
Monasterio Nuestra Señora de la Soledad
Soledad, 58
13670 Villarubia de Los Ojos (Ciudad Real), Spain
Tel/Fax: 926/896208
Note: Hospitality is restricted to religious representatives for spiritual retreats only. Open all year.

Yunquera de Henares

Nuestra Señora de los Remedios
Jeronimos Nuns

The monastery is on the outskirts of Yunquera de Henares, a small town in the plains of the Guadalajara Province, a few km from the town of Brihuega. "It is a very pretty and peaceful countryside," said the Mother Superior. The community was founded in 1564 in Brihuega, but due to the poor conditions of the building, the nuns moved in the present modern monastery in 1971. They once owned some valuable works of art but they were all destroyed during the Civil War. "We were left with very little. We started all over again in a very simple way," she added.

Accommodations
3 beds in 1 double and 1 single room with a shared bath.
Both men and women are welcome but only for spiritual retreats.
Amenities
Towels and linens are supplied.
Meals
All meals are supplied with the lodging.
Cost of lodging
Voluntary contribution
Special rules
Maximum stay 1 week. Closed at Christmas and Easter.
Directions
By car: From Madrid take NII East to Guadalajara. Pass Guadalajara and exit at Torija and follow the signs to Brihuega and Yunquera de Henares.
By train: Get off in Guadalajara and take a bus to Yunquera de Henares.
Contact
Madre Superiora
Nuestra Señora de los Remedios
Avenida Islas Filipinas, 5
19210 Yunquera de Henares (Guadalajara), Spain
Tel: 949/330191

Ávila

Monasterio de Santa Ana
Cistercian Nuns

Contact
Madre Hospedera
Monasterio de Santa Ana
Carretera de Toledo, km 3
Apartado 128
05080 Ávila, Spain
Tel: 920/221666 / Fax: 920/224604
Note: Only women. Sometimes married couples are hosted for a few days of spiritual retreat or meditation. Closed 10 days during the month of October for the annual spiritual retreat of the community (dates vary).

Burgos

Monasterio Cistercience de San Bernardo
Cistercian Nuns of the Congregation of San Bernardo

Contact
Madre Hospedera
Monasterio Cistercience de San Bernardo
Paseo de los Pisones, 60
Burgos, Spain
Tel: 947/205118 / Fax: 947/201678 / Email: ocsosbb@planalfa.es
Note: 9 beds in single rooms for men and women seeking a few days of meditation and prayer. Open all year.

El Parral

Monasterio de Santa María de El Parral
Jeronimos Monks

Contact
Padre Horpedero
Monasterio de Santa María de El Parral
Subida del Parral, 2
40003 El Parral (Segovia), Spain
Tel: 921/431298 / Fax: 921/422592
Note: Hospitality is reserved to men and religious representatives for religious retreats only. Maximum stay 1 week. Voluntary contribution.

Nava del Rey

Convento de los Sagrados Corazones de Jesús y María
Capuchin Sisters

Contact
Anyone who answers the phone
Convento de los Sagrados Corazones de Jesús y María
Calle Rodrigues Chico, 80
47500 Nava del Rey (Valladolid), Spain
Tel: 983/850189
Note: Only groups for spiritual retreats. There are 24 beds in double rooms and dormitories. Larger groups can be hosted inside the convent. Both men and women are welcome. Open year round.

Sahagun

Monasterio de Santa Cruz
Benedictine Nuns

Contact
Madre Hospedera or Madre Abadessa
Monasterio de Santa Cruz
Doctors Bermejo y Calderon, 10
24320 Sahagun (León), Spain
Tel: 987/780078 / Fax 987/780078
Note: There are 38 beds in single and double rooms. Both men and women are welcome but only for religious retreats. Open all year.

San Miguel de las Duenas

Monasterio de Santa María de San Miguel Arcangel
Cistercian Nuns

Contact
Madre Hospedera
Monasterio de Santa María de San Miguel Arcangel
San Bernardo, 20
24398 San Miguel de las Duenas (León), Spain
Tel: 987/467046
Note: 5 beds in single rooms. Only women are welcome and only for religious retreats. Maximum stay 8 days. Open year round, but there is no central heating; winter can be cold. The monastery is often full, contact well in advance.

Segovia

Monasterio San Juan de la Cruz
Discalced Carmelite Friars

Contact
Director del Centro de San Juan de la Cruz
Monasterio San Juan de la Cruz
Alameda de Fuencisla
40003 Segovia, Spain
Tel: 921/ 431349 - 431961 / Fax: 921/431650
Note: The center is a house of religious practice. Both men and women are welcome, but only in groups (minimum 20 people) . Address all requests to the center along with the reason for visit. There are 40 rooms with private bath. Closed from December 20th- January 5th.

Venta de Banos

Abadia de San Isidro de Duenas
Cistercian Monks

Contact
Hermano Hospedero
Abadia de San Isidro de Duenas
34200 Venta de Banos (Palencia), Spain
Tel: 979/770701 / Fax: 979/772003
Note: The monastery is open only to men, women, groups or couples for spiritual retreats. 19 single and double rooms. Closed Christmas, January 1st and January 6th.

CATALONIA

Barcelona

Monasterio de San Maties
Jeronimas Nuns

Contact
Madre Hospedera
Monasterio de San Maties
Bellesguard, s/n
08035 Barcelona, Spain
Monastery: 93/4173666
Reservations: 92/2118240
Fax: 93/2112433
Note: Both men and women are welcome regardless of religion, but only for spiritual retreats. Closed September 30th, Christmas Day, January 26th and Easter.

Monasterio Sant Pere de les Puelles
Benedictine Nuns

Contact
Madre Hospedera
Monasterio Sant Pere de les Puelles
Angli, 55
08017 Barcelona, Spain
Tel: 93/2038915 / Fax: 93/2034830
Note: 10 beds in single rooms. Both men and women are welcome but only for spiritual retreats or meditation. Closed one week a year for the spiritual retreat of the nuns (dates vary).

Poblet

Monasterio de Santa María de Poblet
Cistercian Monks

Contact
Monje Hospedero
Monasteriode Santa María de Poblet
43448 Poblet (Tarragona)
Tel: 977/870089 / Fax: 977/870739 / Email: monespoblet@interbook.net
Note: There are 15 single rooms. Only men are welcome for spiritual retreats. Closed Christmas.

Santa Cristina d'Aro
Monasterio de Santa María de Solius
Cistercian Order

Contact
Padre Hospedero (Padre Jaime)
Monasterio de Santa María de Solius
17246 Santa Cristina d'Aro (Gerona)
Tel/Fax: 972/837084
Note: 8 beds in single rooms. Only men are welcome. They are required to share the daily liturgy with the monks. Maximum stay 1 week. Closed December 25th.

Sant Cugat del Valles
Monasterio Nuestra Señora de los Angeles y Pie de la Cruz
Dominican Nuns

Contact
Encargada de la Hospederia
Monasterio Nuestra Señora de los Angeles y Pie de la Cruz
Virgen del Rosario, s/n
Apartado 124
8190 Sant Cugat del Valles (Barcelona), Spain
Tel: 93/6741745
Note: Open to groups of men and women (up to 30) for spiritual retreats. Visitors must be accompanied by a religious representative (preferably with a reference by the Dominican Order). Representatives of the Dominican Order are welcome anytime. Open all year.

Sant Medir

Monasterio de Santa María de Cadins
Cistercian Order

Contact
Anyone who answers the phone
Monasterio de Santa María de Cadins
17199 Sant Medir (Gerona), Spain
Tel: 972/428077
Note: 12 beds. Both men and women are welcome, but only for spiritual retreats.
Open all year.

Vilobi d'Onyar

Fraternitat de Santa Clara
Hermanas Pobrese de Santa Clara

Contact
Encargada de la Hospederia
Fraternitat de Santa Clara
Aforse, s/n
17185 Vilobi d'Onyar (Gerona), Spain
Tel: 972/474276
Fax: 972/473524
Email: CLARISSES@infomail.lacaixa.es
Note: Open to groups of men and women (up to 30) for spiritual retreats, preferably with a reference from a religious representative, a parish or the Franciscan Order. Closed in June, July and August.

Villagonzalo

Casa de Espiritualidad
Hijas de la Virgen

Accommodations
15 single and 22 double rooms, all with private bath. Both men and women are welcome. Make arrangements well in advance.
Amenities
Towels and linens are supplied.
Meals
All meals are supplied with the lodging.
Cost of lodging
To be arranged depending on the size of the group, length of stay, etc.
Special rules
The Casa de Espiritualidad is open only to groups of 30 and more seeking spiritual retreats or pilgrims to the shrines of Fatima and Guadalupe. Open all year.
Directions
By car: From Merida follow the signs to Villagonzalo (17 kms).
By train: Get off at Villagonzalo or at Merida and take a bus to Villagonzalo.
Contact
Anyone who answers the phone
Casa de Espiritualidad
Madre María, 24
06473 Villagonzalo (Badajoz), Spain
Tel: 024/366720

Sobrado de Los Monjes
Monasterio de Santa María
Cistercian Monks

Contact
Padre Hospedero (mobile tel: 639/938960)
Monasterio de Santa María
15813 Sobrado de los Monjes (La Coruna), Spain
Tel: 981/787509
Fax: 981/787626
Note: There are 30 rooms, open exclusively for religious use. Men and women are welcome. Closed November.

Oseira
Abadia Cistercence Santa María La Real
Cistercian Monks

Contact
Padre Hospedero
Abadia Cistercence Santa María La Real
32135 Oseira (Orense), Spain
Tel: 988/282400
Fax: 988/282528
Note: There are 12 single rooms, open to men and women for spiritual retreats only.

Ferreira de Panton
Monasterio del Divino Salvador
Cistercian Nuns

Contact
Madre Hospedera
Monasterio del Divino Salvador
El Curro, 1
27430 Ferreira del Panton (Lugo), Spain
Tel: 982/456155
Note: 4 rooms for women seeking spiritual retreats only. Closed from November until April.

Viveiro
Monasterio de Nuestra Señorade Valdeflores
Dominican Nuns

Contact
Madre Hospedera
Monasterio de Nuestra Señorade Valdeflores
27850 Viveiro (Lugo)
Tel/Fax: 982/560151
Note: Men and women are welcome, but only for religious use. There are 8 double rooms. Closed September.

Canas

Santa María de San Salvador
Cistercian Nuns

Contact
Madre Hospedera
Santa María de San Salvador
Real, 2
26225 Canas (La Rioja), Spain
Tel/Fax: 941/379083
Note: 10 beds. Open to men and women only for religious use. Guests are required to take part in the liturgy. Open all year.

MURCIA

Guadalupe

Casa de Ejercicios Sagrado Corazón
Esclavas de Cristo Rey Nuns
The institution was built in 1993. It is located in a peaceful spot in the suburbs of Murcia. It hosts groups of men and women seeking spiritual retreats or pilgrims to the shrines in the area.
Accommodations
66 single and double rooms with private bath. Both men and women are welcome.
Amenities
Towels and linens are supplied.
Meals
All meals are supplied.
Cost of lodging
To be arranged when reservation are made. To be hosted, it is necessary to write or call in advance specifying the reason for the visit.
Directions
By car: From Murcia take N301 towards Espinardo, then follow the signs to Guadalupe.
By train: Get off at Murcia then take a bus to Guadalupe.
Contact
Anyone who answers the phone
Casa de Ejercicios Sagrado Corazón
Avenida de los Jeronimos, 1
30107 Guadalupe (Murcia), Spain
Tel: 968/830509

Alloz

Monasterio de San José
Cistercian Nuns

Contact
Anyone who answers the phone
Monasterio de San José
31292 Alloz (Navarra), Spain
Tel: 948/541467 / Fax: 948/541472
Note: Both men and women are welcome but only for spiritual retreats. Open all year.

Huarte-Pamplona

Casa de Oración Nuestra Señora del Pilar
Maríanistas Nuns

The institution is a few kms from Pamplona. Founded in 1960, it is surrounded by a large garden which offers a relaxing atmosphere

Accommodations
60 beds in single and double rooms with private bath. Both men and women are welcome but only for spiritual retreats.

Amenities
Towels and linens are supplied.

Meals
All meals are supplied.

Cost of lodging
To be arranged when reservations are made.

Special rules
Curfew at 10.30 pm, punctuality at meals. Open all year.

Directions
By car: From Pamplona follow the signs to Huarte and the Casa de Oración.
By train: Get off at Pamplona and take the bus to the Casa de Oración.

Contact
Anyone who answers the phone
Casa de Oración Nuestra Señora del Pilar
Calle del Pilar, 7
31620 Huarte - Pamplona (Navarra), Spain
Tel: 948/330139 / Fax: 948/331293

Javier

Centro de Espiritualidad
Jesuit Fathers

The Center of Spirituality is in a beautiful area of Navarra in front of the Sierra de Leyre, not far from the famous Monasterio de Leyre. It hosts groups of men and women seeking spiritual retreats.

Accommodations

160 beds in single and double rooms with bath. Both men and women are welcome.

Amenities

Towels and linens are supplied.

Meals

All meals are supplied.

Directions

By car: From Pamplona take 240 until Yesa and then take NA 5410 to Javier.
By train: Get off in Pamplona and take a bus to Javier.

Contact

Superior Father via telephone, fax or email
Centro de Espiritualidad
31411 Javier (Navarra), Spain
Tel: 948/ 884000
Fax: 948/884259
Email: javier@2000.es

Benaguasil
Monasterio de Santa María de Gratia Dei
Cistercian Nuns
Contact
Madre Hospedera
Monasterio de Santa María de Gratia Dei
Afueras, s/n
46180 Benaguasil (Valencia), Spain
Tel: 96/2730711
Fax: 96/2737704
Note: 5 rooms available to men and women for spiritual retreats only. Open all year.

Benicasim
Casa de Oración Santa Teresa
Carmelite Nuns
The Casa de Oración is part of the compound of the monastery Desierto de Las Palmas. It is managed by Carmelite monks although it is not part of the same building. The present institution is open to nuns of the same order, religious representatives and people wishing to spend a few days of solitude, silence and retreat.
Accommodations
6 single rooms with bath. Both men and women are welcome, but nuns of the same order have priority. Open year round. The casa closes in September, dates vary.
Amenities
Towels and linens are supplied.
Meals
All meals are supplied.
Cost of lodging
To be arranged upon arrival.
Special rules
To be arranged upon arrival.
Directions
By car: Exit A7 at Benicasim and follow the signs to Desierto de Las Palmas.
By train: Get off at Castellon (12 km) or Benicasim (7 km) and take the bus to the monastery.
Contact
Encargada de la Casa
Casa de Oración Santa Teresa
Desierto de Las palmas
15080 Benicasim (Castellon), Spain
Tel/Fax: 964/302467

Benicasim

Desierto de Las Palmas
Discalced Carmelite Monks

The monastery is an important spiritual center. It was founded in 1694 by the Carmelite fathers who were seeking an isolated place to create a "desierto" - literally a desert where they could retreat from the world. They chose this site because it was peaceful. Surrounded by palm, olive and fruit trees, it enjoys a magnificent vista of the sea. The monastery originally consisted of small hermitages (still visible, although some are just ruins). In 1697, a large monastery was built. In 1783 it was destroyed by a storm. A new monastery was erected not far from the original one. During the suppression of the religious orders of the 19th century, the monastery was deprived of most of its artwork. Today the complex consists of 3 sections: the central section is occupied by the church, another by the monks, the third by the Centro de Espiritualidad. Groups and singles seeking spiritual retreats are welcome. Not far form the main building is the Casa de Oración, run by another group of Carmelite nuns.

Accommodations
Centro de Espiritualidad Santa Teresa: The nuns have a program of meetings and retreats which starts in October and ends in September Nevertheless, they accept independent groups and individuals with their own programs. There are 42 single and double rooms with private bath. Both men and women are welcome. Closed from mid-September until mid-October.

Amenities
Towels and linens are supplied.

Meals
All meals are supplied.

Cost of lodging
To be arranged depending on the size of the group and length of stay.

Special rules
To be arranged upon arrival.

Directions
By car: Exit A7 at Benicasim and follow the signs to Desierto de Las Palmas.
By train: Get off at Castellon (12 km) or Benicasim (7 km), and take the bus to the monastery.

Contact
Madre María Dolores Manchon
Desierto de Las Palmas
Apartado de Correo 111
15080 Benicasim (Castellon), Spain
Tel: 964/300786
Fax: 964/305155

Gilet

Convento Santo Espiritu del Monte
Franciscan Friars

The convent is in a secluded site surrounded by pine trees on the mountains near Sagunt, 7 km from the coast and 3 km from the small town of Gilet. "It is a very pretty site for those who like the mountains," said the Friar Hospedero. The convent was founded in the 15th century by the Franciscan Order. "It is not adorned by many works of art because we are a typical simple Franciscan institution." The capital of Valencia is about 30 kms away.

Accommodations

40 single, double and triple rooms, each with private bath. Both men and women are welcome, but only for spiritual retreats. Closed from December 21st until January 12th. Make arrangements well in advance, July is often fully booked.

Amenities

Towels and linens are supplied.

Meals

All meals are supplied with the lodging.

Cost of lodging

To be arranged when reservations are made.

Directions

By car: From Valencia take E6 until Sagunt and follow signs to Gilet and convent.
By train: Get off at Sagunt. There is a bus for Gilet that leaves at 10 am, Monday through Friday. It stops at the convent. The best way is to take a taxi from Sagunt.

Contact

Padre Hospedero
Convento Santo Espiritu del Monte
46149 Gilet (Valencia), Spain
Tel: 96/26220011

Godelleta

Corazon Eucaristico de Jesus
Discalced Carmelite Nuns

Contact

Madre Hospedera
Corazon Eucaristico de Jesus
Carretera de Valencia a Godelleta, km 10
46388 Godelleta (Valencia), Spain
Tel: 96/1800097 / Fax: 96/1800270
Note: 10 beds for men and women seeking spiritual retreats. Guests must have a reference from a religious representative. Open all year.

Onda

Casa de Espiritualidad "El Carmen"
Carmelite Monks

Contact

Director de la Casa de Espiritualidad
C.tra de Tale, s/n
Apartado 53
12200 Onda (Castellon), Spain
Tel/Fax: 964/601394
Note: Open to groups of men and women, but only for spiritual retreats. Open all year. make arrangements well in advance.

Puzol/Puçol

Monasterio Sagrada Familia
Doscalced Carmelite Nuns

The monastery is in a peaceful locale, 1 km from Puzol, 15 kms north of Valencia. Surrounded by trees and meadows, it enjoys a vista of the coast. The community inhabiting the monastery was founded in 1948 and lived in the center of Puzol until 1969 until moving to the new facility. "It is not a classic stone monastery, but a Mediterranean building; it is white and decorated with arches, which match our blue sky," said the Mother Superior. The community works on a regular basis making hosts (averaging 400,000 per month).

Accommodations
A small house with 1 double and 2 single rooms with 1 shared bath. Both men and women are welcome, but only for spiritual retreats. Make arrangements well in advance.

Amenities
Towels and linens are supplied.

Meals
Meals are not supplied. Guests may cook their own meals in the kitchen at their disposal.

Cost of lodging
To be arranged upon arrival.

Special rules
Maximum stay 8 days. Closed in August.

Directions
By car: From Valencia take N340 North towards Sagunt and stop at Puzol. There are signs indicating the monastery.
By train: Get off at Puzol and walk to the monastery.

Contact
Encargada de la Hospedería
Camino de Lidia, s/n
Apartado 17
46530 Puzol (Valencia)
Tel: 96/1420574 / Fax: 96/1424187 / Email: ocdpuzol@teleline.es

INDEXES